THE COUNTRY AND
THE CITY REVISITED

England and the Politics of Culture, 1550–1850

Between 1550 and 1850, the great age of mercantilism, the English people remade themselves from a disparate group of individuals and localities divided by feudal loyalties, dialects and even languages, into an imperial power. Examining literature, art, and social life, and returning to ground first explored by Raymond Williams in his seminal work, *The Country and the City Revisited* traces this transformation. It shows that what Williams figured as an urban–rural dichotomy can now be more satisfactorily grasped as a permeable boundary. While the movement of sugar, tobacco, and tea became ever more deeply interfused with the movement of people, through migration and the slave trade, these commodities initiated new conceptions of space, time, and identity. Spanning the traditional periods of the Renaissance and Romanticism, this collection of essays offers exciting interdisciplinary perspectives on central issues of early modern English history.

Gerald MacLean is Professor of English at Wayne State University. He is author of *Time's Witness: Historical Representation in English Poetry, 1603–1660* (1990). He edited *Culture and Society in the Stuart Restoration: Literature, Drama, History* (1995) and is co-author (with Donna Landry) of *Materialist Feminisms* (1993) and co-editor of *The Spivak Reader* (1996).

Donna Landry is Professor of English at Wayne State University. She is author of *The Muses of Resistance: Laboring-Class Women's Poetry in Britain, 1739–1796* (1990), and co-author (with Gerald MacLean) of *Materialist Feminisms* (1993) and co-editor of *The Spivak Reader* (1996).

Joseph P. Ward teaches History at the University of Mississippi. He is author of *Metropolitan Communities: Trade Guilds, Identity, and Change in Early Modern London* (1997).

THE COUNTRY AND THE CITY REVISITED

England and the Politics of Culture, 1550–1850

EDITED BY

GERALD MACLEAN, DONNA LANDRY,
JOSEPH P. WARD

CAMBRIDGE
UNIVERSITY PRESS

PUBLISHED BY THE PRESS SYNDICATE OF THE UNIVERSITY OF CAMBRIDGE
The Pitt Building, Trumpington Street, Cambridge CB2 1RP, United Kingdom

CAMBRIDGE UNIVERSITY PRESS
The Edinburgh Building, Cambridge, CB2 2RU, UK   http://www.cup.cam.ac.uk
40 West 20th Street, New York, NY 10011–4211, USA   http://www.cup.org
10 Stamford Road, Oakleigh, Melbourne 3166, Australia

First published 1999

Printed in the United Kingdom at the University Press, Cambridge

Typeset in 11/12½ pt Baskerville No. 2   [GC]

A catalogue record for this book is available from the British Library

ISBN 0 521 59201 1 hardback

Contents

Illustrations

Notes on contributors

JOHN BARRELL is Professor of English at the University of York. His books include *The Idea of Landscape and the Sense of Place 1730–1840: An Approach to the Poetry of John Clare* (1972), *The Dark Side of the Landscape: The Rural Poor in English Painting, 1730–1840* (1980), *English Literature in History 1730–1780: An Equal, Wide Survey* (1983), *The Infection of Thomas De Quincey: A Psychopathology of Imperialism* (1991), and *The Birth of Pandora and the Division of Knowledge* (1992).

ELIZABETH A. BOHLS is Associate Professor of English at the University of Oregon. She is the author of *Women Travel Writers and the Language of Aesthetics, 1716–1818* (1995) and of articles on aesthetics, colonialism, and women's writing. Her current research involves identity and place in writings about the British Caribbean between 1770 and 1834.

ELIZABETH HECKENDORN COOK is Associate Professor of English at the University of California, Santa Barbara. She is the author of *Epistolary Bodies: Gender and Genre in the Eighteenth-Century Republic of Letters* (1996). Currently she is working on the intersections of various codes of the natural at the end of the eighteenth century.

ELIGA GOULD is Assistant Professor of History at the University of New Hampshire. He is the author of *Britain and the Atlantic World in the Age of the American Revolution* (forthcoming) which was awarded the Jamestown Prize from the Institute of Early American History and Culture, and articles on British patriotism and imperial identity in *Past and Present* and *The Historical Journal*. He is currently working on the construction of civil society on Britain's imperial periphery during the seventeenth and eighteenth centuries.

ANNE F. JANOWITZ is Reader in Romanticism at the University of Warwick. She is the author of *England's Ruins: Poetic Purpose and the*

National Landscape (1990) and is completing a study of nineteenth-century interventionist poetry, "Labour and Lyric in the Romantic Tradition."

DONNA LANDRY is Professor of English at Wayne State University, Detroit. She is the author of *The Muses of Resistance: Laboring-Class Women's Poetry in Britain, 1739–1796* (1990), co-author of *Materialist Feminisms* (1993), and co-editor of *The Spivak Reader* (1996). Currently she is working on landscape, gender, and field sports in the long eighteenth century.

DAVID LOEWENSTEIN is Professor of English at the University of Wisconsin-Madison. He is the author of *Milton and the Drama of History: Historical Vision, Iconoclasm, and the Literary Imagination* (1990), and *Milton: Paradise Lost* (1993), and co-editor of *Politics, Poetics, and Hermeneutics in Milton's Prose* (1990), and *The Emergence of Quaker Writing: Dissenting Literature in Seventeenth-Century England* (1995). Currently he is co-editing the works of Gerrard Winstanley and *The Cambridge History of Early Modern English Literature: Writing in Britain from the Reformation to the Restoration*.

GERALD MACLEAN is Professor of English at Wayne State University, Detroit. He is the author of *Time's Witness: Historical Representation in English Poetry, 1603–1660* (1990), co-author of *Materialist Feminisms* (1993), editor of *Culture and Society in the Stuart Restoration: Literature, Drama, History* (1995) and co-editor of *The Spivak Reader* (1996). Currently he is editing the English poems on the Stuart Restoration while beginning research on English representations of Ottoman culture.

ROBERT MARKLEY is Jackson Distinguished Chair of British Literature at West Virginia University, Morgantown, and editor of *The Eighteenth Century: Theory and Interpretation*. His most recent book is *Fallen Languages: Crises of Representation in Newtonian England* (1993), and he is currently completing a study of economics, ecology, and literature between 1550 and 1800.

ANDREW MCRAE is U2000 postdoctoral fellow at the University of Sydney. He is the author of *God Speed the Plough: The Representation of Agrarian England, 1500–1660* (1996). Currently he is co-editing (with Stephen Bending) "Green Thoughts: The Writing of Rural England 1500–1800" for Longman Annotated Texts, and working on a historicized study of English satire, 1590–1640.

KAREN O'BRIEN is Lecturer in English Literature at the University of Wales, Cardiff. She is the author of *Narratives of Enlightenment: Cosmopolitan History from Voltaire to Gibbon* (1997). Currently she is working on a study of British poetry and the British Empire, 1650–1800.

RICHARD QUAINTANCE teaches eighteenth-century English literature at Rutgers University, New Brunswick. The present study was completed while he was a Fellow in Landscape Studies at Dumbarton Oaks, working on a book about the politicization of landscaping in the eighteenth century.

NIGEL SMITH is Reader in English at Oxford University and Fellow of Keble College. He is author of *Perfection Proclaimed: Language and Literature in English Radical Religion, 1640–1660* (1988), and *Literature and Revolution in England, 1640–1660* (1994). Currently he is editing the poetry of Andrew Marvell for Longman Annotated Texts.

ROBERT TITTLER is Professor of History at Concordia University, Montreal, where he specializes in early modern urban history. Recent publications include *The Reformation and the Towns: A Study in Politics and Political Culture* (1998), and *Architecture and Power: The Town Hall and the English Urban Community, 1500–1640* (1991).

JOSEPH P. WARD teaches history at the University of Mississippi. He is the author of *Metropolitan Communities: Trade Guilds, Identity, and Change in Early Modern London* (1997). His current research addresses London's influence on early modern provincial culture.

Acknowledgments

Chapter 2 is adapted in part from chapters 1 and 2 of *Metropolitan Communities: Trade Guilds, Identity, and Change in Early Modern London*, by Joseph P. Ward, with the permission of the publishers, Stanford University Press, © 1997 by the Board of Trustees of the Leland Stanford Junior University.

Fellowship support from the Humanities Research Center at Wayne State University helped defray initial costs of preparing the manuscript. Our thanks to Suchitra Mathur, Jodi Wyett, and Laura Wyrick for able research assistance. We are also indebted to Michelle Yucha at the Word Processing Center of Wayne State University for her skilled assistance. Andrew McRae, Richard Quaintance, and Harold Weber provided valuable suggestions for the introduction.

Our thanks to Kevin Taylor for supporting the project in its early stages, and to Josie Dixon for seeing it through so cheerfully. We would also like to thank the (anonymous) readers at Cambridge University Press for their critical wisdom.

Abbreviations and notes on the text

Place of publication for printed works is London unless otherwise stated. Spelling and punctuation in quotations from seventeenth- and eighteenth-century works follow the original. Dates are given Old Style, but with the year regarded as starting on 1 January.

Abbreviated references to works frequently cited in single chapters are indicated in endnotes following the first reference. Endnote references to works frequently cited in two or more chapters are given according to the following abbreviations.

Archer, *Pursuit of Stability*	Ian Archer, *The Pursuit of Stability: Social Relations in Elizabethan London.* (Cambridge, 1991.)
Barrell, *Idea of Landscape*	John Barrell, *The Idea of Landscape and the Sense of Place: An Approach to the Poetry of John Clare.* (Cambridge, 1972.)
Beier, *Masterless Men*	A. L. Beier, *Masterless Men: The Vagrancy Problem in England 1560–1640.* (1985.)
BL	British Library
DNB	*Dictionary of National Biography*
Helgerson, *Forms of Nationhood*	Richard Helgerson, *Forms of Nationhood: The Elizabethan Writing of England.* (Chicago, Ill., 1992.)
Manley, *Literature and Culture*	Lawrence Manley, *Literature and Culture in Early Modern London.* (Cambridge, 1995.)
McRae, *God Speed*	Andrew McRae, *God Speed the Plough: The Representation of Agrarian England, 1500–1660.* (Cambridge, 1996.)

Mullaney, *Place*	Steven Mullaney, *The Place of the Stage: License, Play, and Power in Renaissance England*. (Chicago, Ill., 1988.)
Neeson, *Commoners*	J. M. Neeson, *Commoners: Common Right, Enclosure and Social Change in England, 1700–1820*. (Cambridge, 1993.)
PRO	Public Records Office
Thompson, *Whigs and Hunters*	E. P. Thompson, *Whigs and Hunters: The Origin of the Black Act*. (New York, 1975.)
Turner, *Politics of Landscape*	James G. Turner, *The Politics of Landscape: Rural Scenery and Society in English Poetry 1630–1660*. (Oxford, 1979.)
Williams, *Country and City*	Raymond Williams, *The Country and the City*. (Oxford, 1973.)

CHAPTER I

Introduction: the country and the city revisited, c. 1550–1850

Gerald MacLean, Donna Landry, Joseph P. Ward

I

AFTER WILLIAMS

In revisiting the literary and cultural terrain mapped out by Raymond Williams in *The Country and the City* (1973), this book seeks to connect Williams's analysis of urban and rural spaces with current critical concerns. In many respects Williams's study remains "the indispensable commentary on the poetry of rural life."[1] Literary, social, and art historians, as well as geographers and social and cultural theorists, continue to invoke *The Country and the City* as a necessary starting point for any investigation of the politics of place in the formation of English cultural identity. As recently as 1996, the "incredibly rich literary analysis" of *The Country and the City* was cited, by the geographer David Harvey, for exemplifying the critical relationship between place and space.[2] Certainly, its broad historical scope – reaching across several centuries from the emergence of mercantile capitalism through its transformation by and into industrial capitalism and colonial imperialism – continues to challenge seemingly neater historical periods.

In *The Country and the City*, and perhaps more profoundly in his fiction,[3] Williams created an influential paradigm for conceiving of place and social space, country and city, the rural and the metropolitan, as dialectically related constructs, not fixed and separate entities. Yet however influential Williams's model of country and city has proved over the years, in the disciplines in which it has had most influence, critical thinking has altered in several important respects. However resonant the term "place" may be of rootedness and fixity, no place can ever be wholly abstracted from the social relationships, capital flows, cultural representations, and global forces that late-twentieth-century theorists have come to call "space."

The decades since the publication of Williams's book have seen a great deal of innovative scholarship on the politics of culture, especially the representation of social identities and their constitution in specific geographical locations, places networked within the larger web of capitalist space. As early as 1972, John Barrell was revealing the particularities of the poet John Clare's sense of place, nourished in Northamptonshire on the edge of the Lincolnshire fens. Barrell showed how Clare's sense of space had developed in the old open-field agricultural landscape before enclosure, and how Clare struggled to express an aesthetic of locality against the tides of literary convention and agricultural improvement.[4] In *The Politics of Landscape*, published in 1979, James Turner dealt with the ideological and aesthetic uses of landscape in a sophisticated, theoretically nuanced way that would prove influential.[5] The work of Leonore Davidoff and Catherine Hall on gender within middle-class families and Peter Borsay's study of the distinctive culture of provincial towns represent important developments within social history of the 1980s.[6] Geographers such as Denis Cosgrove and Stephen Daniels have radicalized the understanding of land as landscape by drawing attention to its symbolic dimensions.[7] The early 1990s saw a flourishing of similarly informed studies across the disciplines of cultural, social, literary, and art history.[8]

In the years since *The Country and the City* was published, notions of space have been theoretically developed in ways that challenge Williams's often tacit conceptions. Especially in the work of Henri Lefebvre, David Harvey, and Edward W. Soja, new conceptions of capitalist space have been formulated with regard for poststructuralist thinking across the academic disciplines.[9] If the impact of poststructuralism has most often manifested itself in a suspicion of totalizing theory and an eschewing of scientific or empiricist reductionism, these are critical imperatives that were already at the forefront of Lefebvre's project as early as 1971.[10] One of the tendencies of the new spatialization has been to disrupt "received theory and dominant metanarratives," as Harvey has argued, so it is easy to see why spatial metaphors have proved crucial for much theorizing, regardless of discipline.[11] Emphasizing the inescapability – and duplicity, or at least slipperiness – of signification within cultural practice has rendered untenable the kind of simple distinction Williams was able to make between the "real history" of social relations on the land, and mere ideologies on the other. From the point of view of more recent work, Williams's England, framed by his study window in Cambridgeshire, is itself only another image, a further gloss upon an already deeply layered text of Englishness.[12]

The rise of interdisciplinary work in history, geography, literature, and art history, combined with the broadening of the English literary canon, make a project like Williams's largely unthinkable today. For all its complex specificities, that deeply layered text was itself formulated exclusively within the parameters of literary history, and more specifically within the Cambridge English curriculum, in ways that scholars, including many of the contributors to this volume, have begun to question. The very notion of literature itself has expanded to include the writing of women and racial and ethnic minorities as well as working-class men. The texts of popular culture, including broadsides, pamphlets, newspapers, court records, and other archival materials both visual and verbal, now clamor to be read alongside the formerly canonical works of literature. The enlargement of the literary canon has complicated the field of literary and cultural studies at the same time that a new social history "from below" – focusing upon women, the working classes, colonized peoples, and ethnic and sexual minorities – has become both possible and necessary. Despite the considerable problems of retrieving evidence for the point of view of those "who left no wills, for whom no inventories were drawn up, who had few family papers, no account ledgers or bills,"[13] the popularity of writing history "from below" remains undiminished. Movements toward interdisciplinary work in both literary and historical studies have meant that historians such as J. M. Neeson may now investigate the effects of enclosure by considering the evidence of George Morland's paintings and engravings and John Clare's poetry, while literary and art historical scholars like John Barrell have analyzed what enclosure might actually have meant for Clare's parish of Helpston.[14] Williams would no doubt have approved of such developments.

Few would now consider taking on such categories as "country" and "city" across so many centuries of English history from an exclusively literary point of view. At the same time, the very Englishness of Williams's conceptual framework, which gestures toward the British Empire only in its closing chapters, would today be criticized as insufficiently attentive to questions of imperialism and colonialism. Interdisciplinary work now seeks to account for developments both within and across social history, literary studies, art history, and feminist and postcolonial theory. Any study of the politics of culture needs to challenge both old views and guard against premature orthodoxies.

Yet scholars have paid a price for their distrust of historical grand narratives. Although the new interdisciplinarity achieves argumentative complexity amidst a wealth of detail, it depends upon a retraction of vision from what was possible for Williams. The transition from feudalism to capitalism, the rise of the middle classes and the English novel, the English Revolution that ended in a Restoration of monarchy, the Agricultural and Industrial Revolutions, the making of the English working class, the rapaciousness of the empire machine: large scale explanatory narratives of this sort have come to be seen as too simple, too monolithic, and too ideologically loaded. But what has been proposed instead? Rather than substituting improved explanations for long-term changes, cultural criticism and revisionist history have mainly focused on the local and the particular. As John Brewer once observed, in place of a new grand narrative, they have offered instead many inter-related short stories.[15]

In the spirit of Williams's historical comprehensiveness, though aware of its shortcomings, this book offers a longer vista of early modern English history than is generally available in a single volume. Spanning the traditional literary and cultural periods of the Renaissance and Romanticism, the subjects of this book mark the consolidation of a national identity that, despite enormous local and regional variants, confidently imagined itself ordained to set about ruling the world. How were the English people able to remake themselves from a rough, bucolic island nation, divided amongst themselves by localized feudal loyalties, dialects and even languages, into an imperial power? How can new concepts of spatiality, of socially produced space, help us to envisage how new forms of identity emerged during this period?

II

SPACE, MERCANTILISM, IDENTITY

Williams may have represented the country and the city as dialectically related, an advance over many previous analyses, but country and city nevertheless function dichotomously in his scheme of things. Analytical categories are not the same as descriptive terms. While country and city may continue to describe concrete and specific geographical places, they do so as relational constructs within the social production of space, with its movements of capital, labor, and commodities. What Williams figured as an analytical dichotomy can be more satisfactorily grasped as a series of permeable boundaries. Certainly the explanatory force of a single urban-rural divide has been questioned in the work of Ray Pahl and other sociologists, for whom the very terms rural and urban are regarded as "more remarkable for their ability to confuse than for their power to illuminate."[16] Between 1550 and 1850, as more people traveled and migrated than ever before, differences between urban and rural cultures became less distinct even as they were increasingly reiterated as the social values that constituted Englishness.

During the whole of our period, English people, as well as the Welsh, Scots, and Irish, were perpetually on the move. For the early part of this period, vagrancy was both "the most intractable social problem," particularly between 1560 and 1640, and a crime, "the social crime par excellence," because the vagabond's status itself was criminalized, apart from any actions committed.[17] Vagrancy might be a crime, but "mobility was so pervasive that it was seen as much a natural part of the life cycle as being born or dying."[18] From the 1550s on, the greatest movement of people was from rural areas to metropolitan London and other cities and provincial towns. Poverty and ambition drove many into the suburbs, towns, and cities where they hoped to find work in a cash economy, and perhaps status and influence as well.

Yet at the same time that urban populations were expanding, there emerged a powerful counter-current in imaginative identifications, one that is still very much with us today: increasingly, for those who would be properly English, urbanity itself came to involve a rejection of life in the city for the country estate, house, or cottage. In order to avoid the filth and disease that accompanied city life, those who were very successful could return to the countryside, buy up land, and build themselves monuments to their own achievements. It is worth recalling that Ben Jonson's design in celebrating the ancient family estate of the Sidneys at Penshurst was to repudiate those nouveau mansions that had been "built to envious show."[19] Ironically, as Williams recognized, the Sidneys themselves were relative newcomers to the land, since only half a century earlier Penshurst had been given by Edward VI to William Sidney, tutor and chamberlain of the court. "That is not quite a timeless order," Williams observes, before going on to note that the very consolidation of one's profits from courtiership in an ancient pile made it "easy to complain, with an apparent humanity, against the crude grasping of the successive new men."[20]

The paradox of country life as the desirable end of urban aspirations was often resolved then, as it is now, with the convenience of a suburban residence. Although the London suburbs were socially and economically integrated with the City from at least the sixteenth century, later suburbs became more imaginatively distinct. By 1700, John

Pomfret's poem, "The Choice," which Samuel Johnson thought had been "oftener perused" than any other poem in the English language, celebrates as the best of all possible lives that of an English gentleman of means with "a private Seat, / Built Uniform, not little, nor too great," standing on a rising ground, with fields on one side and woods on the other. But far from being buried in the depths of the country, the narrator wishes to be "Near some fair Town."[21] Thus does a suburban sensibility with a genteel face emerge within polite culture in England. This development must shed new light on the flourishing of middle-class suburbanization over one hundred years later, as evidenced in the architecture, gardening, greenhouses, and house-furnishing manuals of John Claudius Loudon and Jane Webb Loudon in the 1830s and 1840s.[22]

Flows of labor and capital were both internal to Great Britain and, crucially, colonial. From port cities many departed from British shores for colonial ventures, sometimes willingly, sometimes as the objects of transportation or impressment. The movement of commodities not only paralleled but became ever more deeply interfused with the movement of people. Since chattel slaves bore the legal status of commodities, the traffic in African chattel slaves was the most spectacular form of this commodification of human labor.[23] Sugar, tobacco, and African slaves dominated the West Indian traffic, while the East India trade featured tea, silk, and porcelain. As K. N. Chaudhuri argues, these commodities initiated new conceptions of space, time, and identity: "It was not for merchants to explain, much less to speculate on, the abstract unity formed by silk, porcelain, and tea between a great Far Eastern civilisation, warmed by the tropical sun, and the inhabitants of a cold Western hemisphere."[24] But this unexplained, abstract unity bound geographically separate peoples together, plantation chattel slaves and English laborers, transported vagrants and rich merchant adventurers, as well as Far Eastern and North-Atlantic traders. The economics and culture of mercantilism made possible new identities and forms of self-construction that depended on imaginary elements frequently at odds with geography.

Relations between the British colonial project and representations of English cities and countryside began much earlier than Williams's twentieth-century focus implies. The notion of industrial labor discipline originated on the colonial sugar plantation long before its arrival in European factories, for example.[25] And the eighteenth-century landscape aesthetics that shaped and reshaped much of England's rural topography into a picturesque notion of what "the countryside" should look like belonged, as Elizabeth Bohls argues, "to a repertoire of discursive

technologies set to advance the imperial project."²⁶ English landscaped
parks and colonial plantations became not only economically but aesthetically interdependent in the course of the eighteenth century. Such
metropolitan and colonial relations seriously complicate any simple division between the urban and the rural, and these relations begin with
sixteenth-century colonial exploration.

In economic terms, this is the great age of mercantile capitalism, reaching from the Elizabethan explorers and early trading companies that
enjoyed monopoly privileges, such as the East India Company and the
Levant Company, to the era of middle-class family fortunes made by
manufacturing products, such as Cadbury's chocolate, based on the colonial economy.²⁷ Not until the 1560s, during Elizabeth I's reign, did English
poets first seriously begin to imagine the English nation, and the
British Isles, as a whole in terms of geographical space and boundaries.
While reiterating Virgil's line about the Britons inhabiting a world apart,
they also began to look inside the national coastline to examine the aston-
ishing variety of local customs and histories that made up the national
map.²⁸ Cartographers and pamphleteers, as well as poets, contributed
to the construction of new forms of nationhood. The great Elizabethan
chorographical artists and writers followed roads and rivers inland to
discover and describe ancient cities, local heroes, river nymphs, and other
curious spirits of place along the way.

Keeping international trade-routes open frequently meant going to
war in the name of one's country, even as trade offered imaginary alternatives to violent conquest that redefined both *what* that country was and
where it was to be found. Largely through the agency of the press, an
essentially urban civic and political culture – one based on writing and
reading – came to assert itself far beyond the legislative world of the
Court, Parliament, and the great landowners. It became increasingly
possible to be non-aristocratic, and yet nationally powerful beyond one's
immediate place, as studies of provincial towns, English merchants, and
middle-class families, have shown.²⁹ In pursuing these developments, this
book seeks to challenge the courtly, aristocratic, and London-centered
approaches that still tend to predominate in literary and cultural histories of the English in the era before industrialization.

This "long" mercantilist moment, between the Renaissance and
Romanticism, was crucial to Williams's chief concern in *The Country and
the City*: the development of literary forms and structures that both insinu-
ated and resisted attempts to make the newly emergent capitalist relations appear fundamental to English life. Although images of country

life had been invoked for centuries to criticize urban corruption, and to posit a golden age of social harmony that had only recently vanished over the historical horizon, there was a particular urgency to English projections of vanishing rural virtues between the reigns of Elizabeth and Victoria. The mercantilist moment, celebrating imperial expansion and English greatness at home and abroad, depended upon a certain confidence, a certainty of identity as buoyant as the great ships of mercantile trade. This confident assertion of national superiority and resourcefulness, summed up in William Blackstone's description of the English as "a polite and commercial people," would no longer prove tenable beyond the early decades of the nineteenth century.[30] The aftermath of the American War of Independence, colonial and slave rebellions, the French Revolution and the Napoleonic Wars that followed, contributed not only to an agricultural crisis marked by a severe falling-off in agricultural productivity and prosperity, but also a crisis of political confidence in British imperial governance. After mid-century, Victorian imperial ambitions would be couched in a new rhetoric of defensiveness or bellicose bombast. If there had ever been such a thing as mercantilist innocence, it did not survive the era of Romanticism and the coming of the railway.

III
A BRIEF HISTORY, NOT OF TIME BUT OF SPACE

As we have seen, between 1550 and 1850 a profound shift occurred in the balance between the urban and rural populations of England, with particular consequences for the making of social identities. What did this shift mean in terms of physical places and social space? During the sixteenth century, most men and women worked in the agrarian sector and lived in the countryside, while fewer than five percent of them lived in towns. By the middle of the nineteenth century that had changed so dramatically that towns with more than 10,000 inhabitants together comprised roughly half the population of England. While English society was becoming more urban, the relations both among and between towns and their surrounding regions changed as well. Through the seventeenth century, London dominated provincial towns; by the outset of the eighteenth century its population was nearly twenty times that of Norwich, the next largest town, and nearly thirty times that of Bristol, the third largest. During the eighteenth century, the populations of many provincial towns, including several that were little more than sprawling villages, began to rise at an increasingly rapid pace. By the early nineteenth century urban centers such as Manchester, Liverpool, and Birmingham were experiencing growth rates far higher than London's, though their populations were no more than one-tenth that of the metropolis. However, the combination of industrialization and the expansion of internal trade meant that provincial towns not only dwarfed their pre-industrial counterparts, but they emerged from beneath London's shadow.[31]

While there are many obstacles to gauging the metropolitan population with any precision before the 1801 census, the best estimates of the City of London's population in the early years of Elizabeth's reign place it at around 100,000, with an additional 30,000 or so in the nearby suburbs, such as Westminster. Over the next century and a half, the metropolis grew rapidly, if not steadily, until it contained half a million people by 1700, most of them living in suburban areas that had developed in formerly rural parts of Middlesex and Surrey. The relatively high mortality rate in London required huge inflows of immigrants who, responding to population pressures in the countryside, sought better fortunes in towns.[32] The relatively rapid growth of London sparked both praise and criticism from contemporaries. In a sermon published in 1620 in the hope of inspiring King James to renovate St. Paul's cathedral, Bishop John King offered the many marvelous buildings and institutions of London – such as the Royal Exchange, the livery company halls, and hospitals for the poor – as evidence that London had become an "Augustius and majestical city" fit for a great cathedral. But King directed his remarks to a monarch who had already taken steps to stem metropolitan growth from fear that "Soon London will be all England."[33]

The fortunes of provincial towns varied widely during the sixteenth and seventeenth centuries, with most undergoing periods of economic and demographic stagnation, followed by considerable improvements after the Restoration. Leading provincial centers such as Norwich, York, and Exeter continued to dominate important economic regions. Middle-size towns such as Coventry, however, failed to adapt to the emergence of a national distribution network for retail goods centered in London, and consequently saw much of their commercial activity being slowly siphoned away to other towns. Yet where a town's merchants and manufacturers adapted to developing domestic and, increasingly, international markets, then it could continue to prosper throughout the period. The population of Bristol, for example, doubled during the years

1550–1700, and then doubled again during the eighteenth century because its traders successfully expanded their interests beyond nearby ports in France and Spain toward the burgeoning markets in the West Indies and the Chesapeake, thereby encouraging the development of local industries such as sugar refining and the manufacture of tobacco pipes.[34]

Urban growth was made possible by the greater output of raw materials and the steady improvement of the means of transporting them to markets. The growing population in south-eastern counties – and above all in London – contributed to shortages of wood for use in building and as fuel. An increased demand for coal, supplied principally from the Tyneside collieries, in turn encouraged the vast expansion of both mining and shipbuilding in the north-east.[35] Metropolitan growth was thus a catalyst for the urbanization of a region on the other side of the kingdom. At the same time, the higher productivity of agriculture made labor available for a wide array of by-employments in rural areas. The gradual emergence of rural communities that combined agrarian with manufacturing work – a process often referred to as "proto-industrialization" – was well underway in the sixteenth century and continued right into the nineteenth century as domestic and international markets expanded. Entrepreneurs, based in towns, took advantage of the willingness of rural people to supplement their incomes with waged labor to produce a wide array of goods ranging from textiles to nails.[36]

One of the great engines of such demand was the growth of middle-class consumerism, which had emerged during the late seventeenth and early eighteenth centuries largely as a result of increasing profits from commerce, industry, and the professions. In his study of this process in London, Peter Earle suggests that while it is difficult to isolate the specificities of middle-class culture, unmistakeable desires and associated activities emerged: collecting certain kinds of objects – clocks, newspapers, novels – purchasing fire insurance, engaging in tea-drinking, joining social clubs, and for men, the new three-piece suit of coat, waistcoat, and knee-breeches. Peter Borsay's work on the related phenomenon of the "urban Renaissance" of the late seventeenth and early eighteenth centuries demonstrates that in matters of taste and style, London set the example for provincial towns, though there was certainly room for local variations. This emergence of middle-class culture was largely – though not exclusively – urban, since it relied on polite sociability. Urban, indeed urbane, spaces such as coffee-houses, town squares, the meeting halls of scientific societies, lending libraries, spas, and walks, provided the socially mobile with spaces and opportunities to see and to be seen. Although most often tied to specific domestic locations, middle-class culture also embraced many previously exotic forms of behavior, such as consuming tea, cocoa, and coffee – with sugar, of course. Records of circulating libraries and book clubs in towns such as Nottingham, Leeds, Colne, and Bristol, demonstrate from the 1730s onward a shift in interest away from books on divinity and metaphysics toward titles dealing with travel and exploration, suggesting a broadening and secularizing of interests among those whose business concerns were increasingly global.[37]

One of the most enthusiastic observers of the conditions of towns and the proliferation of middle-class culture during the early eighteenth century was Daniel Defoe. While he acknowledged in 1722 that London "sucks the vitals of trade in this island to itself," thereby sapping the prosperity East Anglian port towns such as Ipswich, that had once flourished as regional commercial centers, he also noted the varying fortunes of towns further afield.[38] He found successful models in those places with

some particular trade or accident to trade, which is a kind of nostrum to them, inseparable to the place . . . as the herring-fishery to Yarmouth; the coal trade to New-Castle; the Leeds clothing-trade; the export of butter and lead, and the great corn trade for Holland, is to Hull; the Virginia and West-India trade at Liverpool, the Irish trade to Bristol, and the like.[39]

Since England was still largely rural during the time of Defoe's travels, he had many occasions to comment on life in the countryside. But he always remembered that he was directing his remarks to a middle-class audience. When describing the working conditions and domestic lives of Derbyshire lead-miners, including a family who lived in a cave, yet displayed both manners and consumer durables of pewter and brass, he announced that his aim was "to show the discontented part of the rich world how to value their own happiness."[40]

While the towns of eighteenth-century England provided those who inhabited "the rich world" with a wide array of options for consumption and polite sociability, for laboring people they often offered only economic insecurity. In London and the south, an oversupply of cheap labor depressed real wages from the mid-eighteenth century until at least the conclusion of the French wars. Wandering the chartered streets in "London" (1794), William Blake expressed the desperation that many town-dwellers must have felt, noticing "Marks of weakness,

marks of woe" in every face he met and hearing everywhere a clam-
orous misery:

> In every cry of every man,
> In every Infant's cry of fear,
> In every voice, in every ban,
> The mind-forg'd manacles I hear.[41]

Blake's lines gain power from their appearance during the outset of what
would be several years of food shortages – perhaps accounting for the
"Marks of weakness" and the "Infant's cry of fear" – a time when
Londoners, like city-dwellers across England, were painfully reminded
of their dependence upon the output of the countryside.[42]

In the newer and expanding industrial centers of the midlands and
north of England, laborers fared much better than their counterparts
in the south. But even here there were considerable fluctuations over
time and variations across industries and skill levels.[43] In these areas,
however, economic prosperity led to explosive population growth in
recently rural areas, and to the creation of sprawling slums. Among
the most passionate critics of the growth of industrial towns – and the
economic relations that made them possible – was Friedrich Engels.
Writing in 1844, a century and a quarter after Defoe, Engels deplored
the results of the entrepreneurial processes that Defoe had praised:

The dwellings of the workers are everywhere badly planned, badly built, and
kept in the worst condition, badly ventilated, damp, and unwholesome. The
inhabitants are confined to the smallest possible space, and at least one family usually sleeps in each room. The interior arrangement of the dwellings is
poverty-stricken in various degrees, down to the utter absence of even the most
necessary furniture.[44]

It is as if Defoe's cave-dwelling lead miners have moved themselves –
and their cave – to the city, but have left their manners, their pewter,
and their brass behind. The city has indeed expanded to encompass
the countryside and its residents, degrading each along the way.

Clearly, many of the changes in both country and city often
assumed to have taken place during the nineteenth and twentieth centuries in fact represent late stages in processes of change that had begun
much earlier, in the early modern period investigated in this book.
Between 1550 and 1850, but most conspicuously during the eighteenth
century, the capitalization of agriculture was a project largely undertaken by those landowners whom Pomfret figures as living the ideal life,
those embodiments of "gentlemanly capitalism" who would make their

mark on both countryside and colonies.[45] As P. J. Cain and A. G. Hopkins argue, the "peculiar character of the modern British aristocracy was shaped by merging its pre-capitalist heritage with incomes derived from commercial agriculture."[46] Between 1688 and 1850, City of London financiers and providers of services, great overseas merchants, and merchant bankers, in effect apprenticed themselves to the landed interest, thus creating "a form of capitalism headed by improving landlords in association with improving financiers who served as their junior partners."[47]

Contrary to many literary scholars' continuing fixation upon late eighteenth- and early nineteenth-century parliamentary enclosures as the epitome of capitalist agriculture, recent work by historians attempts to distinguish between the history of enclosure per se and technologies of agrarian transformation. We need to look to the sixteenth and seventeenth centuries for the mass of English enclosures, since by 1700, according to Eric Kerridge, only "about one-quarter of the enclosure of England and Wales remained to be undertaken."[48] Between 1540 and 1700 a "great spurt in production" occurred, ushering in the agricultural developments that would dominate the years between 1560 and 1767.[49] Attempting to reconcile the findings of both agricultural historians and historians of enclosure, Robert C. Allen has identified "two agricultural revolutions in English history," the yeomen's and the landlords'.[50] The yeomen's is the one which Kerridge has examined, a mainly seventeenth-century revolution in productivity brought about by yeomen and small farmers, though its legal basis was laid in the sixteenth century. The landlords' revolution, consisting of the final waves of parliamentary enclosure, but more importantly of engrossment of land and farm amalgamation, began in the fifteenth century but happened mainly during the eighteenth, according to Allen. Rather than increasing output and distributing its benefits widely, as had happened in the seventeenth century, this revolution concentrated benefits among the elite owners of large estates through higher rents and a reduction in agricultural labor. Allen's conclusion is, he claims, "unavoidable – most English men and women would have been better off had the landlords' revolution never occurred."[51] Even recent non-Marxist historians such as J. R. Wordie have admitted that, if the English system did not actively drive people off the land through parliamentary enclosure, it nevertheless prevented people from *getting onto* the land as population grew. In this way, the English system, devised and operated by English landlords, *made available* a labour supply for industry, although it did not *create* it."[52]

The internal travel demanded by commerce, agricultural improvement, and the factory system soon came to be supplemented by the internal travel we now call tourism. In the diverse regions of the first industrialized nation in the world, local identities shaped themselves against the projection of an increasingly imaginary rural English past. For more than a century by 1850, English tourists had been seeking to escape from the squalor of urban areas to picturesque countryside and sublime highland landscapes. At the same time, painted and printed images of rural life became "portable icons of England" for those who had left – "urban dwellers with real or imagined rural origins, colonists and imperial administrators in South Africa or India, soldiers."[53]

At the end of the twentieth century, the English countryside has become, on the one hand, the site of agribusiness or industrialized farming, and on the other, a place of recreation and retreat from cities and towns. Today it is difficult to recapture the early modern sense of suburbs as places where city artisans and merchants both lived and worked. Although suburbs today remain as economically linked to the city as ever, they represent a widespread compromise between the rural ideal and urban economic necessity. The origins of this compromise can be traced to the second half of the eighteenth century, as can the continuing English preoccupation with walking as a leisure activity. Going for country walks is the second most common recreation in Britain today, after watching television.[54] By the end of our period, walking, once the last resort of the indigent traveler, had become a fashionable form of recreation for the middle and upper classes.[55] Vagrants, formerly criminalized for their status as mobile beings, became Romantic figures of freedom in the popular imagination. The weekend gypsy and the suburban *flaneur* began to hover on the edges of imaginative possibility just as the factory worker and the industrial capitalist became new identities signifying the emergence of a modern England.

IV

IDENTITIES AND SPACES

The cultural consequences of England's transformation from an agrarian and largely insular nation into an urban and industrial seat of empire can best be understood through a variety of sources and methodologies. No single category, approach, or method will do justice to what we think we know about the complex relation between space and identity, both as experienced and as represented, in England between 1550 and 1850.

Between the city and the country stands the suburb, and as we have seen, the construction of metropolitan space has necessitated the building of new suburbs and the suburbanization of older rural communities for several centuries. Whether a suburb denotes the expensive green retreat of reluctant city-dwellers, or a cheap supplementary bedroom community for workers who cannot afford to live in town, the twentieth-century suburb has often been the object of scorn and derision. Yet in the late sixteenth and early seventeenth centuries, the emergence of London as a metropolis, and thus the City's very claims to urbanity, depended upon suburban expansion outside the walls of the medieval City of London itself. Joseph Ward identifies the profound interdependence of the City and its suburbs during this period. Countering the assumptions of some historians and many literary critics that London's suburbs were unanimously regarded by citizens as licentious foreign territory, Ward discovers a number of contemporary observers insisting on "the moral integrity of the entire metropolis" in contradistinction to diatribes against the "sinfully polluted suburbs." Ward also offers a new interpretation of the involvement of livery companies and their members in the suburban economy. Only after reformers acknowledged the moral failings of city-dwellers rather than blaming all disasters on suburbanites, and after livery company members were forced to admit their reliance on suburban markets, did Londoners come to imagine themselves as residents of a metropolis.

Despite a great upsurge in mobility, English people in this period had difficulty imagining themselves as travelers unless they went abroad. To be English in England meant being placed, rooted, locally identified. In spite of a mobile gentry actively engaged in a national land market, and vagrants and subsistence migrants taking to the road in unprecedented numbers during the later sixteenth century, to "travel" in sixteenth-century England meant to leave the nation's shores. This discursive framework has obscured the importance of internal travel before the mid-1600s. As Andrew McRae observes, a "powerful discourse of settlement shaped the practices of contemporary administrators and social commentators, and has subsequently informed approaches to historical analysis." Arguing for a recognition of the importance of internal travel in the production of a "capitalist space," McRae aims to recover the shifting range of meanings attached to geographical mobility within England by contemporaries. He discovers that, while "Tudor moralists insistently proclaim the virtues of place, by the early seventeenth century texts increasingly consider the importance of mobility, depicting men and women of middling and lower degree on the move."

Yet the rapid growth of metropolitan London and the phenomenon of cross-country travel in predominantly rural spaces were not the only conditions generating newly emergent forms of English identity in the late sixteenth and early seventeenth centuries. What about life in the provinces? Was provincial urban culture derived from London and court culture, as has often been assumed, or might it have certain indigenous origins? According to Robert Tittler, the commemoration of civic worthies in portraits commissioned by civic authorities represents an ideal test case in this debate. At this time of economic, social, and political upheaval, civic leaders "sought ways of projecting civic virtues, appropriating worthy models of civic consciousness, and tying the town's present identity to its past." In this effort civic portraits proved an important innovation, Tittler argues, by representing civic benefactors as objects "not of self-fashioning," as in court culture, "but of a civic fashioning, projected by the urban leadership of the day toward the putative citizenry in the hope of remodelling the ambient political culture of their specific communities."

Perhaps the most radical innovation in rural culture by the time of the Civil War was the Digger movement for agrarian communism, fuelled by the writings of Gerrard Winstanley, a bankrupt cloth merchant. In April 1649, three months after the execution of Charles I, Winstanley, accompanied by a small group of penniless laborers, began digging, manuring, and planting the common land at St. George's Hill in Surrey, not far from London. As David Loewenstein argues, the Diggers' community, which attempted to transform the earth into "a common treasury for all," was an "acute response to the failures of the Revolution and its experimental Commonwealth." The Diggers' action was not so much a rural escape from economic oppression as a protest aimed at the nearby urban sprawl of London, designed to draw attention to the Diggers' "alienation from the politics and policies of the Interregnum." Not for the first time in English history, and certainly not for the last, symbolic and social action fused on the land, creating "a new kind of social identity based on communal property." Loewenstein contends that the Diggers, though "too radical for the Revolution and the cautious Republic it had generated," nevertheless "boldly challenged and defined the Revolution's limitations, while in their visionary writings they acutely analyzed and represented some of its deepest contradictions."

Robert Markley identifies powerful contradictions also at work in the discourses and practices of forestry, particularly after the Civil Wars. Markley argues that Marvell's poem "Upon Appleton House," when considered in the context of contemporary treatises on forestry and agricultural improvement, both reflects and helps to shape "profound anxieties about the degradation of the environment and the resulting scarcity of essential resources, notably timber." Progressivist historians, such as Eric Kerridge, have celebrated the agricultural revolution as a triumph of productivity through intensification. Ecologists, however, recognize that there can be no intensification of production without the eventual depletion of the resources which such technologies have made available. Markley's reading of Marvell reveals "the tensions between competing ecological and economic models of the land" that are repressed within progressivist narratives of modernity.

If Markley suggested we should re-read triumphalist agricultural history to uncover the ecological other it has repressed, Nigel Smith proposes that we re-think the traditional polarization within intellectual history of "enthusiasm" and "Enlightenment." In the case of Thomas Tryon – vegetarian, follower of the mystic Jacob Boehme, and abolitionist – Smith finds ample evidence of a radical artisanal philosophy based in both mysticism and an experimental and practical engagement with its energies. Tryon's system of bodily self-regulation and rejection of luxury, including plantocratic slavery as well as the excesses of commercial society, is, according to Smith, "nothing other than the elaboration of a radical Puritan agenda, one that had been embryonically formed in the 1650s by others," including Winstanley. Tryon's is "a transformed enthusiasm," anticipating Kant in its critical deployment of contemplative mysticism. Traditional intellectual history has encouraged us to dichotomize enthusiasm and enlightenment, but in Tryon's system, Smith argues, "enthusiasm becomes enlightenment, and seeks to redeem the world from the terror of meat and the sweet violence of sugar."

Defenders of forests, suburban Diggers, and urban vegetarians are forms of seventeenth-century social identity that resonate with late twentieth-century concerns. All three identities suggest something of that imaginative dislocation of identity from specific geographical places we have observed arising from physical mobility, the growing commodification of labor, and the effects of expanding markets. By the mid-eighteenth century, what Anne Janowitz has termed "the coincidence of country and country"[56] was imaginatively in place, but increasingly strained by differences between urban and rural points of view. "Without question," Eliga Gould argues, "appealing to an idealized notion of the country often worked to cloak political activities which had their origin in Parliament and the urban press in the authoritative mantle of England's rural past." Gould's example of such a policy is the elder William Pitt's intrusive and widely resented attempt to reform the English militia during the Seven Years' War, the Militia Act of 1757, which sparked some of "most serious rural riots of the eighteenth century." Subjecting all able-bodied men to a compulsory ballot regardless of their social position or personal wealth, this new law demonstrated the regulatory potential of the rhetoric of patriotism – and its unpopularity. The countryside as imagined from Westminster was a very different place from a countryside full of actual English people, for whom patriotism remained "more a public spectacle or artifact for mass consumption than a virtue to be sustained by personal participation."

On the estates of English grandees, however, efforts were made to keep such rural unrest literally out of sight and beyond the park palings, while inviting the attention of tourists. Collections of engravings of country estates, such as those produced by Jacques Rigaud in the 1730s, began not to be peopled with merely anonymous figures to give scale and perspective to the spot, but with recognizable personages. In such collections, eagerly pored over by object-collecting middle-class urbanites, Richard Quaintance discovers an early form of celebrity chasing. Rigaud's eye "for purchasers ready to be teased by a brush with 'celebrity'," Quaintance observes, "thus bequeaths us a sequence of sketchy on-the-spot portraits of four trend-setting Whig proprietors, their families, and, in their entourages, the leading poet, the leading landscape-designer, and a leading castrato of the moment." The effect of such innovations by Rigaud and the English engravers who followed his lead, Quaintance argues, was to demystify place-making, "leaving English ground visually more accessible to more people" than it had ever been before.

It could be said that expanding "English" ground across the globe and rendering it not visually, but verbally, more accessible to more people than it had ever been before, was the task of the imperial georgic poem. Karen O'Brien takes issue with earlier literary historians who have explained the popularity of georgic verse between 1688 and 1789 purely in terms of literary fashion and changing taste. Instead, O'Brien links the rise of georgic and similarly descriptive kinds of poetry "to a new and growing awareness of the British Empire." She finds "the agricultural landscape of these poems imbued with a sense of spatial and economic continuity with the wider imperial world." In an age suspicious of epic and romance, the adaptability of the georgic middle style "that could rise to national prophecy and rapture or descend to technical detail without breaching generic decorum" proved "highly attractive to poets wishing to communicate the elation of empire, the moral dangers which it could bring, and the mechanics of its implementation."

As important for the imperial project as georgic verse was the discourse of landscape aesthetics. Elizabeth Bohls examines how, in the case of Jamaica's colonial historian, Edward Long, landscape aesthetics "belonged to a repertoire of discursive technologies" that were crucial for imperial expansion and the perpetuation of the colonial sugar industry. Long himself represents a new form of social identity, "that peculiar hybrid, the colonial gentleman planter," as Bohls puts it. "Patterned on the English country gentleman and borrowing his prestige," Bohls argues, yet potentially embarrassed by his unmediated reliance upon a slave economy, the gentleman planter's identity "depends on a central paradox: imposing metropolitan sameness on the very different place that is the colony for the purpose of defending that place's indispensable local difference, namely, the institution of slavery."

Reconfiguring identities back home is, according to Elizabeth Heckendorn Cook, the subject of Frances Burney's last novel, *The Wanderer* (1814), which transposes the georgic mode for female narrative purposes while also georgically recuperating the monarchy of George III. On one hand, Cook finds Burney's "gendered inflection of the georgic mode" an "important – and implicitly feminist – gesture," perhaps even a claim about the future of "actual women in British society . . . bringing together the discourses of literary georgic, landscape aesthetics, natural history and property law." On the other hand, as Cook discovers, it is only "by marking the New Forest as the property of the benevolent Farmer George, and *Father* George – that is, as a doubly patriarchal terrain – does Burney obtain a place for her heroine within it." These "domestications" of the crown forest indicate, Cook argues, that "this terrain is no longer the feudal theater of monarchical charisma and prerogative, nor yet merely a political economist's neutral repository of marketable resources." Instead, as both Burney's and George III's uses of it demonstrate, the crown forest can now serve "as a screen on which to project images of a new society, dramas of reconciliation and transformation, and fantasies of personal, professional, and political identity."

In the figures of the Gypsy and the Jew we can observe equally phantasmatic versions of rural and urban identity, mercantilist fantasies of new forms of social being. Throughout the long early modern period, such figures represented perpetual mobility as a threat to social order.

As Anne Janowitz explains, the "exchange between metropolitan and rural culture that both Gypsies and Jews exemplify is grounded in historical processes at work since the mid-sixteenth century." But by the late eighteenth and early nineteenth centuries, these figures assume a particular urgency in the poetry of William Wordsworth and John Clare that marks a certain historical specificity, and registers the end of the mercantilist moment and the beginning of modern industrial culture. Although, as Janowitz concludes, Jewish peddlers and traveling Gypsy crews might barely be distinguishable from the large numbers of other people displaced through parish exclusion, enclosure, failed harvests, and the press gang, their importance as images in poetry resides in the way they support the imagining of identity in a transitional world – one poised between customary and waged labor.

In the Afterword, John Barrell reconsiders notions of space and identity he initially explored in relation to Clare in *The Idea of Landscape* (1972). Engaging some of the central ideas put forward in the present book regarding the emergence of capitalist space, Barrell goes on to complicate as well as clarify these ideas by analyzing two texts from the 1740s that "offer radically different accounts of space," *The Life and Adventures* of Bampfylde-Moore Carew, and John Dyer's "Commercial Map of England." Carew's "gypsy" narrative might seem pre-industrial and backward-looking, while Dyer's manuscript appears to epitomize the rationalization of commodity circulation; but things are in fact a bit more complicated than that. Attending to the precise configurations of space in each text, Barrell suggests how intricate was the knotting together of metropolis and periphery during the mercantilist era.

NOTES

1 John Barrell, "Sportive Labour: The Farmworker in Eighteenth-Century Poetry and Painting," in Brian Short, ed., *The English Rural Community: Image and Analysis* (Cambridge, 1992), pp. 105–32, this passage p. 132, n. 10.
2 "Militant Particularism and Global Ambition," the first chapter of Harvey's *Justice, Nature and the Geography of Difference* (Oxford, 1996), pp. 19–45, is devoted to a critical appraisal of Williams's use of the terms "environment," "space," and "place"; this passage p. 30.
3 See Harvey, *Justice*, pp. 23–39.
4 See Barrell, *Idea of Landscape*.
5 Turner, *Politics of Landscape*.
6 Davidoff and Hall, *Family Fortunes: Men and Women of the English Middle Class, 1780–1850* (Chicago, Ill., 1987); Borsay, *The English Urban Renaissance: Culture and Society in the Provincial Town, 1660–1770* (Oxford, 1989).

7 Cosgrove and Daniels, eds., *The Iconography of Landscape: Essays on the Symbolic Representation, Design and Use of Past Environments* (Cambridge, 1988).
8 See, for example, McRae, *God Speed*; Nicholas Green, *The Spectacle of Nature: Landscape and Bourgeois Culture in Nineteenth-Century France* (Manchester, 1990); Michael Leslie and Timothy Raylor, eds., *Culture and Cultivation in Early Modern England: Writing and the Land* (Leicester, 1992); John Barrell, ed., *Painting and the Politics of Culture: New Essays on British Art, 1700–1850* (Oxford, 1992); and Andrew Hemingway, *Landscape Imagery and Urban Culture in Early Nineteenth-Century Britain* (Cambridge, 1992).
9 See Lefebvre, *The Production of Space* (1974), trans. Donald Nicholson-Smith (Oxford, 1991); Harvey, *Social Justice and the City* (1973), *Consciousness and the Urban Experience* (1985); and Soja's spirited defense of Lefebvre, "Spatializations: Marxist Geography and Critical Social Theory" in *Postmodern Geographies: The Reassertion of Space in Critical Social Theory* (1989), pp. 43–75.
10 See Lefebvre, *Au-delà du structuralisme* (Paris, 1971).
11 Harvey, *Justice*, p. 9.
12 See Cosgrove and Daniels, eds., *Iconography*, pp. 7–8.
13 Neeson, *Commoners*, p. 11.
14 See Neeson, *Commoners*, and Barrell, *Idea of Landscape*.
15 John Brewer, commentary, seminar on "Culture and Consumption," Center for Seventeenth- and Eighteenth-Century Studies, UCLA, November 1990.
16 Pahl cited in Michael Winstanley, "The New Culture of the Countryside," in G. E. Mingay, ed., *The Vanishing Countryman* (1989), pp. 142–54; this passage p. 142.
17 Beier, *Masterless Men*, p. xxii.
18 Peter Clark and David Souden, eds., Introduction, *Migration and Society in Early Modern England* (1987), pp. 11–48, this passage p. 22.
19 "To Penshurst," in *Ben Jonson: A Critical Edition of the Major Works*, ed. Ian Donaldson (Oxford, 1985), p. 282.
20 Williams, *Country and City*, p. 41.
21 Johnson, *Lives of the English Poets*, ed. George Birkbeck Hill, 3 vols. (Oxford, 1905), I: 302; [Pomfret], *The Choice. A Poem*, By a Person of Quality (1700), lines 5–8.
22 J. C. Loudon's best-known book of many was *The Suburban Gardener and Villa Companion* (1838); his wife Jane not only helped him to edit and produce his own work, but also wrote nineteen books herself, including the popular *The Lady's Companion to the Flower Garden* (1841). See Davidoff and Hall, *Family Fortunes*, pp. 188–92.
23 See David Brion Davis, *The Problem of Slavery in Western Culture* (Ithaca, N.Y., 1966), and Paul Gilroy, *The Black Atlantic: Modernity and Double Consciousness* (Cambridge, Mass., 1993).
24 K. N. Chaudhuri, *Asia Before Europe: Economy and Civilisation of the Indian Ocean from the Rise of Islam to 1750* (Cambridge, 1990), p. 122.
25 See Sidney Mintz, *Sweetness and Power: The Place of Sugar in Modern History* (New York, 1985), pp. 46–52.

26 See Bohls' chapter in this book, p. 180. On the invention of "the country-side" as a generalized aesthetic unity, see Donna Landry, "The Invention of the Countryside: Pope, the 'Idiocy of Rural Life,' and the Intellectual View from the Suburbs," in James E. Gill, ed., *Cutting Edges: Postmodern Critical Essays on Eighteenth-Century Satire* (Knoxville, Tenn., 1995), pp. 301–19.

27 On the Cadburys of Birmingham, see Davidoff and Hall, *Family Fortunes*, pp. 52–9.

28 See Gerald MacLean, *Time's Witness: Historical Representation in English Poetry, 1603–1660* (Madison, Wisc., 1990), pp. 64–126; Helgerson, *Forms of Nationhood*; and Clair McEachern, *The Poetics of English Nationhood, 1590–1612* (Cambridge, 1996).

29 See Borsay, *Urban Renaissance*; Robert Tittler, *Architecture and Power: The Town Hall and the English Urban Community c. 1500–1640* (Oxford, 1991); Robert Brenner, *Merchants and Revolution: Commercial Change, Political Conflict, and London's Overseas Traders, 1550–1653* (Cambridge, 1993); and Davidoff and Hall, *Family Fortunes*.

30 See Paul Langford, *A Polite and Commercial People: England 1727–1783* (Oxford, 1992), p. 1.

31 See Joyce Youings, *Sixteenth-Century England* (Harmondsworth, 1984), p. 66; Roger Schofield, "British Population Change, 1700–1871," in Roderick Floud and Donald McCloskey, eds., *The Economic History of Britain since 1700*, 2nd edn., 3 vols. (Cambridge, 1994), 1: 88–9.

32 See Vanessa Harding, "The Population of London, 1550–1700: A Review of the Published Evidence," *London Journal* 15: 2 (1990): 111–28; Jonathan Barry, Introduction, in Barry, ed., *The Tudor and Stuart Town, 1530–1688: A Reader in English Urban History* (1990), p. 4; A. L. Beier and Roger Findlay, Introduction, in Beier and Findlay, eds., *London 1500–1700: The Making of the Metropolis* (1986), pp. 9–10; and M. J. Kitch, "Capital and Kingdom: Migration to Later Stuart London" in Beier and Findlay, eds., *London 1500–1700*, pp. 224–51.

33 King, *A Sermon Preached at Paul's Cross on Behalfe of Paules Church* (1620), p. 45; James I, cited in E. A. Wrigley, *People, Cities and Wealth: The Transformation of Traditional Society* (Oxford, 1987), p. 133.

34 Among the many surveys of urban fortunes in the early modern period, the best include Peter Clark and Paul Slack, eds., *English Towns in Transition, 1500–1700* (Oxford, 1976), Penelope Corfield, *The Impact of English Towns, 1700–1800* (Oxford, 1982), Barry, ed., *The Tudor and Stuart Town*, and Peter Borsay, ed., *The Eighteenth-Century Town: A Reader in English Urban History, 1688–1820* (1990). See also David Harris Sacks, *The Widening Gate: Bristol and the Atlantic Economy, 1450–1700* (Berkeley and Los Angeles, Calif., 1991), and Ronald M. Berger, *The Most Necessary Luxuries: The Mercers' Company of Coventry, 1550–1680* (University Park., Pa., 1993).

35 See Joan Thirsk, *Agricultural Regions and Agrarian History in England, 1500–1750* (Basingstoke, Hants, 1987); David Levine and Keith Wrightson, *The Making of an Industrial Society: Whickham, 1560–1765* (Oxford, 1991), pp. 1–10.

36 See Michael Zell, *Industry in the Countryside: Wealden Society in the Sixteenth Century* (Cambridge, 1994), and John Rule, *The Vital Century: England's Developing Economy, 1714–1815* (1992), pp. 16–27.

37 See Peter Earle, *The Making of the English Middle Class: Business, Society and Family Life in London, 1660–1730* (Berkeley and Los Angeles, Calif., 1989), pp. 281–2, 336; Borsay, *Urban Renaissance*; Jonathan Barry and Christopher Brooks, eds., *The Middling Sort of People: Culture, Society and Politics in England, 1550–1800* (New York, 1994); John Smail, *The Origins of Middle-Class Culture: Halifax, Yorkshire, 1660–1780* (Ithaca, N.Y., 1994); Margaret Hunt, "Racism, Imperialism, and the Traveler's Gaze in Eighteenth-Century England," *Journal of British Studies* 32: 4 (October 1993): 333–57, and *The Middling Sort: Commerce, Gender, and the Family in England, 1680–1780* (Berkeley and Los Angeles, Calif., 1996), pp. 188–92.

38 Defoe, *A Tour Through the Whole Island of Great Britain*, ed. Pat Rogers (Harmondsworth, 1971), p. 68.

39 Ibid., pp. 68–9.

40 Ibid., p. 462.

41 Blake, *The Complete Writings*, ed. Geoffrey Keynes (Oxford, 1972), p. 216.

42 See Susan E. Brown, " 'A Just and Profitable Commerce': Moral Economy and the Middle Classes in Eighteenth-Century London," *Journal of British Studies* 32: 4 (October, 1993): 305–32.

43 See Peter H. Lindert, "Unequal Living Standards," in Floud and McCloskey, eds., *Economic History*, I: 357–86.

44 Engels, *The Condition of the Working Class in England*, ed. David McLellan (Oxford, 1993), p. 85.

45 P. J. Cain and A. G. Hopkins, *British Imperialism: Innovation and Expansion, 1688–1914* (1993), p. 12.

46 Ibid., p. 24.

47 Ibid., p. 101.

48 Eric Kerridge, *The Agricultural Revolution* (1967), p. 24.

49 Ibid., pp. 336, 328. Kerridge argues that all the "main achievements" of this agricultural revolution "fell before 1720, most of them before 1673, and many of them much earlier still," p. 328.

50 Allen, *Enclosure and the Yeoman* (Oxford, 1992), p. 21.

51 Ibid., p. 21.

52 J. R. Wordie, "Introduction," in C. W. Chalklin and J. R. Wordie, eds., *Town and Countryside: The English Landowner in the National Economy, 1660–1860* (1989), pp. 1–25, this passage p. 19.

53 Elizabeth K. Helsinger, *Rural Scenes and National Representation: Britain, 1815–1850* (Princeton, N.J., 1997), p. 7.

54 Nigel Duckers and Huw Davies, *A Place in the Country* (1990), p. 155.

55 See Anne D. Wallace, *Walking, Literature, and English Culture: The Origins and Uses of Peripatetic in the Nineteenth Century* (Oxford, 1993), pp. 10, 18, 29.

56 Janowitz, *England's Ruins: Poetic Purpose and the National Landscape* (Oxford, 1990), p. 4.

CHAPTER 2

Imagining the metropolis in Elizabethan and Stuart London

Joseph P. Ward

Rapid suburban growth during the late sixteenth and seventeenth centuries encouraged Londoners to think about their metropolis in new ways. In the mid-sixteenth century, around 100,000 people resided in greater London, most of whom lived within the City's square mile. By the end of the seventeenth century, the metropolitan population exceeded half a million, most of whom resided in suburbs and liberties. While some neighborhoods came to be associated with specific activities – such as Westminster with the Court, Spitalfields with weaving, the Bankside with entertainment – every part of the metropolis contained a blend of occupations and social classes. Nevertheless, the development of the suburbs and liberties, the areas in the metropolis that were outside of the City's legal jurisdiction, collectively prompted particularly critical comments from contemporaries.[1] In his *Survey of London* (1598), John Stow decried the encroachment of "filthy cottages" on a common field to the west of the City. He declared such buildings a "blemish to so famous a city" because they formed an "unsavory and unseemly passage thereunto." Others found the suburbs to have been a moral as well as an aesthetic threat because of their residents' illicit activities. A petition to King James I calling for increased government control in the suburbs encouraged the king "to remove many lewd and bad people who harbor themselves near to the City . . . desirous only of the spoil thereof."[2]

Such early modern opinions have encouraged historians and literary critics to assume there were profound divisions among the territories of the early modern metropolis. Historians such as Steve Rappaport and Valerie Pearl who have analyzed London's early modern political stability have contrasted the unruly suburbs with the well-governed City. Rappaport and Pearl have each argued that up to three-quarters of adult men in the City belonged to trade guilds (known as "livery companies") and thereby were citizens ("freemen") of London who participated in a variety of ways in the management of the City's economic, religious, and civic affairs. Such freemen felt threatened by noncitizens, such as native English "foreigners" and "strangers" from other nations, who lived and worked in greater London but avoided responsibility for its government because they lived outside the City.

Similarly, historians of Renaissance drama have stressed the cultural differences between the City and its suburbs. The work of Jean-Christophe Agnew and Steven Mullany assumes that the late sixteenth and early seventeenth centuries, the first great era of public theater in metropolitan London, was a period of profound economic and social dislocation. In their view, because the City's governors dissented from the Crown's support of theater, dramatists were forced to join noncitizens in seeking refuge beyond the lord mayor's reach in the suburbs. The combined economic and cultural freedoms of the suburbs in turn enriched the context of Renaissance drama. As Londoners struggled with the decline of traditional institutions, such as livery companies, in the face of suburban expansion, theater offered them a way to experiment with new forms of representation appropriate to emerging market relations.[3]

This chapter challenges this scholarly consensus in two ways. First, it will place early modern complaints about the suburbs in dialogue with several texts that acknowledged the moral integrity of the metropolis. While some authors sought to place blame for all of London's problems on the suburbs, others argued that no one in the metropolis was blameless. Second, it will offer a new interpretation of the involvement of livery companies and their members in the suburban economy in order to recapture the lived experience of the metropolis. Rather than imagining the suburbs to have been dangerous, foreign territory, many freemen found them hospitable places in which to work and live.

I

By the outset of the seventeenth century, authors often identified London's suburbs as principal locations of licentiousness in greater London, and therefore as the source of God's displeasure with the metropolis. Thomas Dekker's *The Wonderful Year*, a response to the plague of 1603, compared disease to "a Spanish Leaguer, or rather like stalking Tamberlain" who pitched his tents in the "sinfully polluted suburbs" of London. According to Dekker, once the plague progressed across the

suburbs "the skirts of London were pitifully pared off, by little and little."[4] In another discussion of that disaster, Richard Milton argued that
God introduced the plague into the suburbs so that the "City itself seeing the rod so near, should fear betimes." He argued that though God
may have sent the plague to the suburbs as a warning to City residents,
the action was prompted by "the excessive abominations of filthiness
practiced in those places, more than the rest of the City." Milton suggested that the metropolis was an integrated moral system in which "all
the superfluity of extremities, are by the power of a vegetative heat,
wrought to the extremity of the body." As a result of the City's able
government, the "filthy froth of sensual beastliness" was "expelled from
the inner part, and as I may say, the heart of the City" and into the
"utmost skirts and apendant members thereunto." For Milton, the City
was not without its problems, but the direction of the plague's course
revealed that the suburbs were "a fit matter for the first burning of God's
revengeful wrath." In that way, the City would suffer until the suburbs
were reformed.[5]

Despite such arguments, other Londoners hesitated before blaming
the suburbs for provoking God's wrath. In *Christs Teares over Jerusalem*
(1593), Thomas Nashe advised Londoners that they risked a destruction of biblical proportions for their sins. While proclaiming, "London,
what are thy suburbs but licensed stewes," Nashe was also quick to implic-
ate all Londoners in the selfishness, pursuit of fashion, and deceit that
tempted God's displeasure. When he called London "the Sea that sucks
in all the scummy channels of the Realm" and warned that unless London
altered its ways it would share the fate of Jerusalem and Sodom, Nashe
was refering to the entire metropolis, not just the suburbs.[6] In a series
of pamphlets inspired by the plague of 1603, Henoch Clapham counseled Londoners about the epidemic's spiritual causes, and warned them
that fleeing into the countryside would do them little good because God
would strike down sinners wherever they ran. Unlike Dekker and
Milton, Clapham refused to attribute the plague to the corruption of
any specific part of the metropolis, arguing instead that "we have
sinned together, and the hand of God hath come upon us together: let
us therefore humble ourselves together before our lord in fasting and
prayer . . . It is not a change of place, but [a] change of life that must
help us."[7]

In a Paul's Cross sermon responding to a plague outbreak in 1636,
John Squire – the vicar of a Middlesex parish adjacent to the City's

border – noted that during the epidemic more than a thousand people died each week in greater London. But he added that the prayer and fasting of "all the assemblies in the city and suburbs" had encouraged the plague's retreat.[8] Londoners' general awareness of the City's sinfulness is apparent in turner Nehemiah Wallington's interpretation of a fire that destroyed much of London Bridge in February 1633. According to Wallington, the fire was "the will of God" reminding Londoners of the punishment Jerusalem received for violating the Sabbath.[9] Later, the author of a tract inspired by the plague outbreak of 1641 warned Londoners that the disaster was the product of "the multitude of our sins," and suggested that in response London should "put on thy mourning garment, that thy neighbors round about thee may . . . commiserate thee in this thy affliction." While unclear about the identity of London's "neighbors," he suggested that the metropolis was united by sin and affliction and looked to the rest of the country for assistance.[10]

The Civil War encouraged even greater unity between the City and its suburbs. In addition to refurbishing and strengthening London's ancient wall and placing chains across the City's main thoroughfares, Parliament sanctioned the construction of a series of fortresses that encircled the metropolis from the Tower in the east to Westminster in the west. The forts were connected by a continuous line of trenches that joined the suburbs to the City, shielding all of them against royalist intrusions.[11] The parliamentary militia expected all those living within the metropolis to support the war effort. A broadside issued by the committees for the City militia in May 1643 called on those in the "City, suburbs, and parts adjacent" to sacrifice one meal per week and contribute the savings to the militia's collection agents to support the defense of Parliament and the metropolis.[12] Interpretations of disasters later in the century continued to minimize any moral differences between the City and its suburbs and liberties. In 1665, astrologer John Gadbury attributed that year's plague outbreak to God's displeasure with the sins of Londoners, and he warned them that there could be no escape from God's hand: "I believe that the Plague is sent, not so much to afflict the City, as the citizens; the Houses, as the owners of them."[13] The poet "E. N." concurred in two works published that year. One offered counsel to the "willful, wicked, and woeful City of London," and the other cautioned those who planned to escape the plague by fleeing into the country:

> Now therefore hark, ye Gallants of the time,
> You that have counted Godliness a Crime,
> What do you think, or where do y' mean to stay,
> That you from London make such haste away?
> Hear this from me; If you take along
> Your sins with you, you do yourselves but wrong
> To flee away, for you had better be
> Punish'd at first, than to go longer free.[14]

Like Gadbury, "E. N." considered the sins of Londoners in general, and not those of any one part of the metropolis, to be the cause of God's anger.

In a more forceful manner, the Great Fire of 1666 called attention to the moral shortcomings of the City itself. The Fire consumed most of London within the City wall, and much of the area to the west as well, destroying several liberties along the way. In his post-Fire sermon, William Sandcroft, Dean of St. Paul's, began by discussing the destruction of biblical cities and comparing London's experience to the "burning of Jerusalem by Nebuchadnezzar or Titus or (as some as will have it) by both." Fearing the violence of scapegoat-seeking Fire victims, Sandcroft counseled that although some might wish to uncover the "particular sins" that had provoked divine punishment, it was evident that God had passed judgment "upon us All, as an Evidence of his Displeasure for our Sins in general."[15] Robert Elborough supported Sandcroft's argument regarding the nature of the disaster, but went farther than Sandcroft in pointing to the City as the target of God's anger: "Now this and such Fire God threatens to kindle, and that in thee, not about thee, but in thee; not in the skirts, but in the heart."[16] Elborough's metaphors were similar to those employed throughout the discourse of territory and morality in early modern London; his use of "skirts" for the suburbs and "heart" for the City echoed the works of Thomas Dekker and Richard Milton from more than sixty years earlier. But by utilizing that familiar language to isolate the City as the source of "abomination," Elborough brought the discourse full-circle. For many Londoners, the Great Fire ended any assurance that the City was immune to the consequences of immorality that, they may have hoped, were confined to the suburbs.

By the century's end, these concerns had inspired the creation of societies for the reformation of manners. Although such groups were formed throughout England, Robert Shoemaker has shown them most numerous in the metropolis.[17] In 1692, Queen Mary sent a letter to the

JPs of Middlesex, calling for "all constables, church-wardens, Head-boroughs, and all other officers and persons whatsoever to do their part in their several stations" to suppress profanity and debauchery. Seven years later, Josiah Woodward offered a lively account of popular participation in efforts in and around the City to punish those guilty of an array of activities similar to those that had exercised moralists more than a hundred years earlier. "The prosecution of men for their vices," Woodward argued, "has never been reckoned persecution, it being plainly the duty of the magistrate, from the word of God, which obliges him to execute wrath upon those that do evil." The efforts of these reformers were metropolitan in nature. Woodward dedicated his pamphlet to the citizens and inhabitants of the "City of London and the parts adjacent," and he noted that members in both Westminster and the City informed against wrongdoers "in all parts, according to their respective places of abode."[18] The City aldermen indicated their support for such efforts by granting a group of "citizens and inhabitants in and about the City of London" who had prosecuted lewd people the right to nominate two individuals to have the freedom of the City.[19]

The work of the societies for the reformation of manners in the late seventeenth and early eighteenth centuries highlighted the willingness of Londoners to embrace metropolitan ideas of community. The relationship between the City and the suburbs and liberties had at times been strained, with literary sources indicating that disasters during the Elizabethan and early Stuart decades could provoke reformers to direct outbursts of invective at suburbanites. However, throughout the early modern period other contemporary observers insisted on the moral integrity of the entire metropolis, suggesting that diatribes against the "sinfully polluted suburbs" were far from the only reactions to metropolitan development.

II

As open spaces near the City were developed, the Crown took steps to slow the pace of growth. Queen Elizabeth and King James I each tried to curb residential development in the suburbs; efforts to regulate building peaked around 1618.[20] While trying to curb physical development, the Crown considered a new approach to reducing demand for suburban housing. Several proposals to check London's growth are extant among the papers of Sir Julius Caesar, King James's Chancellor of the Exchequer. Two are unsigned and undated, another is undated but from a group calling itself "the foreign tradesmen," and a fourth is from a group of seven Londoners, including aldermen and common councilors, which is dated 30 April 1610. The precise relationship of these sources cannot be reconstructed, but they appear to be part of a debate about the causes and consequences of suburban development.

The plans agreed that unchecked immigration was the main cause of London's problems. The City magistrates' proposal, like the others, complained of the constant arrival of men from across England who were unskilled because they had not completed apprenticeships. Nevertheless, the magistrates asserted, these immigrants were able to find employment in the suburbs.[21] This lack of suburban economic regulation, one of the anonymous petitions claimed, allowed those who had not completed their own apprenticeships to hire and attempt to train other laborers, including apprentices who had deserted their masters, all of whom "taking wives must of necessity need houses." This implied that ineffective economic regulation in areas beyond the lord mayor's jurisdiction undermined the traditional balance between London's economy and its population. The suburban chaos in turn created a cover for criminals.

The anonymous petitioners asserted that although some immigrants worked as porters and laborers, others rejected legal employment and supported themselves through crime. They argued that the flood of immigrants to the overcrowded suburbs enabled criminals to hide from the authorities more easily than they could elsewhere; in addition, criminals found there a steady supply of victims, for they employed bawdy women to trap unsuspecting young gentlemen and apprentices. The petitioners claimed that the criminals' success was evident: they paid higher rents than honest people could.[22]

This description of metropolitan social relations suggested that some gained from the misfortunes of others. According to the foreign tradesmen's proposal, suburban landlords benefited from immigration by erecting sheds on vacant lots, subdividing existing buildings to accommodate immigrants, and increasing their rents whenever they could, without regard to the character or condition of their tenants. One of the anonymous petitions suggested that builders also profited from suburban overcrowding, and so it proposed that the king limit the ability of carpenters and bricklayers to erect or divide houses in the metropolis. The gains of landlords and builders came at the expense of everyone else. The anonymous petitioners and the magistrates all asserted that the suburbs attracted those seeking to produce counterfeit goods for sale at lower prices than those made by honest artisans. Pressured by the combination of unfair economic competition and artificially inflated rents, honest craftsmen were forced to turn to crime and deceit in order to support their families.

All of the proposals thus called for restricting employment opportunities in greater London by tightening the regulation of suburban trade and industry. Each proposal contained provisions allowing those already living in the suburbs to remain if they followed the same guidelines as honest artisans, but they also expressed hope that in the future any immigrant to greater London who had not served an apprenticeship or was otherwise unskilled would be forced to return to his place of origin.[23]

Despite their consensus on general policy, the reformers disagreed over the form of government best suited to economic reform. The City magistrates suggested that King James order those who lived and worked in areas adjoining the City to join the City livery companies associated most closely with their trades and to follow the same rules as freemen regarding the inspection of their work and the training of their apprentices. The other plans outlined the creation of similar yet separate companies in the suburbs. Although they remained vague about enforcing trade regulations outside the limits of City companies, they did not call for the extension of the lord mayor's jurisdiction. Instead, one anonymous proposal asked the Crown to force aliens and traders working as far as ten miles from the City border to join new suburban guilds.[24]

The Crown and the City governors discussed the reform of suburban government periodically until 1636, when Charles I created the New Corporation of the Suburbs of London. The Corporation was designed to regulate the activities of all traders and artisans who worked in areas outside the lord mayor's jurisdiction up to three miles from the City, regardless of whether they already were members of City livery companies. The king placed the Corporation under the rule of a warden and ten assistants for each of four wards, and he promised to alleviate many of the long-standing complaints against suburban interlopers. Those who wished to work in suburban London had to pay an entrance fee to the New Corporation that would then go to the Crown's use. This, along with the need for economic reform, likely explains the timing of the king's initiative. Once in place, the New Corporation faced considerable opposition.

In July 1637, its officers reported to King Charles that "thousands" who would have approved of their government pretended instead to be poor in order to avoid paying their entrance fees. They therefore sought further powers to press their subjects to obedience, and the king granted their request a year later. The City governors' reaction was consistent with their predecessors' claim in 1610 that the City companies could have regulated the suburban economy had their powers been increased. As a result, the magistrates considered the Corporation "very prejudicial" to the City's privileges.[25]

The New Corporation also infringed on the rights of livery companies. Royal charters and letters patent from the Elizabethan period onward typically empowered company officers to regulate their trades for several miles beyond the City's borders. Of course, it remains unclear whether companies succeeded in exercising their mandates. Valerie Pearl has estimated that there were seventy-nine companies operating in seventeenth-century London, but substantial amounts of archival material are extant for fewer than fifty of them, and most of these records generally contain little precise information on the geography of company life. Nonetheless, considerable anecdotal evidence suggests that companies could and often did enforce their ordinances outside the City and, perhaps more importantly, that large numbers of company members lived and worked in the suburbs and liberties.[26]

As the petitions of 1610 suggested, perhaps no occupational group was more involved in suburban development than builders, and so a detailed analysis of their activities may be particularly illustrative of the economic ties between City guilds and the suburbs. Although none of the Carpenters' Company's membership lists have survived, its court records demonstrate its officers' recognition that freemen carpenters worked throughout the metropolis. During the 1610s, they inspected work in suburbs and liberties such as Whitechapel, the Minories, Blackfriars, and "near the Globe play house."[27] In 1613, a committee of London aldermen responded to a complaint brought by the company against the governors of Staple's Inn for their employing a foreign carpenter within the "liberties of London." The aldermen ordered the governors to dismiss the foreigner and to hire a freeman carpenter to complete the project. Although the inn's governors did not concede the legality of the aldermanic ruling, they complied with its intent. In 1628, the company's officers tried to resolve a dispute caused by one carpenter accusing another of supplanting him on a project at extramural Holborn Bridge. The client on this occasion claimed that he had considerable demand for carpenters, and so he simply hired the two carpenters to work on separate projects.[28]

Similar evidence of suburban connections can be found throughout the records of the Tylers and Bricklayers' Company. According to the company's letters patent of 1568, its officers had the right to inspect the use of tiles and bricks within fifteen miles of London. The company's search books survive for the years after 1605, and a comparison of their data with the company's quarterage books, extant for the period 1605–16, indicates that tile- and bricklaying was a metropolitan-wide trade. A sample of the records for the years 1605–6 and 1615–16 reveals that the company's officers inspected work in extramural places, such as Petticoat Lane, Golden Lane, and Chancery Lane, and areas beyond London's borders, such as the Strand, Westminster, and Islington. Among the twenty-three identifiable builders mentioned, thirteen (fifty-seven percent) were working outside the City's wall, including five (twenty-two percent) who were outside the lord mayor's jurisdiction. In addition to supervising tile- and bricklaying, a statute from Henry VII's reign empowered the company's officers to inspect the production and sale of tile, bricks, sand, and lime up to fifteen miles beyond the City's limits.[29] The records of their searches demonstrate that their duties took them across the metropolis and throughout the south-eastern counties. Their influence was apparent from their ability to collect fines from suppliers as far away from London as Lewisham in Kent, Kentish Town in Middlesex, and the manor of Havering in Essex, as well as from those in extramural places such as Bridewell.[30]

The Tylers and Bricklayers' Company's response to King Charles's creation of a new corporation of brick and tile makers in 1636 displayed the importance of the suburbs to its members. The new body, which was based in Westminster, was authorized to supervise production in the cities of London and Westminster as well as in all areas within twenty miles of the City. The officers of the Tylers and Bricklayers' Company responded by claiming that the establishment of the new body only encouraged the deterioration of the quality of bricks and tiles. They charged that brick and tile makers forced tilers and bricklayers to purchase "whatsoever they bring whether good or bad" and also raised their prices. When the tilers and bricklayers complained, the brick and tile makers threatened to call them before the Privy Council, but by 1638, the officers of the City company were ready for such a confrontation. In the event, the Council established a commission to consider their complaints, which subsequently reported that unless Charles overturned the new body, "there can be no reformation, but the said bricks and tiles will still be bad and dear," thereby undermining the king's stated purpose for the Westminster-based corporation.[31]

The Tylers and Bricklayers' officers also participated in efforts to overturn the New Corporation of the Suburbs after 1636. As we have seen, the suburban reform proposals of 1610 had called for the creation of such a company for all artisans and traders in the suburbs in order to protect London freemen from the unfair competition of noncitizens. Contrary to the reformers' assumptions, the members of the Tylers and Bricklayers' Company considered the new suburban guild a threat to their livelihoods. For instance, the company's officers defended the apprentice of one of their freemen who was arrested in Southwark for violating the charter of the New Corporation. Corporation officers justified their actions to the king by claiming that London bricklayers "came and wrought daily in the New Corporation to the great offence of the tradesmen members of this Corporation." However, they also realized that they were stirring up controversy, and so they successfully requested that Charles appoint some of his judges to settle their differences with the freemen. In April 1638, the king postponed the trial of the bricklayers until further efforts had been made to resolve the matter "as shall be reasonable and just."[32]

A petition that ten companies sent to the lord mayor captured the intensity of the opposition of freemen to the New Corporation. It reported that the "greatest part" of the employment of London's builders was located outside the City, and it claimed that since they were restrained by the suburban guild from pursuing their work, the families of builders were being impoverished. They therefore requested the restoration of their right to work in the suburbs and liberties of London. The aldermen found that the petition described a "cause much concerning the freedom and privileges" of the City, and ordered their legal counsel to take steps to relieve the petitioners' complaints. The Tylers and Bricklayers' Company was among the sponsors of the petition, and its officers demonstrated their commitment to the cause by spending more than forty-six pounds on defending the company's rights during 1638 and 1639. The records do not mention the outcome of this particular dispute, which was resolved ultimately with the effective collapse of the New Corporation by 1640, but they demonstrate that during the mid-seventeenth century – a period of rapid metropolitan expansion – members of London's guilds were quick to assert their right to work in the suburbs.[33]

Evidence of the involvement of livery companies and their members in the suburban economy challenges the assumption that those who lived and worked in London's suburbs were primarily immigrants who sought to shelter themselves from the regulations of the City's guilds. In the face of such conflicting data, it should be recalled that the authorship of the 1610 proposals remains uncertain. Two were anonymous, and one claimed to be from the "foreign tradesmen," suggesting that its authors were not members of livery companies. It is possible that they, like the brick and tile makers of Westminster, sought to break away from the control of City companies, and they used the Crown's concern over suburban expansion which had been evident to contemporaries since at least the 1580s to justify their proposals. For these reasons, rather than indicating the diminishing role of City guilds in the economy of London's suburbs and liberties, the reform proposals of 1610 may be evidence of their continued influence.[34]

It was likely in response to such tensions between City companies and foreigners that a group of London magistrates replied to these petitions with a report of their own. The magistrates rehearsed some problems mentioned in the other petitions and proposed that they be rectified by increasing the powers of City companies in the suburbs and liberties. They called for companies to have authority in areas within five miles of the City and for those who traded in such places to be required to join and pay dues to companies. Of course, as we have seen, the City companies already had substantial legal authority outside the City. As leading members of livery companies themselves, the aldermen and common councilors were doubtless aware that their companies possessed considerable influence in the suburbs and liberties.

Although dues paid by interlopers and the geographical extension of company powers into largely undeveloped areas would have enhanced the guilds' influence in greater London, the magistrates seemed rather too eager to claim that suburban development, led by foreigners, was a major threat to the City companies.[35] By blaming interlopers for the apparently chaotic state of the suburban economy, the City magistrates, like the officers of Elizabethan guilds, may have intended their report to deflect criticism from the policies of companies. Since the only identifiable critics of the livery companies had called themselves "foreign tradesmen," perhaps the City magistrates hoped to defend the status quo, a condition that lent livery company members certain advantages over foreigners in the suburbs and liberties.

The activities of the Bakers' Company officers support this hypothesis. In 1604, the Privy Council included the company among the authorities to regulate bread prices. In 1631, the Middlesex JPs arrested fifty bakers "being as well free as foreign, and certain other bakers living in London but serving bread in Middlesex" for violating the assize. The JPs lacked the authority to resolve such matters themselves, and so they sought the assistance of several Privy Council members. This dispute encouraged the Middlesex JPs to propose a new system for enforcing the assize, one that would have eliminated the role of the Bakers' Company's officers. In their defense, the company officers blamed everyone else for the fluctuating price of bread, reserving particular scorn for foreign bakers who lived in suburban London. They complained that foreigners enjoyed advantages over company members who lived in the suburbs and these were "the greatest part of the company" because they avoided paying quarterage and they evaded company ordinances because the officers lacked authority in the suburbs. However, the company's records suggest that the officers overstated this familiar complaint. The company's Elizabethan charter clearly empowered its officers to regulate the baking of bread in suburbs up to two miles from London (an area that included most of the metropolitan area in the early seventeenth century), and the company's records of its officers' actions against foreigners during the period 1631–5 undermined their claim of suburban impotence. Most notably, in 1632 the officers moved against one John Whitehorne of Islington who worked as a baker although, as they alleged, he had not served an apprenticeship in the trade. Whitehorne subsequently stopped baking and turned his shop over to a company member because he knew the "purpose and resolution of and the proceedings of the company against such as was in his case." In this light, the officers' claim of ineffectiveness in the face of suburban economic development appears part of their attempt to deflect criticism that they had allowed their members to charge excessively high prices in those areas. They doubtless preferred to be seen as victims of unfair competition rather than conspirators against the public interest.[36]

III

There was no single attitude toward the suburbs and liberties of early modern London. Some authors condemned them as the sources of vice and corruption in the metropolis that threatened to bring divine punishment on the City. Others recognized them as integral parts of the metropolis and countered those who sought scapegoats in the suburbs by reminding them that City dwellers were not without failings of their own. Economically, the City and its suburbs and liberties were linked by the movement of goods and people. London's livery companies were metropolitan in character, and many of the members lived and worked in the suburbs and liberties. If the livery companies were less efficient in regulating their trades in the suburbs and liberties than they were in the City – and the surviving records preclude a precise analysis of this point – that fact by no means suggests that their members considered the suburbs foreign territory. It was only after livery company members were forced to admit their reliance on suburban markets, and after reformers acknowledged the moral failings of citizens rather than blaming all disasters on suburbanites, that Londoners came to imagine themselves to be residents of a metropolis.

NOTES

1 See Vanessa Harding, "The Population of London, 1550–1700: A Review of the Published Evidence," *London Journal* 15: 2 (1990): 111–28, and M. J. Power, "The Social Topography of Restoration London," in A. L. Beier and Roger Finlay, eds., *London 1500–1700 – The Making of the Metropolis* (London, 1986), pp. 199–223. Since the relationships of the suburbs and liberties were, for the purposes of this discussion, quite similar, the short-hand "suburbs" will refer to all areas in the metropolis that were outside the lord mayor's jurisdiction. This is in contrast to some works that take suburbs to mean areas beyond the City's walls, even if they were within the civic boundary. For example Jeremy Boulton, *Neighbourhood and Society: A London Suburb in the Seventeenth Century* (Cambridge, 1987), focuses on areas that were part of the City's Bridge Ward Without.
2 BL L[ansdowne] MSS 160, fol. 95^r; John Stow, *A Survey of London*, ed. C. L. Kingsford, 2 vols. (Oxford, 1908), 2: 72.
3 Valerie Pearl, *London and the Outbreak of the Puritan Revolution: City Government and National Politics, 1625–1643* (Oxford, 1961), p. 43, and "Change and Stability in Seventeenth-Century London," *London Journal* 5: 1 (1979): 3–34, especially 12–13; Steve Rappaport, *Worlds Within Worlds: Structures of Life in Sixteenth-Century London* (Cambridge, 1989), pp. 46, 62, 187, 231; Jean-Christope Agnew, *Worlds Apart: The Market and the Theater in Anglo-American Thought, 1550–1750* (Cambridge, 1986), pp. 50–5; and Mullaney, *Place*, especially pp. 36 n. 14, and 45. While critical of the approach taken by Pearl and Rappaport, Ian Archer also emphasizes the challenge freemen faced from suburban competition; see *The Pursuit of Stability: Social Reform in Elizabethan London* (Cambridge, 1991), pp. 131–40.
4 Dekker, *The Wonderful Year* (1603), sig. Di.
5 Richard Milton, *Londoners their Entertainment in the Country* (1604), sig. BI.

6 Nashe, *Christs Teares over Jerusalem* (1593), sigs. VI, XI. For the contemporary practice of comparing English towns to Jerusalem, see Patrick Collinson, *The Birthpangs of Protestant England: Religious and Cultural Change in the Sixteenth and Seventeenth Centuries* (Basingstoke, Hants, 1988), especially pp. 28–32.

7 Clapham, *An Epistle Discoursing upon the Pestilence* (1603), sig. C4.

8 Squire, *A Thanksgiving for the Decreasing and Hope of Removing of the Plague* (1637), pp. 10, 21.

9 Quoted in R. Thompson, *Chronicle of London Bridge* (1839), p. 293. For Wallington's providentialist views, see Paul Seaver, *Wallington's World: A Puritan Artisan in Seventeenth-Century London* (Stanford, Calif., 1985), pp. 45–66.

10 *Londons Lamentation. Or a fit admonishment for City and Countrey* (1641), sigs. A2–A3.

11 Norman G. Brett-James, *The Growth of Stuart London* (1935), pp. 268–95; and Victor Smith and Peter Kelsey, "The Lines of Communication: The Civil War Defenses of London," in Stephen Porter, ed., *London and the Civil War* (1996), pp. 117–48.

12 *A Declaration and Motive of the Persons Trusted for Contributing the Value of a Meal Weekly, towards the Forming of some Regiments of Volunteers* (1643). For the background of the militia committee's efforts, see Pearl, *London*, p. 268, and Robert Brenner, *Merchants and Revolution: Commercial Change, Political Conflict, and London's Overseas Traders, 1550–1653* (Cambridge, 1993), p. 452.

13 Gadbury, *London's Deliverance Predicted* (1665), sig. A4.

14 E. N., *London's Sins Reproved* (1665) and *London's Plague-sore Discovered* (1665), p. 7.

15 Sandcroft, *Lex Ignia: or the School of Righteousness* (1666), pp. 3, 6.

16 Elborough, *London's Calamity by Fire Bewailed and Improved* (1666), sigs. B2, C2.

17 Shoemaker, "Reforming the City: The Reformation of Manners Campaign in London, 1690–1738," in Lee Davison, Tim Hitchcock, Tim Keirn, and Robert B. Shoemaker, eds., *Stilling the Grumbling Hive: The Response to Social and Economic Problems in England, 1689–1750* (New York, 1992), pp. 99–120, see p. 100.

18 Woodward, *An Account of the Rise and Progress of the Religious Societies in the City of London, &c., and of the Endeavors for the Reformation of Manners which have been made therein,* "second edition," (1698), pp. 111, 72–8.

19 C[orporation of] L[ondon] R[ecord] O[ffice], Reps. 104, p. 252, and 112, p. 91.

20 Thomas G. Barnes, "The Prerogative and Environmental Control of London Building in the Early Seventeenth Century: The Lost Opportunity," *California Law Review* 58 (1970): 1332–63; R. Malcolm Smuts, "The Court and Its Neighborhood: Royal Policy and Urban Growth in the early Stuart West End," *Journal of British Studies* 30 (1991): 117–49, see pp. 133–5.

21 BL LMSS 169, fol. 130^r.

22 BL LMSS 160, fol. 95^r.

23 BL LMSS 160, fols. 95^r–96^r; 169, fols. 131^r–132^r.

24 BL LMSS 160, fol. 130^r; 169, fol. 132^r.
25 *Calendar of State Papers, Domestic, 1635–36*, pp. 359–60; and see Pearl, *London*, pp. 30–7; Kevin Sharpe, *The Personal Rule of Charles I* (New Haven, Conn., 1992), pp. 406–7.
26 Pearl, "Change and Stability," pp. 12–13. For a detailed discussion, see Joseph P. Ward, *Metropolitan Communities: Trade Guilds, Identity, and Change in Early Modern London* (Stanford, Calif., 1997), chapter 2.
27 G[uildhall] L[ibrary] MSS 7784/6, p. 25, and /8, p. 70. Jacobean letters patent confirmed the company's authority to regulate carpenters who worked in the City of London and in all liberties and suburbs up to two miles from the City border; GL MSS 7784/4, p. 12. On the importance of mobility to early modern building craftsmen and laborers more generally, see Donald Woodward, *Men at Work: Labourers and Building Craftsmen in the Towns of Northern England, 1450–1750* (Cambridge, 1995), especially pp. 119–22.
28 GL MSS 7784/6, p. 61, and /14, p. 32. Other examples of company officers inspecting work sites in liberties are at GL MSS 7784/6, p. 57; /8, pp. 43, 66, 69; and /9, p. 29.
29 GL MSS 4318, pp. 71–2; 3047/1; and 3051/1. In April 1615, a bricklayer named Marshall was fined for poor workmanship near Winchester House in Southwark, which may have been in one of the Bankside liberties. Also, in April 1616, the company fined a lime merchant at his shop in the Clink by St. Mary Overy's Priory.
30 The examples listed were from GL MSS 3047/1, dated December 4, 1606 (Hertfordshire, Kent, and Bridewell); January 1606 (Havering). The Havering search included Romford and also, possibly, "Hornchurch in collier row"; see W. R. Powell, ed., *Victoria County History of Essex* vol. 7 (Oxford, 1978), p. 12, for a map of Havering. For the economy of Havering and its connections to London generally, see Marjorie Keniston McIntosh, *A Community Transformed: The Manor and Liberty of Havering, 1500–1620* (Cambridge, 1991), especially pp. 92–175.
31 GL MSS 4318, pp. 53–69, 113–14, and 122–5. The claim that the Tylers and Bricklayers' Company had been inadequately supervising the production of bricks and tiles is belied by records indicating that more than a third of the new company's members had appeared on the older company's search roll in the early 1630s.
32 GL MSS 4318, pp. 105, 106, 108. These records do not mention any outcome for this dispute.
33 GL MSS 4318, p. 101; 3054/2; 2208/1, fol. 98^r; CLRO Reps. 52, fols. 12^v–13^r; 54, fols. 172^v–73^v. On the slow demise of the New Corporation see Pearl, *London*, p. 37; Robert Ashton, *The City and the Court, 1603–1643* (Cambridge, 1979), p. 167; and Brett-James, *Growth*, p. 244.
34 BL LMSS 160, fols. 95^r–96^r, 97^r, and 169, fols. 131^r–132^r. Foreigners had petitioned the Elizabethan government to enhance their economic interests in London; see Archer, *Pursuit of Stability*, p. 138.

35 BL LMSS 169, fol. 130^r. On the careers of City magistrates, see R. Mark
    Benbow, *Index of London Citizens Involved in City Government, 1558–1603* (1989).
    Sporadically throughout the Elizabethan period, aliens were unjustly
    blamed for crises, thereby absolving London's elite from responsibility; see
    Archer, *Pursuit of Stability*, p. 140.
36 GL MSS 5186; 5196, fols. 7^{r-v}, 20^r–1^r, 48^v, 50^v–51^v.

CHAPTER 3

The peripatetic muse: internal travel and the cultural production of space in pre-revolutionary England

Andrew McRae

To "travel" in sixteenth-century England meant to leave the nation's shores. By close of century, such movement was well-publicized and widely discussed, in terms which tended to stress either heroic endeavor or aristocratic prodigality. Travel within England, though far more common, is considerably less evident in contemporary documents and texts. Historians have long been aware of the realities of mobility, from the gentry spreading across the country through engagement in the land market, to vagrants and subsistence migrants taking to the road in unprecedented numbers during the later sixteenth century. Yet internal travel remains strangely obscured in the literary and historical record, as a result of considerable cultural anxiety about social and geographic mobility. A powerful discourse of settlement shaped the practices of contemporary administrators and social commentators, and has subsequently informed approaches to historical analysis.

This essay is founded on a recognition of the importance of internal travel, and aims to recover the shifting range of meaning attached to the phenomenon by contemporaries. As a study informed by new approaches to cultural history, its principal focus is on representations of travel and travelers. Such an investigation leads less to a handful of central texts than to a generically diverse array of textual fragments, in which writers reflect in various ways on the practices and significance of travel. Hence the broad scope of investigation. If the poetry of Michael Drayton and the prose of Thomas Dekker are involved in a renegotiation of the meaning of mobility, so too are popular pamphlets and royal proclamations. Throughout such texts contemporaries depict the mobile and assess mobility, informed variously by literary and cultural traditions, contemporary circumstances, and personal experience. In the course of the period under consideration (roughly the hundred years preceding the outbreak of Civil War) I will identify a gradual process of change. While Tudor moralists insistently proclaim the virtues of place, by the early seventeenth century texts increasingly consider the importance of mobility, depicting men and women of middling and lower degree on the move.

These developments in discourses of travel are intertwined with shifting appreciations of space and national identity. Social historians have recognized the dangers of focusing only on models of community, noting that a greater awareness of process may prompt a reconceptualization of existing notions of community and space.[1] A consideration of the cultural significance of movement may therefore benefit from more flexible strategies of analysis, alert to a wider range of sources and representations, and engaged with the "profoundly spatialized historical materialism" posited by postmodern geographers and social theorists.[2] In the face of perceptions of space as a mere frame or neutral container for social relations and lived experience, Henri Lefebvre identifies "the production of space," a process dialectically related to changes in the social relations of production.[3] Lefebvre's model, in which space is perceived to be shaped by social, economic, and ideological forces, injects a new dimension into the analysis of the development of capitalism. Traditional marxist narratives tend to treat space primarily as "a physical context, the sum of the places of production, the territory of different markets."[4] The binary relation of country and city dominates such analysis, as it also provided the framework for Raymond Williams's seminal materialist study of literary traditions, *The Country and the City* (1973). The "rise of capitalism" is depicted as a process by which the mercantile imperatives of the city leach the countryside of feudal structures and values of moral economy. By comparison, the notion of spatiality, socially produced space, opens a place in this narrative for broader patterns of mobility and circulation.[5] It directs concern toward the expansion of complex networks for the movement of trade and labor, and the manipulation of space by social and political forces. And it suggests the crucial status of internal travel in the production of a capitalist space.

Lefebvre expresses doubts that the study of texts can offer more than a "reading" of spaces, in a manner that evades "both history and practice."[6] But since the publication of his book in 1974, developments in both historical and literary studies have acknowledged the dynamic function of texts in the construction of discourses, and the implications of discourses in structures of power. It is important to distinguish between physical and discursive impositions of power: between, for example, the forceful enclosure of an estate to the detriment of its tenants, and the emergence of a discourse promoting and justifying enclosure. Nonetheless, the present chapter is concerned principally to trace a history of discursive change, and to situate this development within a broader narrative of social and economic change in England. It is based on the proposition that the production of space may be approached as a process with vital cultural determinants.

I

Orthodox Tudor ideology assumed that geographical stability would accompany social stability. Knowing one's "place" involved observing interlinked codes of values and conduct, including a supposedly rigid political hierarchy, an associated distribution of control over the land, and values of patriarchy which impinged upon both family and commonwealth. The system was spatially underpinned by the model of the manorial estate, a "little commonwealth" knit together by moralized bonds of duty and responsibility.[7] Even an early proponent of estate surveying, which threatened to redefine property relations in alignment with capitalist values, insisted upon the tenant's "love and obedience" and the landlord's "aide and protection," which bound them in a relationship comparable to that between parents and children.[8] Analogous models informed urban life. Relations of service and apprenticeship were absorbed within the familial model; artisans and merchants were exhorted to remain tenants, rather than challenge the power of the gentry; and guilds and corporations espoused ethics of community over individualism.

Within this model of the commonwealth, acceptable forms of movement across the land were those which served interests of unity and coherence. Governmental networks were forged by the gentry and nobility, who traversed their own regions, and traveled to the capital for attendance at Court and Parliament. Although some clearly preferred the social environment of London, they were never allowed to forget the source of their power. One of several royal proclamations on this subject reminded the propertied that they were not "borne for themselves, and their families alone, but for the publique good and comfort of their Countrey" (i.e. local region), and summarily ordered their expulsion from the capital.[9] Further, the state imposed its control across the country through judicial structures, including the provision of circuit judges and central courts. From the reign of Elizabeth I, the Church was also implicated in the maintenance of socio-political power, a project embodied in the placement of clerical hierarchies across the land.

For the lower orders the ideology of settlement was almost entirely repressive. Despite the undeniable realities of geographical mobility, movement was openly sanctioned only within tightly confined parameters. The tenant farmer's trip to the local market, for example, allowed for an orderly exchange of goods, and marked for most people an "economic horizon."[10] Similarly, in Rogationtide ceremonies, the most notable religious processions to survive the Reformation, parishioners "beat the bounds" of their territory, at once endorsing a communal consciousness of place, and invoking a spiritual presence to invigorate the land.[11] Regular convergences upon the manor house were also structured as affirmations of the "little commonwealth." In a sixteenth-century description of the ceremony of homage and fealty, performed at sittings of the manorial court, the tenants promise to "be faythfull and lowly" toward the landlord, and "beare faythe to [him] for the landes and tenementes" they hold.[12] Such attitudes are implicit in Ben Jonson's "To Penshurst," which nostalgically celebrates manorial community in its central image of a feast, to which the families of "the farmer" and "the clown" bring unnecessary offerings of rural produce. The estate is figured as self-sustaining and socially closed, the poem's ideology of "home" fixed by the geographical referents of the great house and manorial land.[13]

A spatiality constituted around the manorial court, local marketplace and parish church is inscribed with values of community and moral economy. It is also a spatiality of localism, immediately recognizable yet strangely opaque to the outsider. Interestingly, two texts of localism, John Stow's *Survey of London* (1598 and 1603) and a collection of proverbs "confined to the soile bounds and territory" of the Hundred of Berkeley in Gloucestershire, compiled by John Smyth of Nibley, have suggested to different scholars the notion of land in early modern England as a "memory palace."[14] Stow's passage through London "amounts to an attentive transcription of the memory-traces impressed upon the city by time and ceremonial circumstance"; Smyth's "landscape was literally used to store information."[15] Such a structure was not necessarily impermeable; many proverbs, in particular, may be easily transferred from one site to another. Nonetheless, the sense of landscape founded upon an accretion of communal traditions remained fundamentally resistant to the flux of internal travel, and opposed to the processes of fragmentation and homogenization which characterize the capitalist production of space.[16]

The realities of movement beyond conservative parameters generated understandable anxiety. Thomas More identified the corrosive spatial economy of the encloser, who becomes the "very plague of [his] native country," thrusting husbandmen "out of their own" to wander "abroad."[17] His perception of covetousness as a force geared toward the erosion of communal space underpinned an outpouring of social complaint. But as More realized, the displaced rode a knife-edge between sympathy and antipathy, offering pitiable symbols of social change, but facing dire consequences when they materialized as masterless men and women. Social critics and legislators united in attacks on "unsufferable swarmes of Rogues and Vagabonds in every street, highway, and place."[18] Accordingly, surveyors of the nation, in the tradition established by William Harrison and Sir Thomas Smith, typically write the placeless out of the social order.[19] Mobility meant classification "as vagabonds and wanderers, as being of no family, of no parish church, of no town, of no shire."[20] Pedlers, chapmen, and carriers, whose activities were instrumental to the formation of a national market, remained on the margins of morality and legality.[21] As late as 1630 a royal proclamation affirmed a commitment to suppress men and women "wandering under the severall names of . . . Glasse-men, Pot-men, Pedlers, Petti-Chapmen, Conyskinners, [or] Tinkers."[22]

It is also worth remembering the challenges that could be made to existing power structures by subverting spatial order. In the rebellions of 1549 one group marched toward London, while another "camped" in the fields of East Anglia, threatening Norwich while provocatively stretching the bounds of an established popular festivity.[23] Similarly, religious radicals challenged the power of the Church and its models of religious community by ignoring church buildings and parish boundaries.[24] The Family of Love was initially propagated by an itinerant artisan;[25] Catholic priests sustained their religion by traveling in disguise between country houses;[26] and the act of "gadding" to hear sermons outside one's parish provided an important form of collective activity for the Elizabethan Puritan movement.[27] Consequently the obfuscation in conservative rhetoric surrounding types of movement is understandable. Placelessness signified rebellion; moralizers launched broadly inclusive attacks on all those "wandryng and gaddyng abroad."[28]

To Thomas Harman, author of the first Elizabethan rogue pamphlet, the phenomenon could be defined by a new word. He explains his nomination of "common cursitors . . . as runners or rangers about the country, derived of this Latin word *curro*."[29] His concluding poem endorses practical and symbolic attempts to arrest the movement:

A Stock's to stay sure, and safely detain,
Lazy lewd Loiterers, that laws do offend,
Impudent persons, thus punished with pain,
Hardly for all this, do mean to amend.[30]

The goal of fixing the problem of the poor by literally fixing them in place impelled a range of social policy, including the provision of badges for licensed beggars in London, laws compelling vagrants to return to their "homes," and the foundation of Bridewell.[31] Harman's concentration on the stocks relishes the capacity of this particular instrument to "safely detain" the wanderer. He chooses an apt emblem of the state's material, legal, and ideological machinery of placement.

II

The violently repressive rhetoric of Tudor moralists highlights the anxiety surrounding manifestations of placelessness. But while such attitudes remained dominant, the reign of Elizabeth was also a period of considerable change in conceptions of the land. An on-going reassessment of the space of the nation, and the relation of individuals to the land, is evident in a range of texts, from the elite genre of chorography to a wealth of popular literature. Given the established authority of discourses of settlement, writers of all such texts required careful strategies of self-justification and subtle acts of negotiation between conflicting claims over the national space. Attention to textual tensions and innovations thus promises to illuminate a development toward new appreciations of spatiality.

The Elizabethan interest in the cartographic and written description of the nation produced texts aiming to reveal the land to its inhabitants. But despite the commitment to descriptive surveys of the nation's spaces, the chorographers' representations of travel betray a marked unease. The classic structure of chorography is a perambulation of the land, on which the reader is guided by a personable narrator. But while traversing the country, the authors simultaneously efface the mechanics of travel. The copious notes prepared by John Leland in the reign of Henry VIII are remarkable for their concern with paths, obstacles and lodgings; however if he had lived to fulfill his promise to fashion from these notes "such a descripcion that it shall be no mastery after, for the graver or painter to make the lyke," Leland would probably have excised much of this detail.[32] Leland alludes to the emergent art of cartography, in which he took considerable interest. In a process explicated by Michel de Certeau, he aimed to replace the circuitous routes of his personal itinerary with a scientific and totalizing discourse characteristic of the modern map.[33]

At least until the seventeenth century, his successors consistently adopted such strategies. In the influential works of chorographers such as William Camden and John Norden, the perambulation of a county frequently means an authorial glide from one settlement to the next, focusing at each stop on local history and the genealogy of land-owning families. The direction of the texts is most commonly determined by river systems; however, the textual movement maintains the ease of a sweep across an abstract surface, rather than a physical navigation of the waterways. The energy of movement is displaced: in Camden's *Britannia*, for example, the Thames "runneth downe [from Oxford] neere unto Ricot, a goodly house"; subsequently, "having fetched a great compasse about [the river] windeth in manner backe againe into himselfe, enclosing within it the Hundred of Henley."[34] Roads are rarely mentioned; nor are they commonly indicated on maps until well into the seventeenth century.

In Michael Drayton's massive chorographical poem, *Poly-Olbion* (1612–13, 1622), the travel is undertaken by the figure of the author's Muse.[35] As the poem works its way across the country, the Muse directs the movement and endows natural features of the land with the power of speech. Her function is consistent with the poem's "almost exclusive emphasis on the land's revelation of itself."[36] The Muse is "industrious" and her labors accumulate a wealth of topographical detail and local information. She reveals the underlying character of different regions: valleys proclaim their fertility; hills uncover their sedimentations of human history; rivers declare their strength. The poem thereby works to occlude the momentum of human travel toward economic integration and the production of homogenized social space. Nonetheless, despite this corporate conception of nationhood, erected around the accumulated mythologies of localism, Drayton at least gestures toward crucially divergent spatial structures. Most notably, in the poem's extensive catalogues of local produce, Renaissance values of *copia* slide into the discourse of a national marketplace, which draws together specialized regional commodities. The Colne River boasts that the "fat soyle" of Essex sends its cheese "to every quarter" of the country; PeryVale claims that her "goodly graine" is in such demand that "chap-men" attend her "How ere I set my price."[37] While productivity is encoded as a natural function of the land, Drayton admits mercantile claims over rural produce, the emergent paths of traffic suggesting human dynamics of mobility which threaten to disrupt the unworldly progress of the Muse.

Authors of descriptive works who felt less constrained by the generic demands of chorography pursued such logic with greater rigor. Thomas Churchyard's *The Worthines of Wales* (1587) focuses from the out-set on the author as a traveler, turning toward his native country late in life to find matter for his "labring pen."[38] Whereas Drayton's Muse sublimates the process of travel, Churchyard's sporadically interjects to goad the flagging author. In georgic imagery used later by Spenser, she exhorts him to "Put [his] hand to [the] Plough," and "purchase praise" through his pedestrian and literary endeavors.[39] Analogous advice is applied to Wales itself, depicted as "a Countrey rich at will," which promises to make the Welsh "full quickly wealthie" if they are prepared to labor in the "sweat of [their] browes." Significantly, this wealth is channeled through routes of traffic, centering on Shrewsbury:

> This Towne with more, fit members for the head,
> Makes London ritch, yet reapes great gayne from thence:
> It gives good gold, for Clothes and markes of lead,
> And for Welsh ware, exchaungeth English pence.

From this perspective the English capital becomes "A fountaine head, that many Conduits serve," in a process of circulation as vital as the flow of rivers to the sea.[40]

Churchyard's presentation of himself and his land shuns generic conventions, in a manner which aligns with contemporary revisions of subjectivity and the author-function. As literary historians have recognized, textual practice in this period became less dependent on royal authority, patronage relationships, and classical legitimation. Within this milieu texts emerged which were strikingly attuned to qualities of individual industry, and prepared to dwell on the purposes and practicalities of travel. Thomas Tusser's *Five Hundred Points of Good Husbandry, United to as Many of Good Housewivery* (1573) affirms the author's own experience of movement, both as a scholar and as a ten-ant farmer troubled by the exigencies of "great rent."[41] Moreover, he challenges the model of stable manorial community, assuming instead a highly mobile population. He advises his reader to "Provide against Mihelmas, bargaine to make, / for ferme to give over, to keepe or to take."[42] In contrast to the localized culture John Smyth claims for the Hundred of Berkeley, Tusser's proverbial ethics are fundamentally placeless. He views the land with a pragmatist's eye, advising the husbandman "To get good plot to occupie," and thereafter simply to "folow profit earnestlie."[43]

While Tusser helped to enshrine thrift as a virtue for the struggler, other writers revitalized traditional images of the wanderer as opportunist and trickster. A sense of unfixed agents exploring the opportunities of space emerges across a range of texts, and is most vividly apparent in pamphlet literature. Several of the jest books which flourished around the turn of the seventeenth century center on peripatetic figures. For example, *Tarlton's Jests* (1638; written about, not by the stage clown) is divided into sections of "court-witty jests," "sound city jests," and "countrey-pretty jests." For Tarlton, wit enables both self-projection and self-preservation, as he moves through a profoundly competitive environment. In one tale, at "a time, when Players were put to silence, Tarlton and his Boy frollickt so long in the Countrey, that all their money was gone," and they could see no way of funding their return to the capital. Since they are unknown at their inn, the boy initiates a rumor that Tarlton is a seminary priest, on the road to spread religious heterodoxy. The innkeeper has him arrested and carried to London: which solves Tarlton's transportation problem. Recognized and discharged by a judge, Tarlton "stood jesting & pointing at [his captors'] folly, and so taught them by cunning, more wit & thrift against another time."[44] The simple honesty of the country innkeeper, troubled by the unknown, is transformed by the jester into a subject of ridicule.

Similar qualities are manifested in pamphlets of rogues and coney-catchers published in the decades after Thomas Harman's assault on "common cursitors." Robert Greene's rogue pamphlets admit a doubleness of vision, as orthodox moralism gives way to delight in the facility of the villain. Thomas Dekker, who extended the genre into the seventeenth century, depicts con men on horseback whose "businesse is weightie, their journies many, their expences greate, their Innes everie where, their lands no where."[45] Another "seemes to have good skil in Cosmography, for he holdes in his hand a Map, wherein hee hath layde downe a number of Shires in England, and with small pricks hath beaten out a path, teaching how a man may easily (though not verry honestly) travell from Country to Country, and have his charges borne." The supposed rogues' map subverts the project of chorography, identifying the residences of gentlemen as sites of potential coney-catching. "Thus doth he ride from Towne to Towne, from Citty to City as if he were a Land-lord in every shire, and that he were to gather Rents up of none but Gentlemen."[46]

The spatiality shaped within such texts was intertwined with changing patterns of social organization. Contextualizing the London pamphleteers requires considering the unprecedented population explosion
in the capital, and the tumultuous growth of extramural suburbs. The
suburbs existed on the margins of civic community as previously constructed. They undermined existing notions of social hierarchy and
spatial organization, and became rather "the preserve of the anomalous,
the unclean, the polluted."[47] This point should not be exaggerated. Joseph
Ward's chapter in this volume demonstrates the ways in which corporate and civic structures ordered life in the suburbs. Other social historians have explored ongoing tensions between traditional ideals of
community and newer forms of social interaction, as London and other
urban centers absorbed increasing numbers of migrants.[48] In many cases
kinship networks or regional ties eased the path of a migrant into social
and economic life. A beggar in an Elizabethan dialogue accordingly
claims that he gained entry to London because the beadle of the beggars was a Northumbrian countryman, and looked favorably upon him.[49]
Yet it is equally clear that "for many newcomers suburban habitation
offered only a precarious foothold in the community."[50] Although conservative commentators continued to invoke the rhetoric of community,
pre-existent models of social and spatial order became naggingly irrelevant, and in the interstices of a besieged ideology there emerged new
models of subjectivity and society.

Analogous productions of space might be discerned in rural areas.
Settlements in forests and wastelands, which were less constrained by
manorial structures than those in arable regions, attracted increasing
numbers of subsistence migrants.[51] Squatters and small cottagers across
the country duly troubled landlords and legislators, concerned partly
by their transient and alienated relation to social space. An Elizabethan
statute decreed that no cottage could be built without four acres of
land, attempting to give even the poorest tenants a stake in the countryside; however, the forces of poverty and the labor demands of rural
industries continued to erode this goal.[52] New approaches to landhold-
ing embraced by those of higher degree further contributed to these
shifts. Surveyors were crucial in this regard, as they traveled the country, offering newly legalistic appreciations of tenurial relationships and
rationalistic standards of land measurement. They challenged notions
of land-holding as a bundle of rights and responsibilities, envisaging
instead an abstract rural space, pliable to the aspirations of the agrarian
improver.[53]

These developments did not simply erase a spatiality of community and shared memory. Social space, in Lefebvre's perception, has a multiplicity "more reminiscent of flaky *mille-feuille* pastry than of the homogeneous and isotropic space of classical (Euclidean/Cartesian) mathematics."[54] In this context a site which highlights the uncertain negotiation between divergent forms of spatiality was the alehouse.[55] This institution had its roots in the medieval village; as numbers proliferated in the sixteenth century, however, it was increasingly associated with the marginal and the mobile. Dekker listed the alehouses' clientele as "cobblers, tinkers, pedlars [and] porters."[56] Alehouses also provided centers within loose networks of credit and exchange. Patrons might expect to purchase food and consumer goods, gather information about the conditions of local travel, and even obtain forged passports to enable wanderers to stay on the road. For the transient and local alike the alehouse offered a realm in which to forge alternative forms of social interaction. In the face of powerful social an l ideological structures of placement, the alehouse stood as a figure and facilitator of circulation.

III

In the early decades of the seventeenth century, internal travel was no longer the subject of unquestioning polemic. Not only were growing numbers of people traveling, but their movement was increasingly accepted and even respected. One commentator, arguing for improvements to the roads and rivers, stressed the benefits which would accrue "by interchange of commodities . . . whereby men everie where may be stirred up . . . to seeke and finde out such commodities whatsoever their Countrie shall affoord and bring forth to the proffiting of themselves and others."[57] Travel within England was also recognized to have · alue as recreation. Henry Peacham advised the thrifty man to consider the benefits of "riding with a good horse, and a good companion in the spring, in the Countrey."[58] John Norden, after his earlier work as a cartographer and chorographer, attempted to make travel more feasible by publishing *England, An Intended Guyde for English Travaillers* (1625), a table showing distances by road between English towns.[59]

Perhaps the most representative writer of these decades of uncertain development and incessant activity is John Taylor, who spent most of his life as a waterman in London.[60] Taylor took to writing in the tradition of Dekker and Nashe, and like them affected a dexterous literary style which embraced both popular and elite traditions. Though he produced poetry and prose on a wide array of topics, his trademark was the pamphlet of travel, which narrated mock-fantastic journeys undertaken on the strength of wagers. Unlike any previous English writer, he pursued travel within the nation as a business. In 1649 he wrote:

> Like to the stone of Sisiphus, I roule
> From place to place, through weather faire and foule,
> And yet I every day must wander still
> To vent my Bookes, and gather friends good will.[61]

He rarely attempts to disguise the imperative which underpins this peripatetic vigor. Not unlike a chapman, he travels "to get money of my book."[62]

On more than one occasion Taylor distinguishes his work from the descriptive project of "learned *Camden*, [and] laborious [John] *Speede*."[63] Whereas the chorographers sweep across the face of the land, Taylor's perambulations are driven by occasion and opportunity, and his texts dwell on the trials and rewards of the traveler. In *The Pennyles Pilgrimage* (1618) he relates a walk from London to Edinburgh. The purpose of the expedition was to rely for his provision solely on the generosity of strangers and casual acquaintances: if the title of "pilgrimage" plays on travel motivated by religious zeal, his pennilessness parodies monastic mendicancy. But while codes of hospitality were still strong in rural England, Taylor rather cadges and cajoles his way by entertainment, thus unsettling the prevailing ethos of noble bounty. In Jonson's "To Penshurst," the lord's hospitality is marked by his preparedness to entertain the king; in Taylor's works, the scruffy star of popular print rails against gentlemen and innkeepers unwilling to give him free board. In due course he acknowledges assistance from people of any rank, and names some places where he came and went as a stranger. Other texts record drunken guides, a hostile welcome when he is "suspected . . . to be a bringer of Writs and Processe . . . to bring men into trouble," flea-infested alehouses, and one confrontation with a suspicious constable, "Who ask'd my Trade, my dwelling, and my name: / My businesse, and a troope of questions more," before taking him to the local Justice of the Peace as an unlicensed traveler.[64]

While his narrations of the vicissitudes of travel sustain a jovial mock-heroic idiom, Taylor becomes more serious when he turns to the business of internal trade. He published a pamphlet detailing the activities of carriers working out of London, and another serving as a directory to taverns in central and southern England.[65] Most importantly, several texts champion the cause of improving the rivers, to allow an easier and cheaper flow of traffic. *Taylor on Tame Isis* (1632) revises the tradition of Tudor river poetry, turning an unashamedly mercantile gaze upon the damage inflicted on the Thames by "stops and locks, / . . . Mils, and hils . . . gravell beds, and rocks."[66] Taylor calculates the benefits of a "cleane and free" river, including the employment of "poore mens industrious paines" on barges, and the distribution of commodities "at cheape rates."[67] While the work remains to be done, the Thames resists the aestheticizing commonly generated by topographical poets, and remains "heavie and disconsolate, / Unnavigable, scorn'd, despis'd, disgrac'd."[68]

Set against centuries of cultural tradition valorizing social and geographical stability, Taylor doggedly espouses circulation. Narratives of his own "toyling trade" as a traveler shade into endorsements of the traffic of goods. He also appreciates the dissemination of news and newsbooks from the capital, the process of the water cycle (in which "nature in a circle runs about"), and even the "right perpetuall motion" of beggars.[69] His poem *The Travels of Twelve-Pence* (1621) applies this perspective to economic exchange. Here a shilling coin describes its "endlesse Journey," facilitating market transactions in the city and passing back and forth through an alehouse as farmers, brewers and artisans mix in the country. While Taylor treats the activity with a measure of ironic detachment, the only truly incomprehensible attitude is that of a miser, who kept the shilling for eighteen years, "day and night / Lock'd in a Chest, not seeing any light."[70] For the shilling as for the poet, stasis is rendered as constraint. Taylor's writing, like the national economic activity typified by the peripatetic coin, is generated rather out of unending movement and exchange.

IV

Taylor witnessed major changes in practices of travel. Traffic on his favored waterways was increasing; the introduction of stage coaches eroded the tyrannies of overland distances; and trade and communications networks became increasingly specialized and reliable. These developments were compounded by new movements in economic theory: most notably mercantilism. As Michel Foucault has argued, in mercantilist thought, "the relations between wealth and money are based on circulation and exchange, and no longer on the 'preciousness' of the metal. When goods can circulate (and this thanks to money), they multiply, and wealth increases; when coinage becomes more plentiful, as a result of a good circulation and a favorable balance, one can attract fresh merchandise and increase both agriculture and manufacturing."[71] Mercantilism thus prompted a reassessment of traditional models of socio-political order. In Gerard Malynes' political vision, *"Bullion* is the very Body and Blood of Kings, *Money* is but the Medium between Subjects and their Kings, *Exchange* the heavenly Mistery that joynes them both together."[72]

After the extraordinary upheavals of the Civil War, appreciations of the riches of space and the dynamics of mobility prompted a fresh wave of textual production, culminating in the pragmatic inquiry of Daniel Defoe's *Tour Through the Whole Island of Great Britain* (1724–6).[73] It would be an exaggeration to claim a revolution in English space, since values of settlement underpinned much of the literature and political discourse of the eighteenth century. The texts and discursive developments considered here, however, achieve an increasingly coherent articulation of innovative notions of spatiality. Their representations of the nation offered to legitimize radically divergent forms of social and economic order.

NOTES

I wish to thank Kristin Hammett, Steve Hindle, David Rollison and the editors of this volume for their comments on this essay. Dr. Rollison also shared with me his valuable unpublished paper, "Exploding England: The Dialectics of Mobility and Settlement in Early Modern England" (forthcoming, *Social History*).

1 See, for example, Joan Vincent, "Agrarian Society as Organized Flow: Processes of Development Past and Present," *Peasant Studies* 6 (1977): 56–65, and *Journal of British Studies* 33: 4 (October, 1996), a special issue on ideas of community in medieval England. James Clifford's critique of modern anthropology might also be considered by scholars of medieval and early modern England; see "Traveling Cultures," in Lawrence Grossberg, Cary Nelson, and Paula A. Treichler, eds., *Cultural Studies* (1992), pp. 96–116.
2 Edward W. Soja, *Postmodern Geographies: The Reassertion of Space in Critical Social Theory* (1989), p. 44. See also Henri Lefebvre, *The Production of Space*, trans. Donald Nicholson-Smith (Oxford, 1991).
3 Lefebvre, *Production of Space*, pp. 34, 36–7.
4 Edward W. Soja, "The Spatiality of Social Life: Towards a Transformative Retheorization," in Derek Gregory and John Urry eds., *Social Relations and Spatial Structures* (1985), pp. 90–127, this passage p. 104.
5 Soja posits the notion of spatiality in "Spatiality," p. 123; see also *Postmodern Geographies*, pp. 79, 120.
6 Ibid., p. 7. Lefebvre nonetheless admits the possibility of "as-yet concealed relations between space and language" (p. 17).

7 John Norden, *The Surveiors Dialogue* (1610), p. 27.

8 Ibid., sig. *2ᵛ, p. 36.

9 James F. Larkin and Paul L. Hughes, eds., *Stuart Royal Proclamations*, 2 vols. (Oxford, 1973, 1983), 1: 357.

10 Alan Everitt, "The Marketing of Agricultural Produce," in Joan Thirsk, ed. *The Agrarian History of England and Wales, Volume IV 1500–1640* (Cambridge, 1967), pp. 466–592, this passage p. 501.

11 See Eamon Duffy, *The Stripping of the Altars: Traditional Religion in England, c. 1400–1580* (New Haven, Conn., 1992), pp. 136–9.

12 John Fitzherbert, *The Booke of Surveying and Improvements* (1523), fol. 31ᵛ.

13 On the significance of "home" in the poem, see Don E. Wayne, *Penshurst: The Semiotics of Place and The Poetics of History* (Madison, Wisc., 1984).

14 Steven Mullaney discusses Stow's *Survey* in *Place*, pp. 15–20. Smyth's proverbs are published in his *Description of the Hundred of Berkeley*, vol. 3 of Sir John Maclean, ed., *The Berkeley Manuscripts* (Gloucester, 1885), pp. 22–33. See David Rollison, *The Local Origins of Modern Society: Gloucestershire 1500–1800* (1993), pp. 67–83.

15 Mullaney, *Place*, p. 16; Rollison, *Local Origins*, p. 71.

16 See Soja, *Postmodern Geographies*, p. 128.

17 More, *Utopia* (1985), pp. 26–7.

18 *Stuart Proclamations*, 2: 185.

19 Harrison, *The Description of England*, ed. Georges Edelen (Ithaca, N.Y., 1968), pp. 94–123; Smith, *De Republica Anglorum* (1583; facsimile edition, Amsterdam, 1970), pp. 20–33.

20 George Snell, *The Right Teaching of Useful Knowledge* (1649), p. 93; quoted in David Underdown, *Revel, Riot, and Rebellion: Popular Politics and Culture in England 1603–1660* (Oxford, 1985), p. 11.

21 See Beier, *Masterless Men*, pp. 89–90, and Margaret Spufford, *The Great Reclothing of Rural England: Petty Chapmen and Their Wares in the Seventeenth Century* (1984), pp. 6–9.

22 *Stuart Proclamations*, 2: 297–8.

23 Diarmaid MacCulloch, "Kett's Rebellion in Context," *Past and Present* 84 (1979): 36–59.

24 The movement of religious radicals, their books and ideas, is documented superbly in Margaret Spufford, ed., *The World of Rural Dissenters* (Cambridge, 1995).

25 On Christopher Vittels, who probably worked as a joiner before taking to the road for the Familist cause, see Christopher W. Marsh, *The Family of Love in English Society, 1550–1630* (Cambridge, 1994).

26 A. G. Dickens, *The English Reformation* (1989), p. 425.

27 Patrick Collinson, *The Religion of Protestants: The Church in English Society 1559–1625* (Oxford, 1982), pp. 258–60.

28 See Beier on vagrancy, *Masterless Men*, p. 3, and Thomas Churchyard, "Of wandryng and gaddying abroad," in *A Pleasante Laborinth called Churchyardes Chance* (1580), fols. 38ᵛ–39ʳ.

29 Harman, *A Caveat for Common Cursitors* (1566), in Arthur F. Kinney, ed., *Rogues, Vagabonds, and Sturdy Beggars: A New Gallery of Tudor and Stuart Rogue Literature* (Amherst, Mass., 1990), pp. 109–53, this passage p. 113.

30 Ibid., p. 153.

31 Beier, *Masterless Men*, chapter 9. In "Exclusion Crises: Poverty, Migration and Parochial Responsibility in English Rural Communities, *c.* 1500–1660," *Rural History: Economy, Society, Culture* 7 (1996): 125–49, Steve Hindle considers the policies of exclusion in rural contexts, focusing on the detailed and imaginative proposals to protect his community from immigrants set forth by Alexander Strange, vicar of Layton, Hertfordshire, 1604–50.

32 John Bale, ed., *The Laboryouse Journey & Serche of Johan Leylande, for Englandes Antiquities* (1549), sig. Dvi^v. His notes are published as *John Leland's Itinerary: Travels in Tudor England*, ed. John Chandler (Phoenix Mill, Gloucestershire, 1993).

33 De Certeau, *The Practice of Everyday Life*, trans. Steven Russell (Berkeley, Calif., 1984), pp. 118–22.

34 Camden, *Britain, Or A Chorographicall Description of the Most Flourishing Kingdomes, England, Scotland, and Ireland*, trans. Philemon Holland (1610), pp. 384, 389.

35 *The Works of Michael Drayton*, ed. J. William Hebel, 5 vols. (Oxford, 1931–41), vol. 4.

36 Helgerson, *Forms of Nationhood*, p. 145; and see pp. 107–47.

37 Drayton, *Poly-Olbion*, 19: 129; 16: 228, 242.

38 Churchyard, *The Worthines of Wales* (1597; facsimile edition, 1876), p. 83.

39 Ibid., pp. 88, 59.

40 Ibid., p. 82.

41 Tusser, *Five Hundred Points*, ed. Geoffrey Grigson (Oxford 1984), p. 4.

42 Ibid., p. 30.

43 Ibid., p. 13.

44 *Tarlton's Jests* (1638), sigs. D4^v–E1^r.

45 Dekker, *Lanthorn and Candle-light* (1609), in *The Non-Dramatic Works of Thomas Dekker*, ed. Alexander B. Grosart, 5 vols. (New York, 1963), 3: 250.

46 Ibid., 3: 291–2.

47 Mullaney, *Place*, p. 22.

48 See especially Archer, *Pursuit of Stability*, and Jeremy Boulton, *Neighbourhood and Society: A London Suburb in the Seventeenth Century* (Cambridge, 1987).

49 William Bullein, *A Dialogue bothe Pleasaunte and Pietifull, Wherein is Goodly Regimente against of the Fever Pestilence* (1573), pp. 3–4.

50 Peter Clark, "Migrants in the City: The Processes of Social Adaptation in English Towns 1580–1800," in Peter Clark and David Souden, eds., *Migration and Society in Early Modern England* (1987), pp. 267–91, this passage p. 278.

51 Joan Thirsk, "The Farming Regions of England," in Thirsk, ed., *Agrarian History* 4: 1–15, and A. L. Beier, *The Problem of the Poor in Tudor and Early Stuart England* (1983), p. 10.

52 *Act for the Protection of Cottagers' Holdings and Rights of Common* (1589), 31 Elizabeth, *c.* 7. Philip Styles discusses this act in relation to subsequent attempts to control mobility in *Studies in Seventeenth Century West Midlands History* (Kineton, 1978), pp. 175–204.

53 Lefebvre discusses the abstract space of capitalism in *Production of Space*, especially pp. 285–7. On surveyors, see McRae, *God Speed*, chapter 6.

54 Lefebvre, *Production of Space*, p. 86.

55 See Peter Clark, *The English Alehouse: A Social History* (1983), especially chapters 6–7.

56 Quoted in ibid., p. 123.

57 Thomas Proctor, *A Worthy Worke Profitable to this Whole Kingdome* (1607), sig. D3^v.

58 Peacham, *The Worth of a Penny* (1647), p. 30.

59 See also *A Direction for the English Traviller*, published four times, 1635–77. The maps and tables of the *Direction* were also used for *A Booke of the Names of all Parishes, Market Towns, Villages, Hamlets, and Smallest Places in England and Wales* (four editions, 1657–77), a work described on its title-page as "very necessary For Travellers, Quartermasters, Gatherers of Breefes, Strangers, Carriers, and Messengers with Letters."

60 On Taylor, see further Bernard Capp, *The World of John Taylor, the Water Poet, 1578–1653* (Oxford, 1994).

61 Taylor, *Wandering, to see the Wonders of the West*, in *The Works of John Taylor the Water Poet Not Included in the Folio Volume of 1630*, 5 vols. (1870–78), 1: 21.

62 Ibid., 1: 1.

63 Taylor, *The Pennyles Pilgrimage* (1618) in *All the Workes of John Taylor the Water Poet* (1630), sig. M1^r. See also *Wandering, to see the Wonders*, p. 2.

64 Taylor, *Wandering, to see the Wonders*, pp. 5, 12; *A Discovery by Sea, From London to Salisbury*, in *All the Workes*, pp. 24–5.

65 *The Carriers Cosmographie* (1637), in *Works . . . Not Included*, vol. 2, and *Taylor's Travels and Circular Perambulations* (1636), in ibid., vol. 3.

66 Ibid., 1: 26.

67 Ibid., 1: 26–7.

68 Ibid., 1: 11–12.

69 Taylor, *The Certain Travailes of an uncertain Journey*, in *Works . . . Not Included*, 2: 20; *Taylor on Tame Isis*, p. 9; *The Praise, Antiquity, and Commodity of Beggerie, Beggers, and Begging* in *All the Workes*, p. 99.

70 Taylor, *The Travels of Twelve-Pence* in *All the Workes*, sigs. G4^r, G5^r.

71 Foucault, *The Order of Things: An Archaeology of the Human Sciences* (1970), pp. 178–9.

72 Malynes, *The Center of the Circle of Commerce* (1623), p. 139.

73 See John Barrell's Afterword to this volume in which he discusses the eighteenth-century spatial perception of John Dyer.

CHAPTER 4

The Cookes and the Brookes: uses of portraiture
in town and country before the Civil War

Robert Tittler

I

In a recent essay on the origins and nature of provincial town culture
of the late seventeenth and eighteenth centuries, Jonathan Barry has
usefully reconstructed the historiographical framework which has
emerged from scholarly consideration of the issue in recent years.[1] As
Barry shows, the prevailing tendency has been to perceive provincial
urban or civic culture as essentially derivative of both the aristocratic
culture of the court and countryside on the one hand and of the
metropolitan culture of London on the other. He himself has suggested
that a number of aspects of civic culture, including traditions of historical writing and civic ceremony, emerged as well from indigenous traditions of urban life, and to suit urban requirements, with far less need to
be appropriated from elsewhere than has commonly been recognized.

Although Barry deals with a period which only begins c. 1640, it seems
likely that the indigenous aspects of the civic culture he describes arose
from an earlier time. In what follows, I have set out to weigh the two
models for the formation of civic culture – the essentially appropriated
and the essentially indigenous – not only in an earlier period (c. 1560–
1640) but also with reference to a cultural genre not often considered
in this context. The study of portraiture affords an interesting opportunity to test out the applicability of these two models, especially with
the quite recent recognition of a small but interesting tradition of civic
portraiture in provincial towns.[2] This tradition yields some striking contrasts to the more familiar aristocratic and royal portraiture of the day,
what one might usefully label the "courtly" tradition.[3]

Civic portraits may be defined as paintings of town benefactors, office
holders, and other local worthies, commissioned or purchased by civic
authorities for display in civic spaces. Those which survive may now
largely be found, not (as with courtly portraiture) in art museums or

58

country houses, but in local history museums and civic halls. The earliest of these date from the last third of the sixteenth century, with several score from before 1640.

This hitherto largely unrecognized source for both the urban and cultural history of that era sheds new light on various aspects of the town/country dichotomy. Because conventions of courtly portraiture were well established for something like a half-century before the emergence of civic portraiture, thus affording ample time for appropriation, the subject itself allows us an ideal means of testing out the two models which Barry describes. In addition, these two traditions of portraiture suggest an interesting application of the idea of cultural self-fashioning laid out by Stephen Greenblatt some years ago.[4]

In order to focus the discussion more clearly, I have chosen to pursue this task by comparing two paintings which are both similar in some respects but also dissimilar in ways which characterize their respective types. The first is the mid-Elizabethan era portrait of William Brooke, tenth Lord Cobham, and his family, of Longleat;[5] the second is the slightly later (*c.* 1600) double portrait of John and Joan Cooke, Mayor and Mayoress of Gloucester.[6]

II

THE BROOKES OF LONGLEAT

The Brookes' portrait, recently displayed in the Dynasties Exhibition at the Tate Gallery, depicts a great many characteristics of English courtly, as opposed to civic, portraiture in this period. Although anonymously done, it bears an inscription identifying the subjects: William Brooke, tenth Lord Cobham, his second wife (Frances neé Newton), their six children, and her sister Joanna Newton. The figures appear in a neo-classical architectural setting which links them to the culture and style of Renaissance humanism. Joanna Newton and the children sit around two sides of a white-clothed table on which are also displayed a number of objects of highly emblematic nature: a pet bird and monkey, a gold-colored goblet, six small pewter dishes, a large serving tray and a still larger pewter serving tray covered with fruit, a fruit knife and what appears to be a servants' bell. A small lapdog peers out from below the table to catch the eye of the smallest child. All the figures are very well- and fashionably dressed, the women sporting elaborate jewellery and elegant coifs. Only Cobham himself remains in plain black.

4.1 Brookes' family portrait.

Though the figures remain somewhat stiff compared to the very best portraits of the day, they have nevertheless been rendered with considerable skill. The brushwork is subtle and finely detailed, shading and shadow are delicately rendered. The posture of the children has been conveyed with grace and ease. The artist had no need to fall back on the cliche of the hand grasping a pair of gloves, and the hands in general have an impressively natural quality to them. The work also displays substantial intellectual depth as the setting, furnishing, and implements suggest a variety of interpretations.

One could have chosen any one of hundreds of examples of courtly portraiture of this era to exemplify the contrasts with the Cooke picture and others like it, though there are not that many which depict a man and his wife. Many courtly portraits would have conveyed a good deal of information about the sitter by the addition of narrative views in the background. The famous Armada Portrait of Elizabeth with the sea-battle over her right shoulder,[7] or the well-known depiction of Thomas Howard, fourteenth Earl of Arundel, against the long gallery of his London house (Arundel House) on the Strand,[8] would stand out particularly in that respect. Other portraits of this type would have made more of the subject's virility, noting especially, for example, the tight-fitting clothing styles which came into fashion later in the century (though Brooke's virility is certainly on display here with six of his children sitting at his table). But this work nevertheless effectively allows us to contemplate the purpose and meaning of the courtly tradition, and it does so in a way wholly in keeping with Greenblatt's analysis of the Renaissance persona.

As Greenblatt's construct of self-fashioning informs us, portraits of this type allowed Renaissance gentlemen to manipulate or refashion their own identity so as to conform to contemporary cultural requirements and aspirations. In the words of Lawrence Stone:

Noblemen and gentlemen wanted above all formal family portraits, which take their place along with genealogical trees and sumptuous tombs as symptoms of the frenzied status-seeking and ancestor worship of the age. What patrons demanded was evidence of the sitter's position and wealth by opulence of dress, ornament and background.[9]

Whether we concentrate on the Brooke family portrait or almost any other courtly portrait of the same era, these aims stand out clearly. Whatever specific iconographical elements or background scenes we may find in individual examples, they virtually all point to the sitter's personal fame and achievement, as he or she wanted it to be viewed. Wealth, success, lineage, courage, manliness or femininity, sophistication and other such desirable attributes are virtually always on display, all elements of the self-fashioning of the Renaissance era.

Most of these aims stand out clearly in the Brookes' portrait, and well they might. As the tenth descendant to come into his family's title, William Brooke (1527–97) was certainly of the ilk who sought to employ portraits in this manner. Son of a wealthy and influential father, the ninth Baron Cobham, William had been educated in Padua, held command of a hundred English troops at Calais (where his father was Deputy), served Sir William Paget and the Marquess of Northampton, and sat twice for Parliament even before coming into the Barony in his own right in 1558. During the reign of Elizabeth his fame and fortune only multiplied, and he went on to serve in a number of senior capacities (including membership on the Privy Council and the office of Lord Chamberlain) and to hold the queen's trust throughout the nearly four decades which remained of his career. His eldest son would inherit his title as eleventh Baron; one of his daughters would marry Sir Robert Cecil.[10] Clearly, Brooke would have had this portrait commissioned himself, with the prime objective of announcing himself to the viewer as a cultivated, virile, affluent, and self-confident gentleman of his time.

III

THE COOKES AND THEIR PORTRAIT

Even before we learn the identity of John and Joan Cooke, it becomes clear that they inhabited a different world from the Brookes'. In addition, we cannot help but note that, if the elements of the Brookes' portrait described above ably typify the mainstream traditions of contemporary portraiture, they also set that tradition apart from the smaller and far more obscure class of civic portraiture represented by the Cookes' portrait. Who, then, were the Cookes? What is their portrait about? What does it try to convey in place of the aristocratic elements of the Brookes' milieu? Why was it done at all, and why in the form we see before us? These questions seem crucial to understanding this portrait type. They hold out promise of a deeper understanding of the civic milieu in which the painting appeared. Let us explore the context and meaning of the Cookes' portrait and see what light it may shine on these issues.

The archives tell us that John Cooke was born in Minsterworth, Gloucestershire, around the 1450s, and that he died in 1528.[11] They identify him as both a brewer and a mercer,[12] both lucrative and influential occupations in that day and age. By discovering the preservative qualities of hops, brewers had managed within the century to produce beer (as well as the more traditional ale) in much larger quantities than before, expanding their potential scale of production, physical plant and wealth. By extending credit to growers of hops as well as grain they were often involved in money-lending activities: in a later time they would be amongst the first private bankers. Mercers were if anything even more successful, certainly at the top of the English merchant hierarchy. Their influence often spread as widely as their trade goods. Involvement in both occupations suggests that Cooke was an extremely enterprizing and well-to-do man indeed. In addition, he was undoubtedly self-made, and a newcomer to Gloucester. His native village of Minsterworth was unlikely to have given him a start in these activities, which by their nature required an urban setting and a substantial base of population.

In addition to these personal attainments, Cooke used his wealth and influence to serve the City of Gloucester in a number of capacities over an active civic career spanning some five decades. Coming up through

IOHN COOKE, MAIOR
OF THE CITIE OF
GLOCESTER
4. TIMES.

4.2 Cookes' family portrait.

the *cursus honorum* of City and Guild organizations in the 1480s, serving twice as Sheriff in the 1490s, and as mayor four times between 1501 and 1518, he can easily be seen as one of the most dominant figures in Gloucester civic affairs in the several decades following that City's incorporation as a County in and of itself in 1483.[13]

As the inscription on his portrait suggests, he was also a generous benefactor to the City at his death. His will tells us that in addition to pious bequests to local churches and for the care of his soul, and bequests of his lands and tenements to his wife, Joan, he contributed widely to civic causes. He gave to support the poor of St. Bartholomew's Hospital, and to repair the great West Bridge of the City and two of its main roads. Finally, both in his will itself and in a conveyance written six days beforehand, he endowed the foundation of a free grammar school in the Parish of St. Mary de Crypt for the "erudicion" of its children.[14] To see that these bequests were carried out he named his wife Joan as sole executor. She, her brother (Alderman Thomas Messenger), and several other prominent townsmen were entrusted, as feoffees, with the foundation of the school. This came to be known as the Crypt School because of its location adjacent to St. Mary de Crypt Church in Southgate Street, where the building still stands.

Joan herself outlived her husband by sixteen years, never remarried, and faithfully carried out his bequests. In 1529 she led the feoffees in purchasing some of the lands belonging to Llanthony Priory, intending the site of those lands, adjacent to St. Mary de Crypt Church, for the school.[15] Nearly ten years later, in the spring of 1538, she managed to secure from the Crown by Letters Patent the right to purchase and hold lands and other resources up to the value of fifty pounds a year as the School's endowment. This allowed the feoffees to purchase from Thomas Pope additional lands of Llanthony Priory, which had by then been dissolved, for the sum of £266 6s. 8d. Added to lands already in hand, this nest egg served as the essential endowment of the institution.[16] Actual construction of the grammar school was completed by 1539.[17]

In addition to her work in seeing the terms of John's will to fruition, Joan left important bequests of her own. By her will of May 1544, she, too, earmarked sums to the Church and for pious bequests, and she, too, left money to keep up one of the main roads out of Gloucester. She also endowed the Cathedral Church of St. Peter's and its High Altar, and also a perpetual chantry to be governed by a board of feoffees. It was probably one of the last to be founded anywhere before the dissolution of such institutions shortly to be announced. She rounded out her bequests by remembering the inmates of three local hospitals and the poor prisoners in the City's gaols.[18] Neither will mentions children, and we must assume that the Cookes remained childless or that their children pre-deceased them.

These wills suggest that both John and Joan Cooke were first and foremost benefactors of their community: John leaving to its various causes the bulk of his considerable fortune, Joan – depicted visually as the dominant and more lively figure – carrying out his bequests and thus completing his work before adding her own. This in itself would suggest something of a different set of priorities from those the Brookes were likely to have had, with a greater emphasis on civic service to the community than on personal self-fashioning. The very fact that the Brookes presumably commissioned their own portrait, and from an artist who would render it with subtlety and sophistication, conveys the same impression. The commissioning of the Cooke portrait is quite another matter and, in fact, what little we know about it provides a crucial clue to the interpretation of the piece.

That is not to say that we know much. Perhaps the most important thing we know is that it was painted long after the death of its subjects, and at the behest of the civic government rather than of the sitters themselves. The first point is explicit, and the second implicit, in the painting's inscription. Nothing in their will suggests a posthumous commission by the sitters themselves, though neither the artist, nor the precise date, nor the cost entailed have come down to us. In addition, the mode of dress, simple as it has been rendered, belongs to a much later period than the lives of either subject. Ruff collars and delicate ruffed cuffs can hardly be earlier than mid-Elizabethan and are probably somewhat later. No record of the portrait's purchase exists in the borough records as they survive up to 1597. Other factors both of style and documentation, as well as the approximate dating of the eleven companion pieces in Gloucester, also point toward the turn of the seventeenth century.[19] We will return to the significance of this chronology below.

Wherever it may be hung it is hard to miss, for this is a striking portrait. Against the merest suggestion of a brown drapery, we see John Cooke, in his scarlet mayoral robe trimmed with ermine, standing rigidly on our left. He seems to be staring blankly into the distance slightly over our right shoulder, and he has extended his right arm, on the left of the picture, across his waist to clasp his wife Joan's right hand. Joan, standing on our right, is also well- but simply dressed, in what appears as a dark-colored (perhaps originally deep maroon), short-sleeved gown, opening in the front to reveal an embroidered underdress. The latter extends beyond the sleeves of her gown, ending in delicate lace cuffs. Her left hand clutches a pair of leather gloves. Both figures wear ruffed collars fashionable from the Elizabethan era, and Joan wears a small beret-like cap of the same time. Her only additional adornment is a curious necklace from which hang four pendants, and a simple chain clasp tying together both sides of her collar. Unlike her husband, she stares right at the viewer and strikes a pose as the dominant figure: she looks younger and more life-like than John, she stands slightly in front of him, and she alone makes eye contact with us.

Two further elements command our attention: an inscribed label in the upper left-hand corner, next to John's head, telling us that he is "MA[ster] Iohn Cooke, Maior of the Citie of Glocester 4 Times", and a much longer inscription, in the form of a poem, which runs in four vertical colums along the bottom few inches of the portrait. It reads as follows:

> Though death hath rested these life mates
> Their memory survives
> Esteemed myrrors may they be
> For Majestrats and wives
> The School of Crist ye Bartholomews
> The Cawseway in ye West
> May wittnes wch ye pious minde
> This Worthy man possest.
> This vertuous dame perform'd ye taske
> Her husband did intend
> And after him in single life
> Lived famous to her end.
> Their bountye & benificence
> On earth remaines allways
> Let present past a[nd] future time
> Still Celebrate yr Praise.

There is no artist's signature or date, and the City Chamberlains' accounts, which would almost certainly have recorded this information, along with the cost of the painting, are missing for all but three years between 1597 and 1635, the period during which the work seems to have been done.

Overall, the portrait conveys to us the charming naivety and absence of formal convention which characterizes the successful folk art of any age, but not by any stretch of the imagination the best of contemporary portraiture.[20] The figures appear lifeless and stiff, though John's more so than Joan's, and it isn't clear if they are meant to be sitting or standing. The brush strokes are broad and lack subtlety. There is very little sense of natural form to their bodies, with the hands being especially schematic. The palette remains limited to four or five colors, and nothing in the picture itself, aside from the inscriptions and John's mayoral gown, tells us much about the subjects' lives.

The Cookes' portrait may perhaps be unusual in that it is a double portrait of a man and wife: one of the very few civic portraits of this or any other time which approach the somewhat more common married couple or family painting of the courtly tradition. Were it not such a compelling piece, and so deserving of further attention in its own right, perhaps some other civic portrait might have been as good a choice for the point at hand. Nevertheless, it exemplifies in virtually all other respects the characteristics of what we must come to recognize as a distinct type of portrait in this era.

The subjects of these civic portraits (with the exception here of Joan Cooke, who held no office of her own) are nearly all cloaked in official rather than personal raiment so as to indicate their civic role as mayor and mayoress. They convey little attempt, as in many courtly portraits, to suggest physical attributes of the human body: strength through musculature, physical vigor or sensuality through close-fitting clothes, or prowess through the addition of horses or weaponry. There is little ornamentation aside from the occasional prop to suggest civic achievement. Except for inscriptions, scenes created to frame the subject, if any at all, are limited in their iconography and imagery, have no clear architectural setting, and virtually never suggest by background description anything to do with the personal achievement of the sitter. Almost all efforts at conveying the subject's character are directed to portraying the sense of age, wisdom, and the weight of civic responsibility.

But if this is intended as a commemoration of civic virtues, why is it painted as much as a half-century or more after the death of its subjects, and why even at a time when Gloucester had already become known as something of a Puritan stronghold? Surely civic virtues were as valued in the lifetimes of the Cookes as after, and yet no one seems to have considered commissioning their portrait any earlier.

In fact, we must recognize that the posthumous nature of this painting is no mere oddity. A good number of the civic portraits which have been identified from before *c.* 1640 are posthumous portrayals, some depicting figures who had been deceased for many decades.[21] The answer to both of these conundra appears to lie in two themes, one associated with the disruption of civic memory occasioned by the Reformation, and the second associated with the urgent need of Gloucester's post-Reformation civic leaders to reconstruct an alternative collective memory, in this case a "civic memory" which served their needs. Let us take up these possibilities in turn.

In its simplest formulation, "civic memory" consists of a collective sense of the past shared by members of a particular civic community. Of course such memories may easily be induced or manipulated, especially in order to fit the requirements of the dominant or ruling element of a particular era.[22] Such memories can be very large indeed. Christendom and the sense of the Christian past shared by all communicants, and the sense of England's past shared by English men and women, weigh in at one end of the scale. On the other end we may find residents of Gloucester and other civic communities, which would also have shared a sense of the past. These locally situated collective memories would have emerged to embrace the town's history, its place in the history of the realm, and its own particular heroes and worthies. In that manner it served as the foundation for the local identity.

Before the Reformation communities like Gloucester would have fostered a collective memory which had much to do with larger identities: being Christian, being English, and so forth. But closely tied with these elements of heritage, part of the local identity would have embraced the particular events, figures, and even material objects with which local residents had long been familiar, many of them with religious connotations. These would have included, *inter alia*, the patron saint of the parish church, religious guild or cathedral; icons, statuary, and images of various sorts; stained glass windows, church plate, and other such items. Noted individuals would have been remembered in the preservation of funerary brasses, in prayers for their souls offered in obits, anniversaries and similar forms, in the periodic reading aloud in the Sunday service of the names on the parish bede roll, and – for the very important – in statuary of themselves in the parish church, in lavish gifts of plate or statuary, and other large items on biblical or related themes.

These commemorative devices played several roles. Obviously, they served in spiritual terms as means of encouraging prayers for the souls of the departed. In addition, they served culturally as a means of constructing a local identity, and they served politically by encouraging respect for the community, its traditions and its leaders. Indeed, they worked in these many ways to foster a civic consciousness in their time and place.

But when most of the doctrinal foundations of the traditional collective or civic memory were disrupted and destroyed in the course of the Reformation, especially in the 1530s and 1540s, much more lay at stake than a rearrangement of the furnishings in the parish church or even a change in approved doctrine. With the iconoclastic destruction of the material elements of the old faith – of the icons and images, the bede rolls and brasses – those changes effectively erased many long-standing and central elements of the civic heritage, and much of the sense of the local past. In a culture with relatively weak traditions of urban identity to begin with, certainly as compared with a number of other Northern European traditions,[23] these were very serious losses. They threatened to disrupt conventions of civic behavior, civil law and order, and the common respect for local civic traditions and leadership.

Especially in the era of rapid economic and social change which characterized the second half of the sixteenth century, when the very population of towns turned over so quickly, civic leaders in many towns strove to reconstruct whatever elements of heritage they could so as to restore the traditional pride, respect, and deference to the civic weal. In so doing they had much less use for the models of courtly or even of metropolitan (i.e., London) culture than we have often assumed. They turned instead to the traditions and foundations of their own milieu, which was both civic and urban. We see this in the polemical use of civic architecture and furnishing,[24] in the enhanced and intense interest in the writing of civic history,[25] and in the rapid adoption of the new Protestant Calendar, in which local traditions of a secular sort could readily be grafted onto the celebration of national events, thus linking the identity of town and nation.[26] We often see it in the encouragement by the civic leadership of many communities, of a religious doctrine which encouraged civic discipline and the perfection of the city as a moral ideal:[27] a pattern which Gloucester certainly exemplified in the era at hand.[28] And in the same vein, we see it as well in the creation, for the first time, of a secular form of civic portraiture, specifically dedicated to the commemoration of civic worthies of both the present and the recent past.

IV

CONCLUSION

Although the tradition of courtly portraiture in the early modern period has not usually been approached from the literary perspective of "self-fashioning," there can be little doubt that it fits comfortably into that construct.[29] As the portrait of the Brookes suggests, the whole genre conforms in one way or another to almost all the elements which have been identified as characterizing such a theoretical model.[30] But what are we to make of civic portraits, which arose later in time and differ in so many respects from the courtly? Do they represent an exercise in self-fashioning at all and does that concept help us to understand their significance? Does civic portraiture appropriate the obvious models provided by courtly portraits, or may we see it as originating more directly from the indigenous cultural traditions and requirements of towns themselves? And finally, what does this contrast suggest about the cultural interaction of town and country?

Although the concept of self-fashioning does not apply as strictly to civic portraiture as to its better-known courtly counterpart, it does apply in some respects. The crucial point is that in the civic tradition it was not the sitters themselves who were engaged in self-fashioning, but rather the civic body, represented by its governing element, which appropriated the sitters' "selves" for civic purposes. This is not to say, of course, that the subjects of these portraits had been above a bit of self-commemoration in their own time. The Cookes did after all work diligently at memorializing themselves in their own lifetimes and in ways open to them at that time. But they did not do so by means of portraiture.

Challenged by the rapid political and social changes of the day – forces which, in Greenblatt's phrase, they well may have "perceived as alien, strange or [even] hostile,"[31] the civic leaders of the post-Reformation era sought ways of projecting civic virtues, appropriating worthy models of civic consciousness, and tying the town's present identity to its past. In this effort civic portraits proved an important innovation, one which had not been as necessary to invoke during times which were more tranquil or static, or while more traditional mnemonic devices continued to serve. The sitters of those portraits, like the Cookes, now become the objects, not of self-fashioning, but of a civic fashioning, projected by the urban leadership of the day toward the putative citizenry in the hope of remodeling the ambient political culture of their specific communities.

These observations suggest that refashioning may have been achieved by visual as well as literary means, and that it may have been pursued by civic bodies as well as by individual men and families on their own behalf. Finally, they suggest the likelihood that at least some aspects of contemporary civic culture were, as Jonathan Barry has proposed for a slightly later period, indigenously urban rather than appropriations of courtly or even metropolitan models.[32]

NOTES

Part of the research upon which this chapter is based has been facilitated by a research grant from the Social Sciences and Humanities Research Council of Canada, to whom I am most grateful. My thoughts on the subject in general have benefited greatly from the comments of David Dean, Karen Hearn, Michael Schoenfeldt, Tim Stretton, Joanna Woodall, and Keith Wrightson. This chapter in particular owes a great deal to Gerald MacLean and Joseph Ward. None of these worthy scholars should by any means be held accountable for any infelicities which may remain.

1 Jonathan Barry, "Provincial Town Culture, 1640–1780: Urbane or Civic?," in Joan Pittock and Andrew Wear, eds., *Interpretation and Cultural History* (New York, 1991), pp. 198–234, especially pp. 201–9.

2 I am engaged in a much fuller exploration of this portrait tradition in early modern provincial towns.

3 On the "courtly" tradition, see such standard works as Lorne Campbell, *Renaissance Portraits* (1990); L. Gent and N. Llewellyn, eds., *Renaissance Bodies: The Human Figure in English Culture, c. 1540–1660* (1990); John Pope-Hennessy, *The Portrait in the Renaissance* (1966); Roy Strong, *Tudor and Stuart Portraits*, 2 vols. (1969), *The English Icon: Elizabethan and Jacobean Portraiture* (1969), and *The English Renaissance Miniature* (1983).

4 Stephen Greenblatt, *Renaissance Self-Fashioning from More to Shakespeare* (Chicago, Ill., 1982).

5 Karen Hearn, ed., *Dynasties: Painting in Tudor and Jacobean England, 1530–1630* (1995), plate 51.

6 "John and Joan Cooke," in Brian Frith, *Twelve Portraits of Gloucester Benefactors* (Gloucester, 1972), cover and see p. 9.

7 Painted anonymously *c*. 1588, in Hearn, ed., *Dynasties*, plate 43.

8 By Daniel Mytens, *c*. 1618, in Hearn, ed., *Dynasties*, plate 140.

9 Lawrence Stone, *The Crisis of the Aristocracy, 1558–1641* (Oxford, 1965), p. 712.

10 See S. T. Bindoff, ed., *The House of Commons, 1509–1558*, 3 vols. (1982), I: 512–13.

11 He reveals the place of his birth in his will, which was proven in 1528, and his approximate birth-date has been inferred from the known dates at which he came to various offices in the City. PRO PROB 11/22/38.

12 Frith, *Twelve Portraits*, p. 9; Roland Austin, *The Crypt School, Gloucester, 1539–1939* (Gloucester, 1939), pp. 14–15.

13 Ibid., p. 15; and see M. Weinbaum, *British Borough Charters, 1307–1660* (Cambridge, 1943), p. xxxviii.

14 The will, proven in the Prerogative Court of Canterbury, has survived in PRO PROB 11/22/38; it is transcribed and published in Austin, *Crypt School*, pp. 136–44. The deed of enfeoffment, dated May 12, 1528, is discussed in ibid., pp. 16–18.

15 Austin, *Crypt School*, p. 28.

16 Ibid., pp. 28–30, 144–57.

17 Ibid., pp. 30–1.

18 PRO PROB 11/31/4, May 1, 1544, 36 Henry VIII.

19 See Frith, *Twelve Portraits*, pp. 7, 10. The work seems almost certainly to have been commissioned by the City of Gloucester, most probably at roughly the same time as the other eleven "Benefactors" portraits to which it bears

strong stylistic resemblance. In further contrast with the Brooke picture, which remained in private hands, the Cooke portrait seems always to have been publicly displayed. The fact that the Chamberlains' Accounts in which we would expect to find payment to the artist recorded are missing for most of this period adds somewhat to the probability of this later dating.

20 Tellingly enough, eleven of the twelve surviving civic portraits from this period in Gloucester are kept in the City Folk Museum: only the Cookes' piece rests in the City Art Museum.

21 For examples, Robert Jannys (d. 1530), John Marsham (d. 1532), and Augustine Steward (d. 1572) of Norwich were first painted in the early seventeenth century; the Bury St. Edmunds benefactor Jankyn Smith died in 1481 but his portrait seems to have been painted much later and acquired by the borough in 1616. Nicholas Thorne of Bristol died in 1545 but his portrait was completed in 1624. See B. Cozens-Hardy and E. A. Kent, eds., *The Mayors of Norwich, 1403–1835* (Norwich, 1938), pp. 42, 48–9; Virginia Tillyard, "Civic Portraits Painted for or Donated to the Council Chamber of Norwich Guildhall before 1887" (Unpublished MA Thesis, Courtauld Institute, London University, 1978), pp. 21, 42–3, 45, 46; A. Moore and C. Crawley, eds., *Family and Friends: A Regional Survey of British Portraiture* (1992), pp. 24, 26–8, 196–7; M. Statham, *Jankyn Smith and the Guildhall Feoffees* (Bury St. Edmunds, 1981), p. 3; Richard Quick, ed., *Catalogue of the Second Loan Collection of Pictures held in the Bristol Art Gallery, 1905* (Bristol, 1905), no. 227.

22 Amidst voluminous scholarship, see especially: Maurice Halbwachs, *Les cadres sociaux de la mémoire* (Paris, 1925 [1952]), *La mémoire collective* (Paris, 1950), and *La topographie légendaire des évangiles* (Paris, 1971); Keith Thomas, "The Perception of the Past in Early Modern England" (Creighton Lecture, London University, 1983); Pierre Nora, "Between Memory and History," *Representations* 26 (Spring, 1989): 7–24; and D. Middleton and D. Edwards, eds., *Collective Remembering* (1990).

23 This theme is pursued at greater length in Lawrence Manley, *Literature and Culture in Early Modern London* (Cambridge, 1995), especially p. 15.

24 See Robert Tittler, *Architecture and Power: The Town Hall and the English Urban Community* (Oxford, 1991).

25 See Robert Tittler, "Corporate Rule and the Civic Memory," in *The Reformation and the Towns: Politics and Political Culture, 1540–1620* (Oxford, 1998), chapter 13; and Barry, "Provincial Town Culture," pp. 211–23.

26 David Cressy, "The Protestant Calendar and the Vocabulary of Celebration in Early Modern England," *Journal of British Studies* 9 (1990): 31–52; and Ronald Hutton, *The Rise and Fall of Merry England* (Oxford, 1994).

27 See especially Patrick Collinson, *The Religion of Protestants* (1982), chapter 4, and *The Birthpangs of Protestant England* (1988), chapter 2; and David Underdown, *Fire from Heaven: Life in an English Town in the Seventeenth Century* (1992).

28 Peter Clark, "'The Ramoth-Gilead of the Good': Urban Change and Political Radicalism in Gloucester, 1540–1640," in Peter Clark, A. G. R. Smith, and

Nicholas Tyacke, eds., *The English Commonwealth, 1547–1640* (Leicester, 1979), pp. 167–88.
29 See Greenblatt, *Renaissance Self-Fashioning*, pp. 1–12.
30 Ibid., p. 9.
31 Ibid., p. 9.
32 Barry, "Provincial Town Culture," *passim*.

CHAPTER 5

Digger writing and rural dissent in the English Revolution: representing England as a common treasury

David Loewenstein

In the Digger writings of the English Revolution, the countryside assumed new symbolic significance. Led by Gerrard Winstanley, the Digger experiment in agrarian communism of 1649–50 strikingly exemplifies the interaction of writing with symbolic and social practice in seventeenth-century England. This short-lived rural initiative, with the visionary writings it generated, was the most daring attempt to create a new kind of social identity based on communal property and ownership of the land during the English Revolution. In *The Country and the City*, Raymond Williams stressed the great potency of these symbolic associations, observing that "on the actual settlements . . . powerful feelings have gathered and have been generalized."[1] In historically specific ways, the Digger settlement on the commons of Surrey became the locus of "powerful feelings" about the countryside and the unsettled nation at large. Such feelings expressed the Diggers' sense of a social revolution in crisis during the English Republic.

The Diggers emerged following a period of extreme economic hardship for the lower classes when unemployment, the disruptions of war, rising food prices, and a series of disastrous harvests in the late 1640s had created famine conditions and "a sad deare time for poore people."[2] Their agrarian community, which attempted to transform the earth into "a common treasury for all" humankind "without respect of persons," was an acute response to the failures of the Revolution and its experimental Commonwealth.[3] The proliferation of "kingly power" during the Interregnum, the failure of the government to address the grievances of the poor, the practice of "buying and selling" the land, the slow progress of law reform, and oppression by local landowners: such conditions were fueling class conflicts and exposing the contradictions and ambiguities of a new Republic "declared to be a free State or Commonwealth" (*Works*, p. 324) by the Rump Parliament in May 1649.[4]

Several major Digger texts challenging London and the powers of England located there will be my focus because these works highlight the contradictions of the Revolution during this volatile period, and because they foreground the tension between the city and the symbolic representation of the countryside sustained by Digger writings and communal activities. A bankrupt cloth merchant who had worked in London during the 1630s and early 1640s, Winstanley was forced to retreat to the country during the economic depression of the Civil War and earn his living as a farm laborer and cowherd. Revelations experienced during a visionary trance late in 1648, which coincided with the climactic events of the Revolution, resulted in his conversion to agrarian communism; however, it was not until April 1, 1649 that he would begin to "act materially" a new "Law of Righteousnesse" (*Works*, p. 195) to free creation from bondage and make the earth a common treasury for all. Accompanied by a small group of poor laborers, he began digging, manuring, and planting the common land at St. George's Hill in the parish of Walton-on-Thames in Surrey – an area where enclosure had hurt the poor.[5] Both communal digging and polemical writing expressed the Diggers' acute sense of rural alienation from the politics and policies of the Interregnum.

Digger activities and writings illustrate the potency of the semi-rural countryside near London as a symbolic resource during this critical period when the new Commonwealth's authority was put to the test. Cultivated by digging, the common and waste lands in the Surrey outskirts quickly became a highly contentious site of rural resistance to the central government in London, and events there were widely reported in contemporary newsbooks. "Our digging . . . is the talk of the whole Land," Winstanley wrote to Lord Fairfax, "some approving, some disowning; some are friends, filled with love, and sees the worke intends good to the Nation . . . others are enemies filled with fury" (*Works*, p. 281).[6] The Digger rural experiment did indeed provoke a good deal of "fury": local landlords and freeholders systematically harassed and beat up the Diggers, pulled down their houses, spoiled their crops, and had some of them arrested and imprisoned. The landowners complained about the Diggers to the Council of State, the Rump's supreme executive body, which directed Fairfax as Commander-in-Chief to investigate the Digger threat to private property. In late May 1649 Fairfax visited the Surrey colony and in subsequent months soldiers stationed in the area (though apparently not acting on orders from Fairfax himself) also cruelly beat the Diggers and destroyed their houses.[7] By August 1649 the original Digger colony was driven off the land. The Diggers relocated on the nearby common at Cobham where they also encountered harassment from landowners, as well as court actions. By April 1650 that community too was suppressed.

On the commons the Diggers were clearly doing more than simply eking out a rural livelihood for themselves. They were performing provocative symbolic actions fundamental to their bold enterprise of social and religious protest.[8] Digging and planting "the plesant fruit trees of freedom" incited the fury of men of property because Winstanley and the landless laborers who followed him were endeavoring "to dig up their Tythes, their Lawyers Fees, their Prisons, and all that Art and Trade of darknesse, whereby they get money under couller of Law" (*Works*, p. 335). Around the Diggers' activities had indeed gathered a series of powerful feelings and associations. The Diggers transformed the land itself into a potent if fragile site of popular agitation – a place associated with agrarian progress, political freedom, and economic equity separate from the center of urban power, worldliness, and capitalism.[9] Historians have tended to suggest that the poorer sort, both rural and urban, were politically inert during the English Revolution.[10] But the symbolic activities and writings of the Diggers suggest that, led by an eloquent spokesman like Winstanley, the laboring poor were not necessarily passive victims and could indeed become sharply critical of the politics of their superiors, including Parliament. The Diggers did not hesitate to question the official policies of the Republic, as well as its agencies and established authorities in London. "I have not flattered Parliament, Army, City, nor Countrey," Winstanley asserts in his *Watch-Word to the City of London*, the same text where, echoing Acts 17: 6, he tells the city that "freedom is the man that will turn the world upside downe, therefore no wonder he hath enemies" (*Works*, pp. 337, 316). Although realistic enough to appeal to powerful leaders like Fairfax and Cromwell, Winstanley's outspoken denunciations of "murdering propriety" (*Works*, p. 453), sometimes issued with prophetic fervor, hardly support the notion that he respected earthly power and authorities.[11]

Because of its size and importance, metropolitan London was an obvious target in Digger writing.[12] As the Republic's capital with a population of 400,000 in 1650, it seemed to Winstanley and the Diggers to be the center of a complex network of power in a nation ruled by a covetous regime whose worldly policies were continuing to fuel class divisions and thwart social revolution, despite the nation's recent political upheavals.[13] In London treacherous forms of antichristian power had

easily assumed new shapes and continued to expand, thereby threatening the fragile rural existence of the Diggers. Hence Digger writings
and symbolic actions in the countryside often dramatize a tension between
country and city that highlights the unresolved social conflicts of the
Revolution – "O thou City, thou Hypocriticall City!" Winstanley cries
out in *A Watch-Word* as he envisages London and indeed all of England
in the clutch of Norman power (*Works*, p. 335). England's central government could respond to the Diggers with "mildnesse and modera-
tion," as Fairfax and his Council of War did on April 20, 1649, when
Winstanley and William Everard were summoned to defend their "work
of Community in the earth" (*Works*, p. 281). But once at Whitehall
the Digger leaders refused to doff their hats to their social superiors,
thereby symbolically expressing their egalitarian convictions in a manner
anticipating the defiant symbolic gestures of the Interregnum Quakers.[14]
Yet as the center of England's power, the city could also represent in
Digger writing a yearning for new freedom for the laboring poor, especially after Parliament had abolished the House of Lords and triumphed
over the king, the Norman successor to William the Conqueror.
Winstanley and his followers issued a series of dense metaphorical
pamphlets challenging and warning the City of London, the Army,
Parliament, Lord Fairfax, and even Cromwell.

The force of such polemical writings partly derives from their visionary mythmaking, which dramatizes the social tensions still unresolved
by the upheavals of the Revolution. Digger writings employ central scriptural myths, such as the Garden of Eden, the Fall and Exodus, the conflict between Cain and Abel, and between the Lamb and the Dragon.
But they invest them with new socioeconomic meanings that vividly
express the material conditions of the oppressed commoners, as well
as continuing class divisions and inequities. As a product of mid-
seventeenth-century radical religious culture, Winstanley rejected
orthodox Protestant theology, emphasizing the Spirit within each
reader above the letter of the Bible. Not only did he interpret scriptural history and texts with great liberty, but he allegorized biblical
myths in socioeconomic and political terms that were historically
specific. The controversial "work of Community in the earth" itself
symbolized the urgent apocalyptic conflict disrupting the nation during the Commonwealth – "a pitched battaile between the Lamb and
the Dragon," Winstanley wrote to Lord Fairfax, in which the struggling
Diggers would "not strive with sword and speare, but with spade and
plow" (*Works*, pp. 281, 286). Even as their radicalism took a religious

form,[15] Winstanley and the Diggers reinterpreted the myth of the Norman Yoke, thereby explaining the origin and continuity of the long process of conquest and seizure of the land with its consequences of social suffering and exploitation. Ever since William the Conqueror introduced the Lords of Manors into England, they argued, the common people had been divorced from the land (much of which had been enclosed) and enslaved by kingly power. This appropriation of the land was then reinforced by an intricate legal system which protected private property and by a cunning professional clergy who perpetuated kingly power by imposing tithes on the people, while using scriptural hermeneutics to confound them.[16]

Central to the Diggers' program for reconstructing society on the basis of communal property was their revision of the Genesis myth highlighted in their first manifesto, *The True Levellers Standard Advanced* (April 1649). This collaborative work – Winstanley's name appears on the title page along with fourteen others – challenges "the Powers of England," and "all the Powers of the World," to restore that state of pristine freedom that pre-existed property rights and class hierarchies:

In the beginning of Time, the great Creator Reason, made the Earth to be a Common Treasury, to preserve Beasts, Birds, Fishes, and Man, the lord that was to govern this Creation; for Man had Domination given to him, over the Beasts, Birds, and Fishes; but not one word was spoken in the beginning, That one branch of mankind should rule over another. (*Works*, p. 251)[17]

Winstanley's revolutionary mythmaking was bold indeed in a political period when England's governors resisted not only rampant sectarian enthusiasm, but any blurring of distinctions between master and servant, landlord and tenant, as well as threats to redistribute wealth and power downward through the social hierarchy.[18] Moreover, by deliberately calling God "the great Creator Reason," Winstanley and his fellow Diggers immediately eschew the more distant, awesome God of orthodox Puritanism – the God the ministry invoked to maintain social control and terrify the poor, so as to keep them submissive and paying compulsory tithes in support of the clerical estate.[19]

At points the Digger manifesto sharply confronts the contradictions of the so-called free Commonwealth (soon to be formally declared by the Rump) in which all just power was supposed to be derived from the people. It blames the present governors of England and their unreformed legal system for bringing great hardships upon the common people of England, thereby preventing the countryside from becoming "a Common Treasury of relief for all" (*Works*, p. 252):[20]

Thou hast made many promises and protestations to make the Land a Free Nation: And yet at this very day, the same people, to whom thou hast made such Protestations of Liberty, are oppressed by thy Courts, Sizes, Sessions, by thy Justices and Clarks of the Peace, so called, Bayliffs, Committees, are imprisoned, and forced to spend that bread, that should save their lives from Famine. (*Works*, p. 256)

To drive home their point about the oppressiveness of laws upheld since the Norman Conquest, the Diggers employ an ominous metaphor. They evoke the harshness of contemporary London prison conditions by characterizing the laws as "the Cords, Bands, Manacles, and Yokes that the enslaved *English*, like *Newgate* Prisoners, wear upon their hands and legs as they walk the streets; by which those *Norman* Oppressors, and these their Successors from Age to Age have enslaved the poor People" (*Works*, p. 259). The imprisonment of the poor in England, however, is not confined to a place like Newgate. They are imprisoned wherever they are in England; their oppression is reinforced by the uncompromising system of laws, judges, courts, and prisons.[21] The powers of England in the new Republic thus live in "mighty Delusion" as they "pretend to throw down that *Norman* yoke, and *Babylonish* power" (*Works*, p. 259). The reality, the Digger writers suggest, is indeed much grimmer and is confirmed by the unsettledness of the new Commonwealth itself.

The tone of *The True Levellers Standard* is often sharp, anticipating the defiant sectarian challenge that extended into the countryside during the early 1650s as the Quaker movement gained momentum.[22] Like the urban prophet Abiezer Coppe, the Ranter who goes to "that great City" London to issue "a terrible Word,"[23] the Diggers direct their warnings at the unrighteous and hard-hearted institutional authorities: "you that are the great Ones of the Earth" (*Works*, p. 266). But the prophets of the countryside also warn the laborers themselves who, working for hire, help to perpetuate England's ensnaring system of buying and selling the land which has created the present condition of economic bondage, inequity, and poverty. The Diggers record another voice, "heard in a Trance," warning of God's imminent judgment and intervention: "*Whosoever labours the Earth for any Person or Persons, that are lifted up to rule over others, and doth not look upon themselves, as Equal to others in the Creation: The hand of the Lord shall be upon that Laborer: I the Lord have spoke it and I will do it*" (*Works*, p. 262). The Diggers themselves act and write according to "the power of the Spirit," though they find themselves living in an age full of spiritual dissembling and duplicity. "Hypocrisie, Covetousness, Envie, sottish Ignorance, and Pride" appear at this moment when it is more common to observe "Forms and Customs, and pretend to the Spirit" (*Works*, p. 263). Their version of Norman tyranny recalls the Israelite captivity; but while echoing the language of Exodus – "*Let Israel go Free*" – and assuming the warning voice of the Lord as they yearn for deliverance, the Diggers also radically redefine social and political oppression in terms of a system of property ownership that must be shattered before a new age of righteousness can begin in the Commonwealth and "the poor may labour the Waste land": "break in pieces quickly the Band of particular Propriety, dis-own this oppressing Murder, Oppression and Thievery of Buying and Selling of Land, owning of landlords and paying of Rents" (*Works*, pp. 265, 264).

When Winstanley published his *Appeal to the House of Commons* in July 1649, Digger disillusionment with the Rump Parliament was even keener and expressed "without flattery" by means of a long series of sharp warnings: "if you free not the Land from entanglement of all *Norman* yoaks . . . seeing power now is in your hand, you will be the first that break Covenant with Almighty God . . . if this freedom be not granted quietly, you will pull the blood and cries of the poor oppressed upon your heads . . . if you neglect this, you will fall as fast in their affections as ever you rise" (*Works*, pp. 310, 305–7). Winstanley evokes a sense of biblical transgression and illicitly coveted possession, combined with a sense of impending divine judgment, as he compares those manorial lords seeking to possess the common lands with King Ahab "that was restlesse till he had *Naboths* Vineyard, and so in the midst of their abundance, yet will eat the bread out of the poores mouthes" (*Works*, p. 307). Naboth refused to part with the vineyard because it was the inheritance of his fathers, much as the poor, victimized commoners of England now consider the land their principal and endangered inheritance.[24] Most ominous is the charge of blood guilt transferred from the king to the new regime itself, which now is in danger of repeating the history of the oppressor and oppressed and the persecution of the righteous that originated with Cain and Abel and culminated in the recent violence of the English Civil Wars: "If . . . the Lords of Manors shall still be Lords of the Common land, and the Common people be still enslaved to them, then you pull the guilt of King Charles his blood upon your own heads; for then it will appear to the view of all men, That you cut off the Kings head, that you might establish your selves in his Chair of Government" (*Works*, p. 307).[25]

Published in August 1649 when the harassed Diggers had moved to nearby Cobham Common, Winstanley's *Watch-Word to the City of London*

and the Armie is the Digger's most forceful prophecy to warn London of
its continuing spiritual crisis. Winstanley addresses London as one of
its "sons" and as "a free Denizen" of the City, and yet he also positions himself as a rural outsider who, having recently been arrested for
trespassing with other Diggers, expresses his sense of alienation from
the center of power and commerce. Because of London's "cheating sons
in the theeving art of buying and selling" he was originally "beaten out
both of estate and trade" and forced "to live a Countrey-life" in Surrey
(*Works*, pp. 315, 317) where he continued to suffer from taxation. After
summarizing how he came to found the Digger experiment in order
"to procure Englands peace inward and outward," Winstanley highlights the Digger commitment to individual human agency, insisting that
words and writings must be accompanied by symbolic actions that challenge class oppression and advance social change: "for action is the life
of all, and if thou dost not act, thou dost nothing" (*Works*, p. 315). Those
ruling the Commonwealth, however, have proven themselves directionless
and blind in the aftermath of the Revolution, despite the destruction
of "the common enemy" – the king – and subsequent promises "made
for freedome" of the poor: like Paul temporarily blinded by a mist (Acts
13: 11), the powers of England "are all like men in a mist, seeking for
freedom, and know not where, nor what it is" (*Works*, p. 316). Recently
the vibrant center of revolutionary activity and discourse, "the mansion
house of liberty" as Milton had imagined it, the City of London has
become the center of England's new Norman bondage and slavery –
"And London, nay England, look to thy freedom; I'le assure thee,
thou art very neere to be cheated of it, and if thou lose it now after all
thy boasting, truly thy posterity will curse thee." When it comes to the
creation of true freedom, Winstanley finds especially distressing the dis-
parity between words and action in the aftermath of 1648–9: "every
one talks of freedome, but there are but few that act for freedome, and
the actors for freedome are oppressed by the talkers and verball pro-
fessors of freedome" (*Works*, p. 317).

A *Watch-Word to the City* includes an idiosyncratic vision of scriptural
history and fratricide expressing the Diggers' distinctive communist perspective on class conflict and oppression. Winstanley reconfigures the
traditional myth of the Fall in terms of the human invention of private
property and enclosure, and the ensuing social discontents and enmity
fostered by the politics of capitalism and the sin of covetousness. The
land becomes a site of mythic struggle dividing the nation into classes,
fueling the tension between country and city, and oppressing creation:

But since the fall of man there from, which came in by the rising up of covetousnesse in the heart of mankind (to which Serpent the man consented) and from thence mankind was called *A-dam*: for this covetousnesse makes mankind to be a stoppage of freedome in the creation, and by this covetous power, one branch of mankind began to lift up himself above another, as *Cain* lifted up himself, and killed his brother *Abel*: and so one branch did kill and steal away the comfortable use of the earth from another, as it is now: the elder brother lives in a continuall theevery, stealing the Land from the younger brother. (*Works*, p. 323)

Addressed to the great urban center of England, the biblical myth of Cain and Abel here is especially evocative since the scriptural Cain was not only a tiller and encloser of the earth, but, after slaying his younger brother, this original "fugitive and . . . vagabond in the earth" established the first urban center: "he builded a city, and called the name of the city, after the name of his son, Enoch" (Genesis 4: 12–17). Scriptural history assumes a fresh immediacy in Winstanley's socio-economic mythmaking, as he challenges the present urban order of England by reminding its rulers that the conflict between Cain and Abel, between "cursed propriety" and righteousness (*Works*, p. 290), persists in contemporary property rights, private ownership, social hierarchy, and unequal power.

Moreover, the consequences of the Fall persist in Norman laws that hinder "the poore from the use of the common Land": in such a world of darkness "is *Adam* fallen, or *Cain* killing *Abel* to this day" (*Works*, p. 323). In Digger mythmaking, the struggle between Cain and Abel is connected with buying and selling the land, which itself has urgent apocalyptic implications for Winstanley, recalling as it does Revelation 13: 17 – "no man might buy or sell, save he that had the mark, or the name of the beast." Winstanley's *Watch-Word* highlights the intensity of the presentday struggle threatening the Digger community: those ministers who encourage local landowners and freeholders to assault and imprison the poor Diggers and to drive away their cows or spoil their crops "prove themselves to be members of the Beast that had two horns, like a Lamb, and yet spake like a Dragon, & so they fulfill that Scripture in Rev. 13.16" (*Works*, p. 334).

Warning the city and England of their great spiritual danger and the need to be alert to the subtle advancement of Norman powers, Winstanley reinforces a sense of immediate social and national crisis by combining an elaborate military trope with the myth of the Norman Conquest. The advancement and hierarchy of the new Norman camp resembles a large army; yet its counselors, officers, and soldiers who overrun the land are actually landowners, ministers, lawyers, and other rich oppressors. Winstanley thereby suggests the ominous expansion of treacherous powers during the new Commonwealth, an expansion threatening the aspirations of England's common people, as well as the rural existence of the poor Diggers. "*William* the Conquerours Army begins to gather into head againe," and though the "chief Captain *Charles*" may now be gone, Winstanley scornfully observes in a passage about its descending ranks:

yet his Colonells, which are Lords of Mannours, his Councellours and Divines, which are our Lawyers and Priests, his inferiour officers and Souldiers, which are the Freeholders, and Land-lords, all which did steal away our Land from us when they killed and murdered our Fathers in that *Norman* conquest: And the Bailiffes that are slaves to their covetous lusts and all the ignorant bawling women against our digging for freedome, are the snapsack boyes and the ammunition sluts that follow the *Norman* Camp. (*Works*, p. 330)

These Norman powers, which Winstanley strives to cast down, have "grown very numerous and big" and their fury is so great – like a flood threatening to engulf the land – that England during the first year of the Commonwealth is more vulnerable than ever before (*Works*, pp. 334, 336).

Winstanley highlights that vulnerability in a subsequent tract, *A New-Yeers Gift Sent to the Parliament and Armie* of January 1650. Here he recalls Civil War history in class terms, thereby reminding the gentry, the central government, and the Army leaders of their outstanding debt to the common people who now murmur against them. During the reign of Charles, "all sorts of people complained of oppression, both Gentrie and Common people, because their lands, Inclosures, and Copieholds were intangled" (*Works*, p. 357). Once in power and "assembled in Parliament," the gentry called "upon the poor Common-People to come and help . . . and cast out oppression," so that Parliament's successes of the Civil Wars owed much to the cooperation and support of the poorer people who now, still living in distress, deserve to share equally in the hard-won victory and benefit from the common land from which they are being excluded. Winstanley's response to the new Commonwealth, whose controversial Engagement he supported as symbolic of a new age of righteous freedom for all classes,[26] therefore remains deeply ambivalent in this text. Although its newest rulers have been provided with a unique opportunity for radical social and spiritual reform – "You have set Christ upon his throne in *England* by your Promises, Engagements, Oathes, and Two Acts of Parliament" – England has also remained a fertile land for the growth of kingly power "to bud fresher out" (*Works*, pp. 386, 359).

Winstanley's vigorous colloquial prose, which we might expect from a writer digging and planting the commons, conveys the resurgence of kingly power despite the regicide, the Act of Parliament abolishing the institution of kingship (17 March 1649), and the Act making England a free state. Reminding the gentry and Parliament of much work yet to be accomplished before all classes can rejoice in the Creation, he compares kingly power and oppression to a great tree whose large roots have grown deep and whose numerous branches block the light of right-eousness from reaching the common land:

you that complained are helped and freed, and that top-bow is lopped off the tree of Tyrannie, and Kingly power in that one particular is cast out; but alas oppression is a great tree still, and keeps off the sun of freedome from the poor Commons still, he hath many branches and great roots which must be grub'd up, before everyone can sing Sions songs. (*Works*, p. 357)

Elaborating the metaphor, Winstanley registers how kingly power has manifested itself in other forms of power and covetousness which darken the Creation and strive against the Spirit: "Now there are Three Branches more of Kinglie power greater then the former that oppresses this Land wonderfully" – "the power of the Tithing Priests," "the power of Lords of Mannors," and "the intolerable oppression" of "bad Laws" and "bad Judges." All these forms of kingly power are "Branches" of the Norman Conquest or Yoke and "branches of the power of darkness it self" (*Works*, pp. 357, 382). Indeed, by letting "the other Branches and root stand," the great tree of kingly power will only "grow again and recover fresher strength" (*Works*, p. 353) as it has since the beginning of the Republic. Its "several limbs and members must be cast out" before "Kingly power," which has become so widely spread in the nation, "can be pulled up root and branch" (*Works*, p. 372). As his trope of the great tree suggests, Winstanley's visionary and figurat-ive language is frequently rooted in the natural world but gains vigor by fusing allegorical and prophetic biblical meanings (in Malachi 4: 1 the Lord shall leave the proud "neither root nor branch"), with socio-historical ones (the "root and branch petition" of December 1640 called for radical reform including the abolition of a Romish episco-pacy "with all its dependencies, roots and branches").[27] The figurative writing of *A New-Yeers Gift* thus conveys Winstanley's acute sense of the interconnectedness of the branches of oppressive power entangling the earth.

Even after his fragile communist experiment in Surrey had collapsed by the spring of 1650, Winstanley boldly challenged Lord General Cromwell himself to continue the arduous task of reforming "the Clergy, Lawyers, and Law; for all the Complaints of the Land are wrapped up within them three, not in the person of a King" (*Works*, p. 505). In his epistle to Cromwell (dated November 5, 1651) prefacing *The Law of Freedom in a Platform of True Magistracy Restored*, Winstanley self-consciously apologized, however, for the "clownish language" of his writing (*Works*, p. 510). The language of his rough-hewn platform, the defeated Digger confesses, may seem, unpolished or "clownish," his text being "like a poor man that comes cloathed to your door in a torn country garment, who is unacquainted with the learned Citizens unselted forms and fashions." By presenting his work in a self-deprecating manner, as he compares it to a poor rustic outsider, the powerless Winstanley managed to express vividly the perspective of the poor, exploited laborer excluded from both the political nation and free use of the English countryside: "take the clownish language," he poignantly advised the godly leader of the Commonwealth, "for under that you may see beauty" (*Works*, p. 510).

In terms of social vision, Winstanley and his fellow Diggers were in many ways far ahead of their age. Indeed, at the most exhilarating moments during their politically and often apocalyptically charged struggle to effect a new agrarian communist order, it seemed to them that "the present state of the old World . . . [was] running up like parchment in the fire, and wearing away" (*Works*, p. 252). Yet neither Digger writing nor action managed to alter the socially conservative course of the Revolution whose first Interregnum regime clearly had little intention of transforming the existing social order so that England might become a "common treasury" for all regardless of class. The Digger movement itself died out within two years of its birth: its visionary ideals regarding the land, illuminated by Winstanley's vigorous prose, were too radical for the Revolution and the cautious Republic it had generated. Yet by investing rural England with such powerful feelings and new symbolic associations, the Diggers boldly challenged and defined the Revolution's limitations, while in their visionary writings they acutely analyzed and represented some of its deepest contradictions.[28]

NOTES

1 Williams, *Country and City*, p. 1; and see pp. 289, 298. Williams, however, does not consider the Diggers.

2 *The Diary of Ralph Josselin: 1616–1683*, ed. Alan MacFarlane (Oxford, 1976), p. 110 (entry for 6 February 1648). On the economic depression and disruptions of the late 1640s, see C. G. A. Clay, *Economic Expansion and Social Change: England 1500–1700*, 2 vols. (Cambridge, 1984), 1: 230; R. C. Richardson, "Town and Countryside in the English Revolution," in R. C. Richardson, ed., *Town and Countryside in the English Revolution* (Manchester, 1992), pp. 1–18, especially pp. 6–8; C. B. Phillips, "Landlord-Tenant Relationships, 1642–1660," in ibid., pp. 224–50 especially pp. 234–5, 245.

3 *The Works of Gerrard Winstanley*, ed. George Sabine (Ithaca, N.Y., 1941), pp. 164, 315. Subsequent references are given parenthetically. On the Republic's failures to provide for the poor in London and throughout the Commonwealth during 1649 and the early 1650s, see Joan Thirsk, "Agrarian Problems and the English Revolution," in Richardson, ed., *Town and Countryside*, pp. 169–97, especially pp. 174–5.

4 Winstanley echoes "An Act Declaring England to be a Commonwealth" of 19 May 1649: see Samuel Rawson Gardiner, ed., *The Constitutional Documents of the Puritan Revolution 1625–1660*, 3rd edn. (Oxford, 1906; rpt. 1979), p. 388. On the Rump's lack of interest in the hardship of the poor, see David Underdown, *Pride's Purge: Politics in the Puritan Revolution* (Oxford, 1971), pp. 282, 284, 329, and Austin Woolrych, *Commonwealth to Protectorate* (Oxford, 1982), p. 7.

5 For Winstanley's visionary trance, see *Works*, p. 190. On the spread of Digger influence to similar rural settlements in central and southern England, see Keith Thomas, "Another Digger Broadside,"*Past and Present* 42 (1969): 57–68, especially 57–60, 65; and *Works*, pp. 439–41, 649–51.

6 For sample newsbook accounts, see Joad Raymond, ed., *Making the News: An Anthology of the Newsbooks of Revolutionary England* (New York, 1993), pp. 392–5. On rural dissent in the early modern period without reference to the Diggers, see the studies in Margaret Spufford, ed., *The World of Rural Dissenters, 1520–1725* (Cambridge, 1995).

7 For hostilities toward the Diggers, see *Works*, pp. 284–5, 344, 367–8, 380, and especially pp. 392–6. See also G. E. Aylmer, "The Religion of Gerrard Winstanley," in J. F. McGregor and B. Reay, eds., *Radical Religion in the English Revolution* (Oxford, 1984), pp. 91–119, especially pp. 100–2.

8 On the importance of such symbolic actions, see Lynn Hunt, "Introduction: History, Culture, and Text," in Lynn Hunt, ed., *The New Cultural History* (Berkeley, Calif., 1989), pp. 1–22, especially p. 16.

9 On the city's usual association with progress, see Williams, *Country and City*, p. 297.

10 See, for example, Lawrence Stone, *The Causes of the English Revolution* (1972), p. 145; and Brian Manning, *The English People and the English Revolution*,

1640–1649 (1976). Buchanan Sharp summarizes recent historians of the Revolution, including Stone, Manning, and David Underdown who have suggested that the poorer sort were passive compared to the godly middling sort. See "Rural Discontents and the English Revolution," in Richardson, ed., *Town and Countryside*, pp. 251–72, especially p. 252; see also pp. 260–1, 267–9.

11 For the view that Winstanley "always had a respect for [earthly] power and its personal and institutional manifestations," see J. C. Davis, *Utopia and the Ideal Society: A Study of English Utopian Writings, 1516–1700* (Cambridge, 1981), p. 182; see also pp. 183, 190.

12 On London and liberty in the 1640s, see Lawrence Manley, *Literature and Culture in Early Modern London* (Cambridge, 1995), chapter 10. See also Keith Lindley, "London's Citizenry in the English Revolution," in Richardson, ed., *Town and Countryside*, pp. 19–45.

13 For discussion of why a social revolution did not accompany political revolution in London, see Valerie Pearl, "Change and Stability in Seventeenth-Century London," *London Journal* 5: 1 (1979): 3–34, and "Social Policy in Early Modern London," in Hugh Lloyd-Jones, Valerie Pearl, and Blair Worden, eds., *History and Imagination: Essays in Honour of H. R. Trevor-Roper* (1981), pp. 115–31.

14 See the newsbook report of the Diggers in Andrew Sharp, ed., *Political Ideas of the English Civil Wars, 1641–49* (1983), p. 207; and Raymond, ed., *Making the News*, pp. 392–3.

15 See Barry Reay, "Radicalism and Religion in the English Revolution: an Introduction," in McGregor and Reay, eds., *Radical Religion*, pp. 1–21; and Christopher Hill, "The Religion of Gerrard Winstanley," *Past and Present Supplement*, no. 5 (1978). For the unconvincing view that Winstanley was a secularized saint, see C. H. George, "Gerrard Winstanley: A Critical Retrospect," in C. R. Cole and M. E. Moody, eds., *The Dissenting Tradition* (Athens, Ohio, 1975), pp. 191–225.

16 On the debate whether the manorial system was introduced into England by the Normans, see Phillips, "Landlord-Tenant," p. 224. On the continuous process of enclosure and the appropriation of the land, see Williams, *Country and City*, pp. 96–7.

17 Compare Genesis 1: 26.

18 On the Rump's resistance to social radicalism, see Woolrych, *Commonwealth to Protectorate*, p. 8.

19 For Winstanley's provocative use of "the Spirit Reason," see *Works*, pp. 104–5.

20 On the Rump's shortcomings with regard to legal reform, see Underdown, *Pride's Purge*, pp. 275–80, and Blair Worden, *The Rump Parliament, 1648–1653* (Cambridge, 1974), pp. 114, 116, 139, 152.

21 On radical responses to the legal system during the 1640s and 1650s, see Manning, *English People*, pp. 269–74. For the metaphor of England as a prison with the intricate laws as its materials and the lawyers as its jailors, see Winstanley's *A New Yeers Gift*, in *Works*, p. 361.

22 See Derek Hirst, "The Failure of Godly Rule in the English Republic," *Past and Present* 132 (1991): 33–66, especially 36, 38.
23 See Coppe, *A Fiery Flying Roll: A Word from the Lord to all the Great Ones of the Earth* (1649), title page and "Preface."
24 See 1 Kings 21: 1–16.
25 See Stephen Baskerville, "Blood Guilt in the English Revolution," *The Seventeenth Century* 8: 2 (1993): 181–202.
26 See G. E. Aylmer, "England's Spirit Unfoulded: or, An Incouragement to Take the Engagement: A Newly Discovered Pamphlet by Gerrard Winstanley," *Past and Present* 40 (1968): 3–15.
27 See Gardiner, ed., *Constitutional Documents*, pp. 137–44.
28 See Underdown, *Pride's Purge*, pp. 280–1, 284; and Margaret James, *Social Problems and Policy during the Puritan Revolution: 1640–1660* (1930), chapter 6. For valuable comments on Winstanley's revolutionary writings in terms of agrarian complaint literature, see McRae, *God Speed*, pp. 124–31.

"Gulfes, Deserts, Precipices, Stone": Marvell's "Upon Appleton House" and the contradictions of "nature"

Robert Markley

Literary critics and historians traditionally have assumed that the pressures of demographic growth and technological innovation transformed seventeenth- and eighteenth-century England from a quasi-feudal into a capitalist society and, in the process, reshaped the landscape in unprecedented ways. The progressivist implications of this narrative, however, have been challenged by recent cultural and ecological historians who have called into question the underlying values and assumptions that structure accounts of revolutionary change in the early modern period – notably the separation of "nature" from "culture" and the championing of modern, technologically sophisticated societies at the expense of their primitive antecedents.[1] In this chapter, I shall consider landscape as a manifestation of "ongoing dialectical relations between human acts and acts of nature" in order to reread Marvell's "Upon Appleton House" as a text which both foregrounds and mystifies the mutually constitutive discourses of literature and political economy.[2] Previous critics have discussed Marvell's use of pastoral and georgic traditions; in extending their work, I shall suggest that the poem's ambiguities both reflect and help shape profound anxieties about the degradation of the environment and the resulting scarcity of essential resources in the seventeenth century, notably timber.

As the writing about forests in Marvell's time demonstrates, timber was essential for building and repair work, shipbuilding, transportation, and providing fuel for industries such as iron smelting and glass-making.[3] John Evelyn's concern in his influential treatise, *Sylva* (1664), about what he called the "impolitick diminution of our Timber," is only one manifestation of his culture's efforts to come to terms with processes of intensification – defined by Marvin Harris as "the investment of more soil, water, minerals, or energy per unit of time or area, [as humankind's] recurrent response to threats against living standards." As Harris argues, "intensification is always counterproductive" because "new and more efficient means of production . . . sooner or later lead to the depletion" of the resources which such technologies and practices have made available.[4] Historicizing Marvell's poem by locating it within the context of seventeenth-century literature on forestry and agricultural improvement allows us to explore the tensions between competing ecological and economic models of the land that are repressed within progressivist narratives of modernity. Seventeenth-century writers did not share twentieth-century conceptions of environmentalism, but their moralistic laments about the corruption of nature as well as their urgent calls for reforestation both testify to and seek to transcend the grim logic of intensification. This logic, in turn, underlies the ironies that Marvell both foregrounds and attempts to transcend in "Upon Appleton House," a poem that redefines the pastoral and georgic conventions on which it draws.

I

The political conflicts of mid-seventeenth century England, as Jack Goldstone argues, result from economic and environmental crises that came after a century and a half of population growth, diminishing returns on capital investment, inflation, and competition for what seemed to contemporaries increasingly scarce resources.[5] Between 1500 and 1650, the population of England increased from approximately two million to five million, prices rose six hundred percent but wages only three hundred; timber prices went up fifty percent more than the general rate of inflation.[6] As Joan Thirsk says, "men made war upon the forests, moors, and fens with a zeal which they had not felt for some three hundred years."[7] The most visible and contentious sign of the "corruption of nature" – manifest in "a generall scarcitie and penury" – was the disappearance of England's forests.[8] For centuries, woodlands had been "intensely managed as a valuable self-renewing resource" and arboriculture had been seen as the triumph of civilization over the desolate and wild forest. But despite numerous conservation and reforestation Acts passed by the Tudors, only eight percent (three million acres) of England and Wales was cultivated woodland by the late seventeenth century; another eight percent was covered by forests, parks, and commons.[9] In 1611, Arthur Standish published, under the king's imprimatur, *The Commons Complaint* to remedy "the generall destruction and waste of wood."[10] Standish outlines concisely the socioeconomic significance of timber shortages:

there is not Tymber left in this Kingdome at this instant onely to repaire the buildings thereof another age, much lesse to build withall: whereby this greiuance doth daily increase. The reasons are many: first, the want of fire . . . without the which mans life cannot bee preserved: secondly, the want of Timber, Brick, Tyle, Lime, Iron, Lead and glasse for the building of habitations; Timber for the maintaining of husbandry, for navigation, for vessels, for bruing and the keeping of drinke, and all other necessaries for housekeeping: barke for the tanning of Leather, bridges for trauell, pales for parkes, poles for Hops, and salt from the Wiches. The want of wood is, and will bee a great decay to tillage, and cannot but be the greatest cause of the dearth of corne, and hindereth greatly the yearely breeding of many cattell by reason that much straw is yearely burned, that to the breeding of cattell might be imployed: the want of wood in many places of this kingdome, constraineth the soyll of cattell to be burned, which should be imployed to the strengthening of land, and so doth the want of hurdles for the folding of sheepe, and the want of wood causeth too many great losses by fire, that commeth by the burning of straw, so it may be conceived, no wood, no Kingdome.[11]

Standish clearly understands the economic consequences of ecological stress. The scarcity of timber sets off a chain reaction of consequences, hindering building and repair work and forcing the use of other resources – dung for fuel, for example – which depresses agricultural productivity. His formulation, "no wood, no Kingdome," is not a simplistic lament for vanishing forests, but an acute analysis – borne out by rising prices – of timber shortages that, he argues, can be remedied only by encouraging landowners to undertake an aggressive program of reforestation.[12]

The timber crisis of the seventeenth century illustrates the extent to which agrarian reformers, no less than poets, grappled with contradictory images of nature. Nature, on the one hand, is the fallen, postlapsarian realm of scarcity and labor and, on the other, the divinely ordered handiwork of a beneficent God that can be made to yield infinite profits.[13] For reformers such as Walter Blith, "Man himselfe . . . by his sinne procured a curse upon the Land, even Barrenesse it selfe, which by the sweat of his browes must be reduced, if he will eat bread."[14] Blith's emphasis on human sin, however, does not hinder his millenarian vision of an England restored to a near paradisal state by agricultural improvement. As Andrew McRae notes, "Blith's rallying call for national regeneration through agrarian improvement" was based on values that transcended political antagonisms between supporters of the Commonwealth and monarchy by promoting an ideology of improvement that depended on the efforts of enlightened landowners.[15] Gervase

Markham's popular treatise *The English Husbandman* (1613; fourteen editions by 1683) "sheweth how to make the fruitfull more fruitfull," and its sequel, *Markhams Farwell to Husbandry* (1620; eleven editions by 1684), "how to make the Barren most plentifull."[16] Assuming that the stability of property rights will encourage enterprising landowners to invest in capital and technology, Markham promises a geometrical increase in the productivity of a land redeemed not by "sweat" but by careful management: "all grounds being made able and apt for Tillage," he declares, "the Kingdome may afford to sowe for one Bushell that is now, hereafter five hundred."[17] England, then, can simply produce its way out of socioeconomic crises.

During the Civil Wars, faced by frightening prospects of a "generall Famine," writers advocating improvement take on a messianic fervor and often an authoritarian cast. The author of *A Designe for Plentie* advocates "a Law made, and put in force by Authority for a generall and universall Plantation" of fruit trees, compelling landowners to plant twenty apple, pear, walnut, or quince trees for "every five pounds per annum of plantable land" they own.[18] Other writers associated with the Hartlib circle, notably Blith and Ralph Austen, argue that large plantations of fruit trees to feed and provide fuel for the poor are essential to a program for national prosperity. Even these reformist plans, however, rely on stalwart defenses of property rights and visions of huge profits to persuade readers to manage their woods productively. Ralph Austen, like Markham and Blith, sees reforestation, particularly the planting of fruit trees, as a universally beneficial project. The poor will be delivered "from *Idlenesse, Beggery, Shame*, and consequently, *Theft, Murther*, and (at last) *the Gallowes*," while reaping "Positive advantages: Meate, Drinke, Clothing, Riches, and Profits, to themselves and others." Landowners who plant fruit trees will find that "after a few years, they y[ie]ld great profits, with little cost and labour."[19] In such visions of tree-farming triumphing over poverty, laziness, and ignorance, Austen and his fellows subsume the competing interests of different readerships – "the humble ploughman, the thrifty yeoman, the entrepreneurial innovator [and] the retired lord" – within an ideology of improvement that promises vastly increased yields of crops and timber.[20]

This ideology mediates among and seeks to transcend political as well as class divisions. Reformers and royalists alike invoke visions of a perpetual increase in timber production to alleviate the conditions that produce social unrest. After 1660, the rhetoric of government mandates "for a general and universall Plantations" give way to assertions that emphasize how the planting of fruit and timber trees is a capitalist enterprise, a money-making venture of entrepreneurs doing their patriotic duty to ensure a steady supply of timber. As Evelyn puts it succinctly, "our Forests are undoubtedly the greatest Magazines of the Wealth, and Glory of this Nation; and our Oaks the truest Oracles of its Perpetuity and handiness, as being the only support of that Navigation which makes us fear'd abroad and flourish at Home."[21] The planting of trees, particularly oaks, not only perpetuates individuals' wealth but ensures a coherent national identity that depends on naval strength and international trade to protect England against threats from abroad and "a generall scarcitie and penury" at home. Trees make possible the difference that is the nation.

Given the mutually constitutive discourses of improvement and property, it is hardly surprising that the literature of forestry reinscribes the values associated with the landed gentry. Moses Cook, who managed the Earl of Essex's estate, invokes images of arranged marriages and human sexual reproduction to describe readying acorns for planting:

if the Acorn hath had a convenient quantity of heat and moisture (but if too much of either of these, that is deadly to all seeds) then the seed spears forth . . . For Nature, if once set in Motion, will rather cease to be, than alter its course; for Nature hates violence, neither can the seed receive this precious sperm without these two, Father and Mother; and these two must have a sutable Agreement between them.[22]

As this gendered imagery suggests, arboriculture is marked by patrilineal values familiar to seventeenth-century gentlemen, notably the peaceful begetting of heirs. The legal and familial preservation of the estate thus is linked symbolically as well as practically to the propagation of trees. But with duties come responsibilities. Cook harangues his betters for neglecting their woods and thereby decreasing the value of their land. Those "persons of Quality" who let old timber stand as an "Ornament to their Ground," are, he suggests, as foolish and unfashionable as those who "wear a Garment very Old, with half a skirt, a piece of a Sleeve, and all the Trimming off."[23]

By turning ideals of fashion and entrepreneurial know-how against the indolence of the upper classes, Cook links gentlemanly self-image to the care of the estate. But the prerequisites of privilege are themselves subordinated to an ideology of national improvement which assumes that nature is marked irrevocably by its potential exchange-value. In imagining the infinite extension of the profitability of arboriculture into the future, Cook both assumes and reinforces the stability of property relations and the elasticity of use-value. By minimizing the ecological impact of massive tree-planting on grain and livestock, he emphasizes his faith in the survival of estates and families to enjoy the monetary rewards of their forbears' diligence as well as the ability of agricultural production to outstrip population growth. Conservation goes hand-in-hand with conservative social values. Like Blith, Evelyn, and Austen, then, Cook can describe the benefits of agricultural management only by invoking literary – that is, imaginary – models of a harmonious and infinitely productive nature as the means to overcome the crises of intensification that have plagued humankind since the expulsion from Eden. By redeeming humankind and the environment from the ravages of sin and neglect, arboriculture subsumes pastoral idealizations within an ideology of self-sustaining progress.

II

In important ways, the ironies of "Upon Appleton House" and the self-ironies of its speaker exploit and reshape the literature of agricultural improvement.[24] NunAppleton is a working estate as well as a bucolic retreat, and his speaker's contemplation of the workers as well as the woods allows Marvell to explore his culture's contested views of the natural world. At times, in describing the grounds, the poet invokes traditional images of a pristine nature, a golden age before the Fall into scarcity, warfare, and Hobbesian competition; at others, he distances himself from such idealizations to comment ironically on a seemingly universal desire to escape to pastoral visions of a harmonious world. Such ironies both excite and seek to contain contemporary anxieties about the corruption of nature and the devastation of its resources. If Marvell questions his own fantasies of pastoral retreat, he also wittily interrogates the values and assumptions of a georgic virtue which unendingly exploits nature for profit.

At the beginning of the poem, the speaker commends Lord Fairfax for living modestly in his retirement. Unlike many of his peers, Marvell's patron disdains the luxury and extravagance of those who, to build their estates, "unto Caves the Quarries drew, / And Forrests did to Pastures hew" (lines 3–4).[25] In contrast to this despoilation of nature, NunAppleton preserves a balance between human desires and natural resources. On Fairfax's estate, "all things are composed . . . / Like Nature, orderly and near" (lines 25–6), and in his house itself "ev'ry Thing does answer Use" (line 62). These images identify the retired

General's "Honour" with his refusal to succumb to the excessive practices – indiscriminate quarrying and hewing – that create luxury,
surplus-value. Because NunAppleton, in this regard, is not "defac'd"
by art but, by nature, "laid so sweetly wast, / In fragrant Gardens, shaddy
Woods, / Deep Meadows, and transparent Floods" (lines 77–80), the
estate becomes a standard of value – an idealized vision in which desire
and use-value are equivalent.

The phrase "Like Nature," then, suggests that nature is both the
origin of value, a standard against which the deviations of art and
luxury are measured, and a "wast" which is incomplete, imperfect, fallen
– the corrupt world of Protestant theology – that requires art, labor,
and capital to transform it into a simulation of its prelapsarian condition. Nature is marked simultaneously by its pastoral and georgic
reconstructions, shaped by the contrasting fantasies of absolute and
exchange-value. In these imagined registers, use-value must be both
exhaustive – to use stone or trees to build ostentatious estates is to use
them up, leaving caves and pastures in their places – and infinitely extend-
able into a future that transcends the moral and environmental consequences of past degradations.[26]

As pastoral ideal and georgic landscape, NunAppleton is described
ironically in images of the war from which Fairfax has retired. Much
of the middle of the poem extends a metaphor of the natural world as
a battleground; memories of the Civil War are encased and preserved
in georgic description. If "The *Gardiner* [has] the *Souldiers* place,"
Fairfax's estate nonetheless is the site of a continuing campaign, however metaphysically playful, represented by mowers who "Massacre the
Grass along" (lines 337, 394). Marvell's wit connects the martial hero-
ism of Fairfax to a vision of the war hero retired to pastoral virtue and,
more subtly, allows the reader to acknowledge and distance herself from
the recognition that the Civil War has been a conflict over scarce resources
as well as over opposing theological and political views. "What luck-
less Apple," the speaker asks, "did we Last, / To make us Mortal, and
The[e]" – the "*Paradice*" of England itself – "Wast?" (lines 327–8). The
apple, in one respect, is the bitter fruit of humankind's knowledge that
someone's brow has to sweat for others to eat. A world given to "Wast"
needs mowers and fishermen to maintain standards of living.

As he observes the efforts of these laborers, the speaker is moved to
distinguish himself from them, to separate intellectual labor, such as
language tutoring, from physical drudgery. This division of labor on
Fairfax's estate provides the basis for a gentlemanly faith in the ability

of labor and technology to enhance nature by laying out intricate gardens and hedged-in woods that coyly promise to efface the marks of human intervention. The "doubled desire" of technology is to make the grounds at NunAppleton "Like Nature," a simulation which exists beyond the corrupting forces of history and environmental decay.[27] The world restored to its pristine form, however, is an idealization that Marvell exploits and burlesques in such self-images as the *"easie Philosopher"* imagining himself "some great *Prelate of the Grove*" (lines 592–3). The intellectual labor of imposing poetic order on a chaotic world remains distinct from manual labor, but such distinctions cannot rescue either nature or the poet from the effects of a metaphorical warfare that is necessary to the preservation of the estate.[28]

In a poem fraught with theatrical and metacritical images, Marvell uses the ironies of his speaker's position to question those pastoral fictions that seek to transcend a corrupt world by transforming nature into a timeless ideal. The escape to a green thought in a green shade depends, it seems, on our giving in to reveries of an unmediated access to a pristine nature. The speaker imagines nature before human exploitation as

> A new and empty Face of things,
> A levell'd space, as smooth and plain
> As Clothes for *Lilly* strecht to stain.
> The World when first created sure
> Was such a Table rase and pure.   (lines 442–6)

This stanza presents the image of a pristine nature in negative ("empty") and artificial images, Lely's blank canvases. The "Table rase and pure" may anticipate Locke in offering an idealized world open to communal exploitation, but it is an ideal which exists only in imagination or in art, and which borders on political delusion:

> For to this naked equal Flat,
> Which *Levellers* take Pattern at,
> The Villagers in common chase
> Their Cattle, which it closer rase;
> And what below the Sith increast
> Is pincht yet nearer by the Beast.   (lines 449–54)

The notion of a nature available to all – "a levell'd space" – invites the political fantasies, and dangers, represented by the Levellers, whom Fairfax had suppressed in 1649. These lines resonate with the assumptions and values of Blith and other agricultural reformers; if agricultural improvement results from managing labor and technology so that output is by "the Sith increast," then the Levellers threaten to return the land to inefficient practices, to a state of being "pincht" to scarcity.

Marvell's irony, in this respect, does not extend to challenging the prerogatives of ownership.[29] The benefits of agricultural production by "the Sith increast" are contrasted with an environmental degradation that is displaced onto the villagers; by exercising their traditional grazing rights "in common," they allow their livestock to "rase" and pinch the resources that ultimately determine social hierarchy and order. If the villagers nonetheless remain within the economy of estate management, the Levellers fail to recognize that the divisions of property that create social distinctions also define nature. The blank space of a "Table rase and pure" exists outside of a history of human actions (the division of labor, the spiriting away of Isabella Thwaites from the nuns, and Parliament's resistance to the king's threats to property) which secures the moral, natural, and patrilineal order. The fantasy of a "naked equal Flat," in this regard, is a negation of humankind's efforts to redeem a fallen world. The Levellers' ideal therefore must give way to the rights of ownership that have been secured earlier in the poem by Marvell's account of William Fairfax's rescuing of his bride-to-be in 1518. The transformation of NunAppleton from a sterile Catholic enclave to the Fairfax family seat establishes a history of patrilineal succession which guarantees the proper stewardship of natural resources in Marvell's time and presumably into an indefinite future.

Nature emerges in "Upon Appleton House" as an effect of both the poet's imagination and the ideology of improvement. When the speaker retreats to the woods of the estate, he is among trees of a "green, yet growing Ark, / Where the first Carpenter might best / Fit Timber for his Keel have Prest" (lines 484–6). The forest is a refuge from a corrupt world, as the allusion to the story of Noah suggests. Yet its status as a haven must be secured by the labor of a primordial "Carpenter," who is directed by God to fell trees and build an ark in order to survive the inundation of a corrupt world. Within seventeenth-century Protestant theology, the divinely-sanctioned labor of resource extraction becomes the means to redeem a fallen world. Even the woodpecker measures "the Timber with his Foot" to decide which trees should fall (line 540). Such images of nature as a means to overcome the consequences of the fall – sin, scarcity, political unrest, and unproductive labor – are treated without irony by other writers in the mid-seventeenth century and routinely transformed into ringing paeans to human ingenuity and national greatness. For Evelyn and Cook, writing after the

Restoration, the oak is the "Royal Tree" identified with allegiance to the Stuarts. It is, as Cook's "unpruned Verses" indicate, both a commodity and symbol of the nation's strength:

> Oak-Walls our Seas and Island do inclose,
> Our Best Defence against our Foreign Foes.
> No thing on Earth but Oak can Time Redeem,
> No Wood deserving of so high Esteem.[30]

Oaks can redeem time precisely because they are a renewable resource, a means to ensure the continuity of an idealized nation that is not facing timber crises, inflation, Dutch adventurism on the high seas, and so on. The fictions of an endlessly exploitable nature and a stable and always prosperous England are mutually reinforcing.

In contrast to such overt royalist mythologizing, Marvell's ironies exploit the superimposition of corrupt and idealized images of the natural world to reinforce the ambiguities of a theology that assumes humankind's originary alienation from a prelapsarian nature. The *"tallest Oak"* falls by the *"feeble Stroke"* (lines 550–1) of the woodpecker because the tree has

> A *Traitor-worm*, within it bred.
> (As first our *Flesh* corrupt within
> Tempts impotent and bashful *Sin*.)
> And yet that *Worm* triumphs not long,
> But serves to feed the *Hewels young*,
> While the Oake seems to fall content,
> Viewing the Treason's Punishment.   (lines 554–60)

Like all humans, the oak is "first . . . corrupt within," and this corruption is a catalyst for historical and ecological processes of decay that otherwise would be "impotent." This is the paradox of originary alienation: for nature to fall, nature must have already fallen – both morally, as an index of humankind's sin, and ecologically, as a resource always marked by exchange-value, always in the process of exceeding the ideal of a pure use-value. Nature is "corrupt," in other words, because it cannot exist prior to its exploitation.

Even as Marvell plays with superimposed images of a corrupt and idealized nature, though, he distances his readers, and the speaker, from the implications of postlapsarian ecology; without such ironic images as worms punished for treason, the idealized forest – as the *negation* of a fallen nature – would threaten to give way to darker views of environmental degradation. Taken as evidence of humankind's insatiable demands on the environment, the spectacle of falling oaks hardly inspires "content." In Michael Drayton's *Poly-Olbion* (1612–13, 1622), the "bigge and lordlie Oakes" of Blackmore Forest fall victim to "mans devouring hand, with all the earth not fed."[31] The destruction of the forest has grave ecological consequences in a land "Where no man ever plants to our posteritie": "when sharp Winter shoots her sleet and hardned haile, / Or suddaine gusts from Sea, the harmlesse Deere assaile, / The shrubs are not of power to sheeld them from the wind."[32] A vibrant ecology is reduced to winter winds howling through the seventeenth-century equivalent of clearcuts. If Marvell, writing from the ordered retreat of NunAppleton, seeks to displace anxieties about environmental degradation, Drayton casts his massive poem in the voices of rivers and ecological regions subject to humankind's ravenous desires. The River Frome's complaint about the devastation of Blackmore Forest, in an important sense, suggests that ecological violence must be repressed within the tradition of great house poetry in order to define the landscape by the artificial demarcations of ownership.

Given the ironies that structure his descriptions of NunAppleton, Marvell can bring the poem to artistic and ideological closure only by invoking an imaginary construct to redeem a fallen nature. In the final stanzas, nature becomes the effect of an ordering principle, represented by Marvell's pupil, Mary Fairfax. The virginal young woman is the imaginative guarantee of a natural order that she seems both to embody and transcend:

> 'Tis *She* that to these Gardens gave
> That wondrous Beauty which they have;
> *She* streightness on the Woods bestows;
> To *Her* the *Meadow* sweetness owes;
> Nothing could make the River be
> So Chrystal-pure but only *She*;
> *She* yet more Pure, Sweet, Streight, and Fair,
> Then Gardens, Woods, Meads, Rivers are. (lines 689–96)

Mary becomes the repository of those patrilineal values that presumably will secure the continuation of the Fairfax line and the integrity of the estate.[33] As a symbol of the family's dynastic hopes, she embodies an imagined future of virtuous prosperity because she "with Graces more divine / Supplies beyond her Sex the Line" (lines 737–8). The patrilineal fantasy of endless propagation reinforces, and is reinforced by, images of the natural world contracted to the boundaries of the Fairfax estate and thereby transformed into both a pastoral retreat and an idealized estate that will provide ample income for the family indefinitely into the future.

Exhibiting the order that Mary's virginal body symbolizes, Nun-
Appleton can be identified with an ideal realm that, in a postlapsarian
world, can take shape only as the imaginary projection of virtue from
– and onto – a fallen nature. In complimenting Fairfax, Marvell calls
attention to the transformative powers of both the estate and his own
poetic imagination:

> 'Tis not, what once it was, the *World*,
> But a rude heap together hurl'd,
> All negligently overthrown,
> Gulfes, Deserts, Precipices, Stone.
> Your lesser *World* contains the same,
> But in more decent *Order* tame;
> *You, Heaven's Center, Nature's Lap.*
> *And Paradice's only Map.*
>
> (lines 761–8)

In a disordered world of "Gulfes, Deserts, Precipices, Stone," Nun-
Appleton assumes the status of an iconic representation – "*Paradice's only
Map*" – of what humankind has lost through sin, warfare, and bad husbandry. But in a poem that places Appleton House within the contentious
history of England's Civil Wars and the Reformation, "*Heaven's Center*"
remains a fiction attainable only in and through poetry – or in and
through a political economy that both acknowledges and represses the
fact that there can be no nature untouched by desire, scarcity, and
competition. The "more decent *Order*" of the carefully managed estate
can distance the poet and his readers from nightmarish visions of "a
generall scarcitie and penury" but it cannot banish them entirely. In
"Upon Appleton House," as in *Poly-Olbion*, humankind is continually,
if implicitly, threatening to destroy the very conditions that, through our
labor, we idealize and seek to recreate.

III

There's an afterword. There always is with land. In 1679, Fairfax's cousin
Brian Fairfax (1633–1711) wrote a poem, "The Vocal Oak. upon cutting down the Woods at NunAppleton," that survives in manuscript.[34]
Written in anger ("Facit indignatio Versus"), the poem is the mono-
logue of an oak which rehearses the fall of the estate (settled on Mary
and her husband, the Duke of Buckingham, in 1666) from pastoral purity
to despoilation. The poem begins by invoking a prelapsarian time "when
Learned Druid taugh[t.] / Then it was Sacriledg to cut a Tree, / To
wound an Oak, to Offend a Deity." This idealized past is characterized

by a sanctification of use-value when "Vestal Virgins . . . nere did . . . desire / To Cut more wood then fed the Sacred Fire." Thomas, Lord Fairfax is the heir to this tradition; according to the vocal oak, "Hee did me defend / From the injurious hand of Foe, or Friend," so that NunAppleton, when it was the retreat of the retired general, seemed to exist in a timeless present outside the logic of estate management, of pressures to turn timber into capital. The poet, though, imposes a Christian, metaphysical order on this idealized past because his late cousin, "like some Religious Hermit," devoted himself to studying "diviner things then Druids knew." Yet, as the subtitle of the poem suggests, the Christian virtues identified with the oaks on the estate have been jettisoned by "the hand of Luxury and Pride." The poem ends with a moralized lament for the destruction of the woods to satisfy the immoderate desires of a corrupt age:

> How many stately Oks must bye a Fan,
> What Lands a dish from China, or Japan.
> How many Acres of this flowry mead
> Must bye a flowred satin for a Bed.
> What Mannors morgagd to supply a feast.
> What Trees, and Houses eaten by a Guest,
> Till all's reduc'd at last to what wee see,
> Painted in Landskips, and in Tapistry.

Oaks and entire estates are consumed in frantic efforts to convert putatively stable use-values to surplus-value, to the luxuries that turn nature into art, flowery meadows into flowered bedspreads. The economic usefulness of Evelyn's trees as bulwarks of national identity gives way to a nostalgic evocation of oaks as symbols of a past that, with the death of Fairfax in 1671, and the passing of the estate to Mary and Buckingham, seems irrevocably gone. In a world of "Luxury and Pride," resources are capitalized: "Oakes are mown down like grass at [Luxury's] command." The vocal oak signals the passing of a mythologized landscape into art, paintings and tapestries, even as its lament reinforces the divisions between nature and culture, past virtue and modern excess, that structure seventeenth-century accounts of nature's fall.

In 1700, harassed by creditors, the widowed and childless Mary wanted to sell NunAppleton, but the deed of settlement from her father prevented alienation of the estate.[35] She wrote to the heir presumptive, her cousin, the fourth Lord Fairfax, to persuade him to allow her to sell. When he refused, her lawyer maintained that NunAppleton was subject to the late Duke of Buckingham's debts, and since Mary, now

over sixty, might yet have children he contended that she indeed could
sell the estate. To forestall her designs, her cousin claimed small parcels
of land on the estate to scare off potential buyers. He succeeded. After
the deaths of the principals and years of legal wrangling, NunAppleton
finally was sold in 1710 by the widow of the fifth Lord Fairfax to pay
off debts on her family's estates. The purchaser was William Milner,
alderman of Leeds, and the price was £8,000. Brian Fairfax protested
vigorously.

In formalist criticism, the fate of NunAppleton is irrelevant to
Marvell's achievement; in New Historicism, the legal context allows us
to interpret the poem as an effect of power displayed; for Marxists, the
Duchess's problems are evidence that the land was already capitalized;
and for feminists, the legal battles testify to the subjection of women to
the laws of primogeniture. If these approaches locate Marvell within
complex histories of seventeenth-century culture, in an eco-economic
criticism yet to be written the land itself must be historicized in (if such
a thing is possible) non-androcentric terms. NunAppleton cannot be
reduced to a discursive site, a symbol of stability or appropriation, a
table rased and pure, or a pristine ecology. The land, after all, has never
been natural.

NOTES

1 See Bruno Latour, *We Have Never Been Modern*, trans. Catherine Porter
  (Cambridge, Mass., 1993), especially pp. 99–104; Shane Phelan, "Intimate
  Distance: The Dislocation of Nature in Modernity," in Jane Bennett and
  William Chaloupka, eds., *In the Nature of Things: Language, Politics, and the
  Environment* (Minneapolis, Minn., 1993), pp. 44–62; Alice E. Ingerson, "Tracking
  and Testing the Nature-Culture Divide," in Carole Crumley, ed., *Historical Ecology: Cultural Knowledge and Changing Landscapes* (Santa Fe, N. Mex., 1994),
  pp. 43–66; and Carole Crumley, "The Ecology of Conquest: Contrasting
  Agropastoral and Agricultural Societies' Adaptation to Climactic Change,"
  in Crumley, ed., *Historical Ecology*, pp. 183–201.
2 Carole Crumley, "Historical Ecology: A Multidimensional Ecological
  Orientation," in ibid., pp. 1–16, this passage p. 9. On the notion that natural and social "totalities" are continually degrading the very conditions
  that brought them into being, see Richard Levins and Richard Lewontin,
  The Dialectical Biologist (Cambridge, Mass., 1985), especially pp. 133–42, 272–85.
3 See John Rogers, "The Great Work of Time: Marvell's Pastoral
  Historiography," in Claude J. Summers and Ted-Larry Pebworth, eds.,
  On the Celebrated and Neglected Poems of Andrew Marvell (Columbia, Mo., 1992),
  pp. 207–32; Douglas D. C. Chambers, " 'To the Abyss': Gothic as a
  Metaphor for the Argument about Art and Nature in 'Upon Appleton

House'," in ibid., pp. 139–53; Turner, *Politics of Landscape*, pp. 61–83; Annabel Patterson, "Pastoral versus Georgic: The Politics of Virgilian Quotation," in Barbara Lewalski, ed., *Renaissance Genres: Essays on Theory, History, and Interpretation* (Cambridge, Mass., 1986), pp. 241–67; Anthony Low, "New Science and the Georgic Revolution in Seventeenth-Century English Literature," in Arthur F. Kinney and Dan S. Collins, eds., *Renaissance Historicism: Selections from English Literary Renaissance* (Amherst, Mass., 1987), pp. 317–47; Alastair Fowler, "Georgic and Pastoral: Laws of Genre in the Seventeenth Century," in Michael Leslie and Timothy Raylor, eds., *Culture and Cultivation in Early Modern England: Writing and the Land* (Leicester, 1992), pp. 81–90; and Douglas Chambers, " 'Wild Pastorall Encounter': John Evelyn, John Beale and the Renegotiation of Pastoral in the Mid-Seventeenth Century," in Leslie and Raylor, eds. *Culture and Cultivation*, pp. 173–94.

4 John Evelyn, *Sylva, or a Discourse of Forest Trees*, 3rd edn., *"much inlarged and improved,"* (1679), p. 1; Evelyn, in this edition, includes praise of Cook's work (see n. 22 below), pp. 59, 66, 79, 239–40. Marvin Harris, *Cannibals and Kings: The Origins of Cultures* (New York, 1977), p. 4.

5 Jack A. Goldstone, *Revolution and Rebellion in the Early Modern World* (Berkeley, Calif., 1991), pp. 63–167. Goldstone's "structural/demographic" model of history rejects a simple Malthusianism to argue that Marxian notions of the "material bases" of labor and economics must include ecological and demographic pressures. The implications of Goldstone's account for a cultural ecology of early modern England, I want to emphasize, supplement rather than invalidate materialist histories of the period.

6 On inflation see, C. G. A. Clay, *Economic Expansion and Social Change: England 1500–1700*, 2 vols. (Cambridge, 1984), 1: 43–50; on timber prices, see Oliver Rackham, *Ancient Woodland: Its History, Vegetation and Uses in England* (1980), p. 164.

7 Joan Thirsk, ed., *The Agrarian History of England and Wales, Volume IV 1500–1640* (Cambridge, 1967), p. 2.

8 Godfrey Goodman, *The Fall of Man, or The Corruption of Nature* (1616), p. 49.

9 Keith Thomas, *Man and the Natural World: Changing Attitudes in England 1500–1800* (1983), p. 198.

10 Standish, *The Commons Complaint* (1611), p. 1. Two years later, Standish published a further polemic on reforestation, *New Directions of Experience to the Commons Complaint* (1613), which reprints the King's address "To all Noblemen, Gentlemen, and other our loving Subjects," encouraging them to promote "projects for the increasing of Woods; the decay whereof in this Realme is Universally complained of," sigs. A2^r–A2^v.

11 Standish, *Commons Complaint*, pp. 1–2.

12 On the problems of harvesting and transporting timber that exacerbated the degradation of forests close to navigable rivers, see N. D. G. James, *A History of English Forestry* (Oxford, 1981), pp. 118–24; on the various conservation Acts passed during the sixteenth and seventeenth centuries, see pp. 125–8.

13 On nature in seventeenth-century natural philosophy, see my *Fallen Languages: Crises of Representation in Newtonian England, 1660–1740* (Ithaca, N.Y., 1993), especially pp. 96–130.

14 Walter Blith, *The English Improver Improved*, 3rd edn., "*much augmented,*" (1652), pp. 5–6.

15 McRae, *God Speed*, p. 228.

16 Markham, *Markhams Farwell to Husbandry* (1620), p. 4.

17 Ibid., p. 4.

18 *A Designe for Plentie* (1653), pp. 2, 4. This anonymous pamphlet, apparently written in the 1640s, was published by Samuel Hartlib, as part of his program for agricultural reform. See McRae, *God Speed*, pp. 159–68.

19 Austen, *A Treatise of Fruit-Trees* (Oxford, 1653), pp. 1, 3. On Austen and Blith, see Charles Webster, *The Great Instauration: Science, Medicine, and Reform 1626–1660* (New York, 1976), pp. 465–83.

20 McRae, *God Speed*, p. 3.

21 Evelyn, *Sylva*, p. 234.

22 Cook, *The Manner of Raising, Ordering, and Improving Forest and Fruit Trees*, 2nd edn., (1679), p. 35. Evelyn praises Cook's efforts as the gardener for the Earl of Essex: "The Gardens [at Cassiobury in Hertfordshire] are likewise very rare, & cannot be otherwise, having so skillfull an Artist to Governe them as Mr. Cooke," *The Diary of John Evelyn*, ed. Edmund S. de Beer, 6 vols. (Oxford, 1955), 4: 200.

23 Cook, *Manner*, p. 120.

24 See Michael Wilding, *Dragon's Teeth: Literature in the English Revolution* (Oxford, 1987), pp. 138–70; A. D. Cousins, "Marvell's 'Upon Appleton House, to my Lord Fairfax' and the Regaining of Paradise," in Conal Condren and A. D. Cousins, eds., *The Political Identity of Andrew Marvell* (Aldershot, Hants, 1990), pp. 53–84; Jonathan Crewe, "The Garden State: Marvell's Poetics of Enclosure," in Richard Burt and John Michael Archer, eds., *Enclosure Acts: Sexuality, Property, and Culture in Early Modern England* (Ithaca, N.Y., 1994), pp. 271–89.

25 Quotations from "Upon Appleton House" are from *The Poems and Letters of Andrew Marvell*, ed. H. M. Margoliouth, 3rd edn. rev. Pierre Legouis, with E. E. Duncan-Jones, 2 vols. (Oxford, 1971) and will be cited parenthetically.

26 In his rereading of Marx, Derrida argues for the "coimplication" of use-value and exchange-value: see *Spectres of Marx: The State of the Debt, the Work of Mourning, and the New International*, trans. Peggy Kamuf (New York, 1994), p. 162. On Marxism and ecology see the essays in Ted Benton, ed., *The Greening of Marxism* (New York, 1996).

27 On this "doubled desire," see Don Ihde, *Technology and the Lifeworld: From Garden to Earth* (Bloomington, Ind., 1990), especially pp. 75–6; on the idealization of time see Derrida, *Spectres of Marx*, pp. 154–5; and Latour, *We Have Never*, p. 68.

28 Turner, *Politics of Landscape*, pp. 76–7; on Marvell's self-irony, see Annabel Patterson, *Pastoral and Ideology: Virgil to Valery* (Berkeley, Calif., 1987), p. 156; and Marshall Grossman, "Authoring the Boundary: Allegory, Irony, and

the Rebus in 'Upon Appleton House,'" in Claude J. Summers and Ted-Larry Pebworth, eds., *"The Muses Commonweale": Poetry and Politics in the Seventeenth Century* (Columbia, Mo., 1988), pp. 191–206.

29 See Wilding, *Dragon's Teeth*, pp. 155–63.

30 Cook, *Manner*, p. 49.

31 *Poly-Olbion* in *The Works of Michael Drayton*, ed. J. William Hebel, 5 vols. (Oxford, 1931–41), 4, 2: 62, 64. On Drayton's "profound disgust at the exploitative desires of humanity" and his view of "forests not as economic resources, but rather as coherent and vibrant geographical regions," see McRae, *God Speed*, pp. 259–60; see also Helgerson, *Forms of Nationhood*, pp. 143–6; and Simon Schama, *Landscape and Memory* (New York, 1995), pp. 153–74.

32 Drayton, *Poly-Olbion*, vol. 4, 2: 69–71.

33 On the role Maria Fairfax plays in the poem see Lee Erickson, "Marvell's 'Upon Appleton House' and the Fairfax Family," *English Literary Renaissance* 9 (1979): 158–68; and Turner, *Politics of Landscape*, pp. 74–8, who sees the issue of procreation as the unifying theme of the poem. See also Derek Hirst and Steven Zwicker, "High Summer at Nun Appleton," *Historical Journal* 36 (1993): 247–69.

34 BL Egerton MSS 2146. I am grateful to Kathryn King for transcribing this poem. Turner, *Politics of Landscape*, p. 137 discusses several lines of this poem.

35 Clement R. Markham, *A Life of the Great Lord Fairfax* (1870), p. 408. The account of NunAppleton that follows is drawn from pp. 404–6.

CHAPTER 7

Enthusiasm and Enlightenment:
of food, filth, and slavery

Nigel Smith

> When an English barbarian hangs up a black slave in an iron cage
> in the deepest forest, so that for days birds of prey eat him alive
> piece by piece, turning his torment into infernal torture – would
> it not be better for humanity if Carolina, where this occurred, were
> more enlightened and would learn to honor the rights of humanity?
>
> Andreas Riem, *Uber Aufklärung* (1788).[1]

> The flesh of all Animals and Beasts is gross, succulent, and full
> freighted with many impurities and uncleanesses . . . to say noth-
> ing of the Bestial and revengeful passion of their Mind, which after
> Deaths painful stroke centers in the Blood and Spirits, and those
> violent encroaching Spirits do never fail to incorporate with their
> Similies in the Eaters.
>
> Thomas Tryon, *Tryon's Letters* (1700).[2]

Religious Enthusiasm and the Enlightenment are two major features in
the landscape of eighteenth-century cultural and intellectual history with
roots in the ferment of the previous century: the former in the triumph
of Puritanism during the Civil War and Protectorate, the latter in the
rise of the new natural philosophy. And in their different ways both were
to have a major impact on the great intellectual upheavals that accompanied the political revolutions of the later eighteenth century.

Yet both are usually considered to be separate categories, pointing
in opposite directions. Enthusiasm, with its simple claims for the direct
personal experience of the Holy Spirit, seems diametrically opposed to
the Enlightenment critique of superstition and inhumane behavior
founded in rationalist and mechanistic thought. This is certainly how
the Enlightenment thinkers liked to think of their relationship to
enthusiasm, picking up on longstanding definitions of enthusiasm as not
merely heretical and irrational, or as a species of melancholy, but even
as insanity. The much-voiced fear of enthusiasm among eighteenth-
century authors, not least of all Jonathan Swift, in his famous satire of
the Puritans, the *Discourse on the Mechanical Operation of the Spirit*, has been

generally accepted by modern commentators. We tend to think of the Enlightenment as hostile to enthusiasm.

This stereotypical view has been challenged in the scholarship of the past two decades. Building on Christopher Hill's understanding of mid-seventeenth-century radicalism, Margaret Jacob has argued in several publications for a connection between the skeptical ideas of the enthusiasts and the rational critique of traditional religion and society cultivated among the eighteenth-century's guardians of Enlightenment, the freemasons and pantheists.[3] Some support with respect to the attack on priestcraft has been given to Jacob's view by more recent publications.[4] But Jacob's picture remains a sketchy one, providing not evidence of a genuine tradition so much as a series of loosely associated concepts: a join-up-the-dots notion of cultural transmission. A more formidable, though brief, attempt was offered by J. G. A. Pocock, whose little-noticed article of 1980 offered a sophisticated view of the relationship between the metaphysical notions of mid-seventeenth-century enthusiasts and the rationalism and deism of the eighteenth century.[5] In Pocock's view, the deist John Toland emerged not merely as the transmitter of English republicanism to the eighteenth century, but also the crucial figure in the rationalizing of enthusiastic cosmologies. But Pocock's essay remains speculative, its findings unrealized in concrete examples of enlightened enthusiasts or enthusiastic enlighteners. We are left instead with a proposal for how the map of intellectual history might look were Pocock's proposals for revision to be adopted.

There is, however, a case for seeing the coincidence of Enthusiasm and Enlightenment as conjoined in the writings and practices of particular individuals before the "deist moment" of Toland's career, and a hundred years before the Enlightenment agenda had matured.

Benjamin Franklin said that for a while in his earlier career he had been a "Tryonist," that is to say, a follower of Thomas Tryon (1634–1704), the vegetarian and follower of the mystic Jacob Boehme. This itself is a testimony to Tryon's exploitation of the printing press, for Franklin became acquainted with Tryon's ideas through reading the vegetarian's two most famous works. Tryon's books seem to have constituted the backbone of an eighteenth-century vegetarian canon, so much so that Joseph Ritson could later regard him as its father figure.[6] Tryon also made a considerable impact during his lifetime. Aphra Behn is supposed to have been persuaded not to wear animal skins by Tryon, and that most influential of eighteenth-century physicians, George Cheyne, who ministered to and corresponded with Samuel Richardson, was introduced to Boehme's writings by Tryon.[7] Keith Thomas notes that the respect for all parts of creation, a view associated with Hume and Kant, was being voiced by Tryon long before their time.[8]

Tryon's roots are typical of the middling sort who made up the radical Puritan churches of the mid-seventeenth century. His entry into literacy from a humble social origin has many parallels among his contemporaries and near-contemporaries, but of Tryon we know a great deal more. He was born the son of a tiler and plasterer, who had him carding and spinning wool by the age of six. When Tryon was ten, he persuaded his father to let him keep sheep, and by swapping a sheep for lessons from a literate shepherd, he was able to gain rudimentary skills in reading and writing. Toward the later stages of his teenage years (corresponding with the last years of the Commonwealth and the early days of the Restoration), Tryon moved to London where he became apprenticed to a barrel-maker. His master belonged to a Baptist conventicle, and Tryon followed suit, remaining in the conventicle for three years, and becoming, so he later claimed, a prominent member of the congregation. During this time, the young Tryon managed, by working very long hours, to earn enough money (the considerable sum of fifty-six shillings per week) to be able to pay for books and for lessons in further literary and philosophical subjects. He studied by remaining awake long into the night: by my estimation he was able to function on three hours sleep a night. This is a remarkable story of the achievement of a considerable mastery of the written and printed word, turning Tryon from a shepherd into a highly original critical thinker and practitioner. In his memoir, he claims that he was immersed during these formative years in alchemy and astrology, and there is further evidence that he knew the writings of Heraclitus (and hence Pythagoras), Aristotle, Hobbes, Rochester, and possibly also Montaigne. At some point during the 1660s, he came upon the writings of Jacob Boehme, and it was these that transformed his awareness, fusing his practical skills, his religious enthusiasm and his knowledge of philosophy into a complete and profoundly new system.[9]

Abstinence must have been at the center of Tryon's strict self-regulation. It re-emerges in his mature vision as the center of a system of recommendations:

Despise not the Rules for promoting Health and Temperance, the ways of God and Nature are plain and simple, but mighty in operation and effects, the Body is an Instrument to the Soul, and being out of tune no harmony can be expected in the Microcosm.[10]

Thus, bodily purity was to be respected, so that for Tryon, separation came to mean strict vegetarianism, a total abstinence from meat and fish. The body and its needs were to be strictly regulated. The European pursuit of luxury "sets open the *Gates of Venus* to many lewd Practices." Gross bodies, swollen with heavy food, overeating, and drunkenness, are distended in one sense, and over-extended (i.e. erect) in the sexual: "one great *over-grown Christian* shall spend as much in *one Day*, to gratifie his Lusts or Vanity, as an *Hundred or Two* of his poor *Slaves* can get by their sore Labour and Sweat."[11]

The origins of such abstinence are founded upon a respect for nature that is very close to the mystical pantheism of Gerrard Winstanley: "This whole Visible World is nothing else but the Great Body of God."[12] Boehme's notion of the natural world as the "outspoken" and eternal moment of creation is reflected in Tryon's description of the organization of the senses, which itself finds further parallels in Winstanley:

And these secret and wonderful Operations cannot be performed any other way, but only by the five great Princes or compleat governors, called Senses; the Creator hath appointed each of them its province and government, who are always ready and on their Guard to defend the Tree of Life, that is, that nothing should be communicated to the Central parts of Nature that should be injurious or hurtful.[13]

And Tryon insists that this knowledge may only be acquired through "Experimental acquaintance," a phrase that relates both to the tradition of self-analysis for the sake of exploring the workings of God on the individual believer, and the new sense of inductive observation of the natural world.[14] Tryon's notion of "experimental acquaintance" relates centrally to religious enthusiasm, and is connected, as it was for many Puritans, with a fear of human invention.[15] Thus, the order of Tryon's discourse is randomly experimental, as the divine works through him and through creation:

The Curious may expect these Axioms should be more methodically placed, but as I wrote them down as they sprang up in my Mind, so I have observed Posies, [sic] That a careless mixture makes the whole more pleasant to the Eye and Radolent, then if every sort of Flowers and fragrant Herbs were put together by themselves. Read and practice, turn thy Eyes inwards, and wait at Wisdom's Gates, separate thy self from the Ways of the Multitude, and the Lord from whom alone proceeds every good and perfect Gift, gives thee understanding in all things.[16]

As a true follower of experimental theology, Tryon also believed in the importance of the witness of dreams and visions to the extent that he devoted one entire volume to the subject.[17]

Vegetarianism was one feature of the enthusiastic diaspora of the 1650s. Whereas Winstanley's followers ate vegetables because they had no choice, and meat is plentiful in Winstanley's imagined utopia, other radicals observed biblical injunctions to refrain from eating blood. This was the case with Thomas Tany and Roger Crab, the most well-known vegetarians of the Interregnum years.[18] Tany and Crab's follower, Captain Robert Norwood, was a vegetarian whose dietary abstinence is supposed to have led to an untimely death (DNB).

But Tryon is different from these enthusiasts because his system is founded so completely and extensively not in biblical injunctions alone but in an eclectic mysticism founded in Boehme's own eclectic mysticism. A purified diet, such as Tryon considered vegetarianism to achieve, resulted in an enlightenment of perception, where the true nature of creation would be apparent:

all whose Eyes shall be enlightened to understand the Mysteries of Nature; Cleanness in Foods being a thing of greater moment and value than the World usually imagines for they are the very Being, Substance, and as it were, the Original of the Microcosm Man, and in them are contained all the true Properties of him, having a Simile in all particulars, with the Qualities, Principles and Fountain-Spirits, and being taken into our Bodies, they are separated in our Stomachs by the curious and cunning Chimistry of Nature, whereby they afford Support and Nourishment.[19]

Pure, vegetable food is lighter than meat, and therefore does not clog the body, making it "gross" and "heavy." And by eating meat, we also imbibe the violent spirits of the beasts, since Tryon's cosmos is permeated with the sympathies of Hermetic teaching:

The flesh of all Animals and Beasts is gross, succulent, and full freighted with many impurities and uncleanesses . . . to say nothing of the Bestial and revengeful passion of their Mind, which after Deaths painful stroke centers in the Blood and Spirits, and those violent encroaching Spirits do never fail to incorporate with their Similies in the Eaters.[20]

There is not so much a distinction here between the raw and the cooked, as a knowledge of the different states of "perfection" that different vegetables and fruits reach in their natural states of growth. Plantains need not be cooked in pies or tarts because in their natural state they have already reached a state of sufficient richness, and to go beyond this is to risk blocking the circulatory system of the body: "if baked with

Sugar, Spices and the like lose their natural operation, and thereby become hot, and apt to obstruct the Passages, and tire the Appetite and Stomach, generate evil Juices, dull Spirits and thick Blood."[21]

A mystical system of tastes supports Tryon's explanation of the natures of different vegetables and fruits. All tastes "proceed and arise from the four grand Qualities . . . so that there are but four perfect Tastes, they being the Radix of all others, as the seven Notes are the Basis or Foundation of all Musical Harmony."[22] As with his comments on philosophy, Tryon manages to combine the well known and commonplace with the unexpected, a knack that may help to explain the popularity of his housekeeping manuals and health guides.[23] The range of cosmic reality in which he sets his recommendations on diet may surprise us, but it will have made sense to the many who read almanacs. Pineapples are thus dignified with "Celestial energy" because they are "under the Sun and Venus, in the Sign Leo."[24] Alchemical concepts are used to explain the nature both of food and of digestion: "The Sal Nitral Vertues or Oily Body in Vegetables, is not only more clean, sweet and fragrant, but much easier separated in the Stomach, and doth administer both dry and moist Nutriment in a clean and easie Method."[25]

The consumption of food is also intimately related to climate. Cold countries are full of traps for unknowing but freezing people. Tryon experienced the cold winters of the mid-1680s, and commented accordingly:

This immoderate Cold locks up the Pores of mens Bodies, and drives the natural Heat more Central, which occasions great Appetite and Drought, whence follows much and excessive Eating and Drinking of gross, fatt, succulent Foods, and strong Drinks . . . The way to prevent these mischiefs is, for the Rich to observe Sobriety and Temperance and for the poor to use Discretion in their Diet, for a pint of Milk with a quarter of a pint of Water, thickned with one Spoonful of Flower and heated just to Boyling, and then putting into it a few Crums of Bread, (all which will not cost above a penny) shall give any person as nourishing a Meal as the best Surloyn of Beef or Capon.[26]

In this way, Tryon's teaching begins to look very much like the account of "higher appetite" in Milton's *Paradise Lost* Book 5, where enhanced purification for unfallen mankind is explained in terms of a rarefying of digestion. Unfallen man, so long as he remains in that state, will become refined so that he becomes more like an angel, eating more refined substances.[27] In an unsigned epitaph, Tryon is remembered as a kind of unfallen, Miltonic Adam, redeeming Eden with his vegetarian idealism, which is seen as part of a communion with angels:

Such refin'd Notions to the World he gave,
As Men with Angels Entercourse might have
Shewed how to live on cleanest Food,
To abstain from Flesh, and Fish, and Blood.
Harmless his Life was, as his Food,
Both Patriarchal Primitively Good.[28]

Inner purity was matched by demands for an outer cleanliness, so that
Tryon's system features two kinds of circulation. The proper regulation
of the body was to be fostered by the frequent use of running water to
bathe and wash, and for the purposes of effective sanitation: people "ought
to ease themselves in a vessel of Water."[29]

Where some of the gentlemen scientists associated with the Royal
Society, such as John Evelyn, published plans to cure London of pollu-
tion and started with designs based on the city as a whole, Tryon reveals
his Puritan heritage by starting with the individual. The temperance
in this sanitary practice is measured by the fact that while violent action
is not recommended, stasis is to be avoided so that putrefaction or infection of healthy bodies may be prevented: "Be careful that you do not
sit on Common house of Easement, which oftentimes proves of evil con-
sequence, and infects the Party with Diseases of various kinds."[30]

Vegetarianism was not the end of Tryon's vision, however central it
was to his temperate teachings. Tryon's mature work involves an entire
vision of an ideal productive organization of society that constitutes an
attack upon the economics of western Europe and the colonies belonging to west European nations, especially the English. Tryon's temperance solutions are effectively put to work as solutions to the problems
that commercial society and imperialism had created for the well-being
of people.

In the first instance, and with some reference back to his own childhood, the under-usage and improper usage of children in family-based
systems of economic production is seen as an offense to God. The "Asian"
system – it seems as though Tryon has a knowledge of Indian family
organization – makes all children in a family educated in a particular
skill so that they may contribute to the well being of the family. All help
to feed everyone in the family and duress is avoided.[31] In western Europe,
this system once prevailed in the cottage industry that produced cloth,
and that, in the case of the wool industry, was the worthy staple and
backbone of the English economy.

But the quest for large profits and luxury goods has resulted in a fall
into decadence at home, and colonial plantations. The plantations, though

not evil in themselves, use one people brutally as a slave class in order to force production of luxury and unnecessary goods. Slave women especially are made to work harder than the men and at tasks entirely unsuited for their bodies. This is an inhumane use of people (it obviously offends the rules of charity as laid out in the Gospels), and it violates the entire system of nature and natural beneficence of which man is a part. The solution is to make white people as well as imported African slaves productive with their labor in the running of the colony. Thus white and black children must be educated together in the skills of producing cotton cloth.[32] The duress of the plantation, which looks through Tryon's eyes like an early and brutalizing kind of factory, should be eliminated in the recreation of the cloth industry in the colony. Additionally, rotation of crops should be introduced to avoid making the land infertile.[33] The land is a body too and so should be cleansed, properly regulated, and opened to a mixed agriculture, rather than subjected to the "forcing" of single crops (sugar and cotton) in the plantation.

The use of black slave labor turns white children to a life of luxury, disobedience, and even dissoluteness, while the slaves themselves are subjected to such harsh conditions during transportation and in the colony that they die in alarmingly great numbers: hardly a sound economic proposition, says Tryon, since the planter is bound to buy more of them every year. The plantation – and Tryon had extensive experience of Barbados, having lived and worked there for two periods in his life – is thus the home of abuse and self-abuse. It is indeed a living hell. As a Behmenist, Tryon believes that creation is permanently occurring as the godhead "outspeaks" from its "abyss" into the external world. Man has the choice to live through the light or dark principles, the two spiritual states by which the "outspoken" world is created from the godhead. By choosing the dark world, man refuses his "Paradisal Estate" and precipitates his "Imagination into the Centre of Wrath and Fierceness," the qualities of violence and disruption in the Behmenist cosmos.[34]

Most remarkable of all, in one work, Tryon gives voice to a black slave whose wide-ranging critique of the ways of Europeans and their treatment of slaves in the plantations is devastating, and amounts to a Behmenist demolition of "white" reason. Tryon and the slave become one in an instance of cross-racial sympathy, just as Tryon's occultism assumes the sympathies between similar objects in creation. Where Aphra Behn in *Oroonoko*, takes into the world of the slave concepts of honor derived from early modern Europe, Tryon appears to accept the perceptions of slaves (based on his own "Experimental acquaintance" in Barbados) and to make them work as an intimate part of his vegetarian vision. And the fusion of the two perspectives is apparent in the uncertain way in which the dialogue between the slave and master is written: it begins as merely "The Negro's Complaint," and then develops into a dialogue proper.

Carnage becomes a kind of extended trope by which the ill treatment of the Africans is registered. Planters buy poor-quality meat and rotten fish for their slaves, so that for the most part starving or stealing are the only alternatives.[35] In a horrifying vision of deprivation and depravation, Africans are described exhuming recently buried dead horses in order to eat the carrion, while any living thing – cats, dogs, rats, and mice – will suffice as food. And all of this, says the slave, is the result of the west European quest for luxury, which itself results in the decadence of the Europeans:

You say, *You are required to observe Purity, and the natural Rules of* Cleanness, *and to avoid all appearance of Evil*: Which indeed is no inconsiderable point in Nature and Religion, but as far as we have been able to observe, you practise the quite contrary; for not only your Words are very unclean for the generality, but also in your *Foods* and *Drinks* you make no distinction, but rich provoking Food in excess, and all strong intoxicating Drinks, you desire with greedness, which over-heats the whole Body, and irritates the fierce wrathful bestial Nature, whence all *wanton, vain* and *unclean* Thoughts and Imaginations are generated.[36]

By the same token, the colonial Europeans turn their bodies into dead meat by means of a dangerous superfluity of ailments, so that they *"pamper their Carkasses,* and indulge . . . with things that are not needful, nor convenient."[37] Swearing, and other verbal "debauchery," such as "Jesting, Lying, Vapouring," are condemned, along with the drunkenness and gluttony of festive culture. The slave's critique suggests that Europeans should be glad to revert to a kind of Adamic state, for clothes are equated with pride, and by being either over-dressed or hidden indoors, Europeans wither away. Their pursuit of luxury and wealth is a search for death. Accordingly, the economy of the plantation involves a perverse form of sacramentalism. Sugar is sweet, tobacco is poisonous, both are harmful, both are produced though the sacrifice (that is, the blood) of the slaves.[38]

In instances where it's beginning to look as though Tryon believes African culture embodies the *priscia theologia* he so values, the slave points out that Africans distinguish between clean and unclean beasts, and that they have a relevant proverb: when any one swears, they must "*Wash their Mouthes with Water.*"[39] This embodies in a figure Tryon's literal agent of purification and sanitation. But there is also an element of either naivety or extreme cleverness on Tryon's part, for earlier the slave complains about a purely vegetarian diet – "a few *Potato's* or *Yam's,* and these without either Butter or Bread."[40] Either Tryon's thinking is inconsistent or the slave is an authentic African carnivore, who accepts a mixed but temperate diet.

The element of relativism in Tryon's thought is made obvious by the ironic framework in which the master's replies to the slave are placed. The master produces a list of racial commonplaces that belong to un-enlightened early modern Europe: that blackness is an emblem and representation of sinfulness, that in their nakedness Africans are close to beasts, that Africans being unlearned in European terms, and having no professional classes or culture, or machines of war, are uncivilized. Neither do they have a leisure culture, and a use of sexuality as pleasure rather than for procreative, and hence productive, purposes.[41] Just as Tryon can accept that it is rational for some people from non-European cultures to eat their dead relatives to prevent their corpses from putre-fying or becoming carrion, so the slave attacks the rationality of the European Christians for their inhumane morality: "Is it possible that *rational men,* much less such illuminated *Christians,* as you account your selves, should thus be taken with things that are so much *below* the Dignity of humane Nature, to boast of your *Evils,* and glory in your *Shame?*"[42] The rationality (and Tryon would have disputed the applicability of the category) of interest has perverted the Europeans. Sometimes Tryon writes of self-interest in the simple sense of moral selfishness, but in other places he is clearly meeting head-on the interest theory that was so valued by those English writers who defended the ideals of aggressive commercialism.[43]

It is the slave's hope that in perceiving these truths, the planters will be persuaded to treat the slaves humanely, and according to religion and "common Equity." To do so will end slavery, converting it to mutu-ally agreed arrangements of servitude. As the Africans willingly agree to be the servants of the Europeans, so the master is miraculously per-suaded by the slave.

Tryon's writings, and what we know of his practices, are nothing other than the elaboration of a radical Puritan agenda, one that had been embryonically formed in the 1650s by others, put to work against the consequences of burgeoning commercial and colonial society. It is a deeply learned vision, one that appears to be cognizant of the full range of

intellectual innovation during Tryon's lifetime. It is a transformed
enthusiasm in which the energies provided by the immediacy of the
indwelling Spirit are reimagined as a programmatic overcoming of the
terrors of worldliness, be it meat-eating, luxury, or slavery. The career
of Immanuel Kant has been described as one where mysticism (in the
form of an engagement with Swedenborg's writings) had to be engaged
with and rejected in order for Kant's metaphysics to be formulated.[44]
Similarly, Tryon critically engaged with contemplative mysticism in order
to put it to critical and practical use. Unlike Kant, he sought not for
aesthetic categories, but for the obliteration of the imagination, the source
of all sin. Jane Shaw has recently argued that Enlightenment definitions of enthusiasm were the chief means by which the rationalists defined
their own activity.[45] But in Tryon, enthusiasm becomes enlightenment,
and seeks to redeem the world from the terror of meat and the sweet
violence of sugar.

NOTES

1 Andreas Riem, *Uber Aufklärung* (1788), trans. Jane Kneller, in James
 Schmidt, ed., *What is Enlightenment? Eighteenth-Century Answers and Twentieth-
 Century Questions* (Berkeley, Calif., 1996), p. 170.
2 Tryon, *Tryon's Letters, Upon Several Occasions* (1700), p. 87.
3 See Jacob, *The Radical Enlightenment: Pantheists, Freemasons and Republicans* (1981),
 and *Living the Enlightenment: Freemasonry, Politics and Eighteenth-Century Europe*
 (Oxford, 1991).
4 Justin Champion, *The Pillars of Priestcraft Shaken: The Church of England and
 its Enemies, 1660–1730* (Cambridge, 1992).
5 Pocock, "Post-Puritan England and the Problem of the Enlightenment,"
 in Perez Zagorin, ed., *Culture and Politics from Puritanism to the Enlightenment*
 (Berkeley, Calif., 1980), pp. 91–112.
6 See Timothy Morton, *Shelley and the Revolution in Taste: The Body and the Natural
 World* (Cambridge, 1994), pp. 13–30.
7 See B. J. Gibbons, *Gender in Mystical and Occult Thought: Behmenism and its
 Development in England* (Cambridge, 1996), p. 186.
8 Thomas, *Man and the Natural World: Changing Cultural Attitudes in England,
 1500–1800* (1983), p. 170.
9 See Tryon, *Some Memoirs of the Life of Mr. Tho. Tryon* (1705).
10 Tryon, *Wisdom's Dictates* (1696), sig. A3^r.
11 Tryon, *Friendly Advice to the Gentlemen-Planters* (1684), p. 164.
12 Tryon, *Tryon's Letters*, p. 65.
13 Tryon, *Tryon's Letters*, p. 119. Compare, for example, Gerrard Winstanley,
 Fire in the Bush (1650) in *The Law of Freedom and Other Writings*, ed.
 Christopher Hill (1973), pp. 220–1.

14 See Lotte Mulligan, *et. al.*, "Winstanley: A Case for the Man as He Said He Was," *Journal of Ecclesiastical History* 28 (1975): 57–75.

15 See Winstanley, *Fire in the Bush*, pp. 220–1.

16 Tryon, *Wisdom's Dictates*, sigs. A3$^{\text{r-v}}$.

17 See Tryon, *A Treatise of Dreams and Visions* (1689); and see also his *Pythagoras his Mystick Philosophy Reviv'd* (1691). These works contain the best Behmenist accounts of the interpretation of dreams and visions in the period.

18 It has been argued by Alexander Gordon in his *DNB* entry on Tryon that the fact that Tryon eventually set up as a hatter, and that Crab was also a hatter, may mean that Tryon was at some point under the influence of the older man.

19 Tryon, *Letters*, p. 85.

20 Ibid., p. 87.

21 Tryon, *Friendly Advice*, pp. 10–11.

22 Ibid., p. 5.

23 See Tryon, *Health's Grand Preservative* (1682), 2 editions; *The Way to Health, Long Life and Happiness* (1683), 7 editions; *The Good Housewife made a Doctor* (1685), 3 editions; *The Way to make all People Rich* (1685), 2 editions; *A New Art of Brewing Beer* (1691), 3 editions; *A Pocket Companion* (1693), 2 editions.

24 Tryon, *Friendly Advice*, p. 8.

25 Tryon, *Letters*, p. 91.

26 Tryon, "A Philosophical Account of this Hard Frost," in *Modest Observations on the Present Extraordinary Frost* (1684), p. 4. Strike food like this did not work.

27 See Milton, *Paradise Lost* (1667), 5: 404–20.

28 Tryon, *Some Memoirs*, sig. L5^{r}.

29 Tryon, *Wisdom's Dictates*, p. 102.

30 Ibid., p. 102.

31 Tryon, *Tryon's Letters*, pp. 184–5.

32 Ibid., p. 184.

33 Ibid., p. 189.

34 Tryon, *Friendly Advice*, p. 27.

35 Ibid., pp. 103, 107.

36 Ibid., p. 168.

37 Ibid., p. 165.

38 See Tim Morton, "Trade Winds," in Kate Flint ed., "Poetry and Politics," *Essays and Studies* (1996), pp. 19–41.

39 Tryon, *Friendly Advice*, p. 167.

40 Ibid., p. 97.

41 Ibid., pp. 190–2.

42 Ibid., p. 192.

43 Ibid., p. 77. See also Albert O. Hirschman, *The Passions and the Interests: Political Arguments for Capitalism before its Triumph* (Princeton, N.J., 1977).

44 Hartmut Böhme and Gernot Böhme, "The Battle of Reason with the Imagination," in Schmidt, ed., *What is Enlightenment?*, pp. 426–52.
45 Shaw, "Religious Experience and the Formation of the Early Enlightenment Self," in Roy Porter, ed., *Rewriting the Self: Histories from the Renaissance to the Present* (1997), pp. 61–71.

CHAPTER 8

"What is the country?": patriotism and the language of popularity during the English militia reform of 1757

Eliga Gould

In recent years, scholars have rediscovered one of the more compelling images of early modern Britain, that of the English, Scots, and Welsh as a "nation" bound together by a broad-based, often enthusiastic commitment to a set of shared political and religious values. In studies ranging from David Cressy's analysis of religious holidays under the Tudors and Stuarts to Linda Colley's magisterial survey of the eighteenth-century invention of the British nation, patriotism has come to provide historians with a powerful device for uncovering what ordinary men and women thought both about themselves and about their place within the world at large.[1] But if patriotism often represented, in Colley's words, a "highly rational" and "creative" posture for "all classes" and "both sexes," it could also serve hack journalists, aspiring politicians, and would-be reformers of all sorts as an extraordinarily effective way to popularize novel, frequently burdensome initiatives ranging from the first halting attempts to reform the poor laws to the growing demand for establishing a "better police" in the principal cities of Britain and Ireland.[2] To paraphrase Raymond Williams's famous analysis, we might well say that the same sentimental resonance which made loyalty to one's "country" such an effective refuge for populist "scoundrels" like John Wilkes also ensured that patriotism would provide one of the more potent forces for regulation and social reform in England during the second half of the eighteenth century.[3]

This chapter examines one of the earliest manifestations of patriotism's regulatory potential, the elder William Pitt's intrusive, widely resented attempt to reform the English militia during the Seven Years' War. Enacted just before the formation of the Newcastle-Pitt ministry, the Militia Act of 1757 supplied the metropolitan press with compelling proof of the new administration's determination to prosecute the war with France on a patriotic basis.[4] Yet the new law contained a number of deeply unpopular provisions, the most objectionable of which subjected all able-bodied men to a compulsory ballot regardless of their social position or personal wealth. Where the militia's primary burden had traditionally fallen on the landed gentry, both the Act of 1757 and its various successors shifted the main responsibility for the militia squarely onto the shoulders of those least able to afford it by making every able-bodied man equally eligible for the militia ballot and requiring landless laborers to pay the same £10 penalty for hiring a substitute as broad-acred gentlemen.[5] Although the new law eventually enabled Parliament to raise some 15,000 soldiers in England and Wales, the initial attempts during the summer of 1757 to ballot men sparked some of the most serious rural riots of the eighteenth century. Many of the men who were eligible for actual service continued to regard the measure as little more than a novel scheme to force "the poor . . . to defend the rich."[6]

In many ways, this opposition to militia service was not all that surprising. What was remarkable was the response that it received in the metropolitan press. Although the virtual insurrection which greeted the new Act was impossible to ignore, Pitt's apologists in the London and provincial presses proved adept at deploying an idealized notion of the "country" both as a way to mask the extent of this rural opposition and as a device for affirming the patriotic character of those units which actually were raised. In a sense, the mid-century language of patriotism served to enlist the unchanging values of rural England on behalf of ideas that had less to do with actual conditions in the countryside, than with the country as it was imagined by politicians at Westminster and their supporters in the urban press. As we shall see, this triumph of "perspective," to borrow another of Williams's analytical categories, was not quite as complete as Marxist historians might have once expected.[7] Still, with its claims to popularity, the measure which Parliament approved in 1757 resembled nothing so much as a calculated attempt to use the patriotic commitment to personal military service as a way to enhance the reach of Britain's "fiscal-military state."[8]

I

The unpopularity of Pitt's militia must have come as a surprise to many, since the Whigs' patriot critics had long depicted the absence of such an institution as one of the more conspicuous emblems of the government's disregard for the liberties of the English people. As oppositionists liked to point out, the Whigs' hostility to the militia was inconsistent

with the provisions in the English Declaration of Rights which named
the right to bear arms among the fundamental laws which no monarch
might revoke.[9] "Liberty . . . is the Birthright of every Englishman, and
ought to be defended by all," was how the Tory polemicist, John
Shebbeare, put the issue in his notorious *Letters to the People of England.*
(1755). According to Shebbeare, "every Law, which can deprive you of
defending that celestial Right is . . . an Infringement of your just
Privilege, and a Violation of the Constitution."[10] The editor of a collection of addresses submitted during the war's opening year made the
same point, noting that the costs of the regular army and the constitutional danger of foreign mercenaries meant there was no reason
to doubt the "popularity" of reforming the militia.[11] Whatever Court
Whig apologists might say about the advantages of having a professional
army, their opponents were sure that denying ordinary subjects the right
to defend themselves threatened the very foundations of Britain's
"matchless constitution."

These general assumptions about the militia's popularity reflected
a number of more specific considerations, the first of which involved
the conviction that an efficient militia was essential for safeguarding
Britain's standing among the principal "imperial" states of Europe. By
enabling the government to protect the coasts of England without the
assistance of foreign auxiliaries, an effective militia promised to liberate
the country from what was widely perceived as the Whigs' excessive
commitment to the continental alliances which had been the centerpiece of British foreign policy since the Glorious Revolution. For many
of those who supported Pitt's militia reform, the Jacobite rebellion of
1745 provided an especially vivid reminder of the dangers of relying
exclusively on professional troops. Not only had the regular army been
unable to prevent Charles Stuart's Highland band from reaching Derby
during the autumn of 1745, but many of the Dutch, Swiss, and German
auxiliaries brought over to help quell the insurrection had refused to
undertake offensive operations, thereby forcing the government to
withdraw troops from Britain's hard-pressed allies in the Netherlands.
In the concise words of a bill proposed at the height of the crisis, "a
well-constituted militia" represented "the natural and constitutional
defence of this Kingdom and the best security for both King and
people."[12] "If we had such a Militia," queried one commentator in early
1746, would "this Rebellion . . . ever have happen'd?"[13] "The truth is,"
wrote another, that the Jacobites had come so close to succeeding because
none of the king's loyal British subjects had it "in their Power to

appear in Arms either in their own Defence, or in Defence of the Government."[14]

What made the prospect of reviving the militia especially enticing, though, was the belief that such a measure would place the defense of the realm in the hands of a different class of men from those who tended to enlist in the regular army. To be sure, the supporters of the legislation, which was eventually passed in Parliament in 1757, took care to avoid any suggestion that the new militia might eventually rival or even supersede the professional establishment. Nonetheless, most of the militia's projectors assumed that having an efficient force in the counties of England and Wales would rectify one of the worst effects of a standing army by permitting men from the "middling" and more respectable of society's "lower" ranks to acquire the training necessary to defend themselves, their families and, of course, their king and country. Indeed, the case for reform owed a good deal to the proposition that men with a vested interest in preserving Britain's "matchless constitution" would fight with greater conviction than those who enlisted for life terms and served for pay alone. "I speak to the nobility and gentry, the traders and yeomanry of this kingdom, to all those who are possess'd of property, and have something to lose, and from the interest of their respective shares, are equally concern'd in the preservation of the whole," was the way Edward Wortley Montagu envisaged the militia in 1759.[15] As an anonymous pamphleteer had explained during the Jacobite Rebellion a decade and a half before:

The Hireling, who goes to the Field only to earn his daily Wages, has but weak Motives to risk his Life in the Defence of his Country. His Notions of Liberty are but confused and cold; whereas, the Housekeeper's must be supposed to be animated with a Different Spirit; his Knowledge of the Happiness he enjoys under our happy Establishment, fires him with Zeal for its Preservation; the Thoughts of his Property, his Wife and Family, animate his Courage in their Defence.[16]

The problem, of course, was that it was not at all clear whether men like this would actually be willing to make the sacrifices which militia duty was bound to entail.

Not surprisingly, the Court Whigs who had long opposed efforts to revive the militia in England were especially quick to point out the institution's authoritarian potential. As the Duke of Argyll had assured the Upper House during the 1730s, there was no military reason why the government might not revive the county regiments, but he was confident that "laying the whole militia of the kingdom under a necessity of marching to exercise once or twice every week, would raise a most terrible disaffection against the government; and the disaffection would be the more terrible, because the disaffected would not only have arms in their hands, but would have some sort of skill in using them."[17] The Dean of Gloucester, Josiah Tucker, struck an equally skeptical note in his lengthy polemic against Pitt's prosecution of the war, warning that the gentry who officered the militia would have to assume broad "*discretionary*, nay *military* Powers" in order to prevent it from becoming a "headless Mob."[18] In the words of Robert Henley Ongley, Member of Parliament for Bedford, it seemed "that many Persons have of late been captured by the Sound of the Word, without duly attending to the Nature of the thing."[19]

The course of events would show that there was a good deal to justify such concerns. Yet the likelihood that not everyone would relish being balloted for the militia did less to diminish the issue's popular appeal than we might suppose. One of the clearest indications of this imperviousness involved the preoccupation of many patriots with the paired categories of "manliness" and "effeminacy." As scholars have frequently noted, the often misogynistic use of such terms can be understood partly as an attempt to reaffirm traditional gender relationships in the face of widespread anxieties over the role of women in contemporary English society.[20] At the same time, though, the tendency to discuss matters of national politics in terms of a generalized crisis of masculinity was calculated to influence the conduct of men as well. Although patriots like John Shebbeare were confident that many would volunteer for militia duty, the terms in which they depicted the issue effectively removed the legitimate grounds for refusing to do. In the words of a pamphlet ostensibly addressed to the common men of Norfolk during the autumn of 1757, "those who would at such a Time call upon Substitutes, to defend their Sweethearts, their Wives and Families, deserve richly, that my pretty country-Women should find Substitutes to serve for them in a more pleasing Duty."[21]

Another pamphlet, also addressed to the people of Norfolk, attributed the opposition to the militia to an "effeminate" diet of foreign luxuries.[22] Once a reformed militia took hold, however, patriots were quite sure that the English would lose their "effeminacy," and "the military virtues, and the manly exercises, [would] become fashionable, and the nation which now seems immersed in debauchery and corruption, [would] think seriously and be once more, what it has often been, the terror of Europe."[23] Even after the English riots of 1757, Pitt's apologists continued to insist on the militia's popular credentials. "Let it not be said," urged one of the patriot minister's anonymous correspondents during the autumn of 1757, "that the national honour and credit, are matters of no concern, to the common people."[24] In the words of George Townshend's preface to Sir William Windham's influential *Plan of Discipline for the Norfolk Militia*, the new force would quickly show "how easily an healthy robust countryman, or a resolute mechanic, may be taught the use of arms."[25] According to another piece, also written by a militia officer during the last year of George II's reign, the effects of militia service would eventually spread to the rest of English society:

The knowledge of Arms will grow fashionable, and the lower Sort of people, now so into Ease and Luxury, will awake as from a Dream, and be familiariz'd to a military Spirit. The sons will catch it of their Fathers, and our Villages, instead of being alarm'd at the Sight of a Soldier, will soon become the best Nursery of them, and will abound with men willing to defend their Country at home, and to supply his Majesty's Fleets and Armies abroad.[26]

II

The new law received a very different response from the ordinary men and women who were expected to shoulder the militia's unwelcome burden. In practically every parish where the local magistrates attempted to implement the new militia ballot, there was some sort of violent demonstration.[27] In one Hertfordshire village, a crowd armed with clubs and staves surrounded a meeting of the deputy lieutenants, threatened them with violence, and eventually forced them to surrender the lists of eligible men.[28] There were reports of similar occurrences in Cambridgeshire, where a gathering of both men and women attacked the house of a magistrate who had attempted to ballot men at Royston, refusing to leave until he agreed to give them three guineas and insisting that he sign a pledge promising not to enforce the militia laws for the rest of the year.[29] In November, a belated attempt to draw up lists of eligible men in Gloucestershire threw the entire countryside "for eight or ten miles" around Cirencester into "the utmost confusion."[30] And crowds in Yorkshire proved so successful at intimidating the parish constables that the county's superior magistrates despaired of ever bringing the leading perpetrators to justice.[31]

In many ways, the riots triggered by the Militia Act of 1757 resembled what students of English popular culture would regard as a familiar conflict between long-standing custom and an innovative parliamentary statute.[32] The militia's plebeian opponents certainly seem to have regarded their own actions in this way. During the riot at Royston, for example, the crowd made it look as though they had the law on their side by forcing two constables to accompany them in their march.[33] Several days later, a similar encounter took place in Lincolnshire, where a crowd entered the county seat, "compell'd the Chief and Petty Constables to deliver up all their Lists," and proceeded to shred them, "forcing some of the Constables to joyn" in the destruction.[34] And no fewer than twenty-eight constables appeared at the head of a large crowd in Yorkshire, all of whom "expressed great Loyalty to his Majesty," but who also made it clear that they looked upon the present "Bill as taking their Liberties from them" and insisted "that they would not consent to this Law."[35]

As far as Britain's Whig rulers were concerned, popular challenges to a parliamentary statute were always cause for alarm. The disturbances which convulsed the English countryside during the autumn of 1757 were no exception, with politicians and commentators holding forth on the likely effects of "suffering a giddy and riotous populace to stand in opposition to an Act of Parliament."[36] What was unusual about the resistance to the new militia was that it placed the government in the uncomfortable position of having to compel the men who were sup-posed to serve in it to undertake an action which ultimately depended on their voluntary consent. Indeed, the more perceptive observers noted that the attempt to reform the English militia posed a fundamental challenge to the libertarian foundations of the British constitution. As Lord Chancellor Hardwicke observed in a particularly revealing letter to his son:

This is a law, which it is impossible to cram down the people's throats by force. You can never raise a militia by the compulsion of a standing army . . . It dif-fers from other cases. Troops may defend, and keep up a turnpike. But, in this instance, the final acts are to be done by the people themselves person-ally. They are to *subscribe* their names and *take oaths* before the Deputy-Lieutenants. No force can make them do that, if they stand out; nor can any body do it for them. They may indeed be convicted, and be imprisoned or fined, for their refusal, but is it possible to imprison or prosecute 1000 or 500 men in a county at once? . . . Force must support it at last; and force is inad-equate to the present case.[37]

Hardwicke's problem actually had two parts. The first concerned the landed gentry who were responsible for drawing up lists and balloting men on the parish and county level. Even those who had opposed the

measure while it was still under consideration as a bill in Parliament
recognized that once it had been enacted into law, they were under a
general obligation to try to enforce it. This is not to suggest that many
gentlemen relished the idea of taking steps which were likely to result
in disturbances like the ones that occurred during the autumn of 1757.
At the height of the riots, Lord Chancellor Hardwicke was startled to
discover that the part that he had played in defeating the militia bill
the year before had made him one of the only politicians in England
with a legitimate claim to be "popular."[38] But even Hardwicke had no
doubt as to where his duty lay. "Tho' I was originally against the Bill,"
remarked the Whig peer, "yet now it is a Law, I talk as much for
it, and against the opposition to the execution of it, as anyone."[39] As
the Tory historian of the Roman Empire, Edward Gibbon, would later
recall of his own experience as an officer in Pitt's militia, the fact
that the "country gentlemen" in Parliament had given the measure
their sanction meant that most felt they had no choice but to support
it. "When the king's order for our embodying came down," Gibbon
noted in his autobiography, "it was too late to retreat and too soon
to repent."[40]

As for the ordinary men singled out for service, many of the militia's
staunchest supporters seem to have hoped that this sense of patriotic
obligation would eventually produce the same results as it had among
their landed superiors. As a measure of these hopes, the government
initially responded to the riots with what amounted to a series of attempts
to persuade those who were expected to serve in its ranks. During the
spring of 1758, Parliament took the unusual step of enacting a new law,
a principal goal of which involved simplifying the oaths of allegiance
in order to make the militia's defensive function more readily apparent to the enlisted men.[41] At the same time, the local gentry frequently
published written explanations of their own. In Hertfordshire, for example, the county magistrates arranged to have a broadsheet printed
and distributed to farmers attending local markets in order to counter
"false representations of the Act."[42] Similarly, during the autumn of 1757,
newspapers in Ipswich, Cambridge, and Gloucester carried official man-
ifestoes meant to reassure the general public about the limited terms
of actual service.[43] Elsewhere, magistrates referred rioters to the text of
the Act itself, and in at least one instance persuaded a crowd to admit
"that an Act of Parliament never had deceiv'd them, nor was likely ever
to do so."[44] Indeed, Pitt himself was quite sure – or so he claimed in
the Privy Council – that "a proper disposition in the Lord Lieutenant

and Deputy Lieutenants to explain the Act" was all that was necessary to persuade the people to serve in the regiments of their constituent counties.[45]

The problem was that the English people already understood the militia's central provision perfectly well. In Lincolnshire, angry rioters claimed that the new Act showed "that the gentlemen just kept Poor men alive to fight for them," and several magistrates received an anonymous letter wondering "which of you Buntin' Ars'd Coated fellows" were prepared to maintain the families of those whose "ticket" happened to be drawn in the militia ballot.[46] In a similar manner, an anonymous note posted at Halifax warned potential recruits that "you [are] soon to be trepann'd out of your liberty & all that is Dear," while crowds elsewhere insisted that the Militia Act was nothing more than a scheme to force the poor to defend the rich, that the new law would reduce honest countrymen to the same condition as regular soldiers, and that they would "rather be hanged in England, than scalped in America."[47] As the author of a pamphlet on the militia observed in early 1758, "our daily bread being dear, husbandry work very cheap, and the labourers required to fight, or learn to form the hollow-square, for little or nothing, are [all] esteemed intolerable hardships!"[48] "The friends of the Bill cannot now say, that, the Gentry have been the authors of its failure," Lord Royston noted with evident satisfaction, "for *it is* the work of their *favorites and friends* the οἱ πολλοί – the *People*."[49]

Indeed, the disturbances caused by the Militia Act suggested that the patriotism of the English people was not all that different from that of the Court Whigs, whose stated preference was for a system of political obligation based on the payment of taxes to support a professional army. In the East Riding, for example, the crowds who forced the deputy lieutenants to suspend the Militia Act during the autumn of 1757 insisted that they would happily "serve [the king] in any other way against all enemys whatsoever."[50] Elsewhere, observers noted that the common men claimed to be "willing in time of publick danger to fight for their King & country," but that they objected to being compelled "to desert their families" in order to serve on the same terms as soldiers in the regular army.[51] Even after Parliament had removed some of the main popular grievances in 1758, the militia's emphasis on personal service remained the subject of recurring complaint. In the words of an anonymous note addressed to the constables of Hambleden in Buckinghamshire: "supose we are farmer leaber or wat not, we must leaves our wives and familys and all our callings for that one damd wimse of yours when

there is leteren [i.e., loitering] felers enouf goes about the country such
as Jipses and others trampers."[52] British patriots might decry the
Hanoverian regime's dependence on standing armies and foreign
auxiliaries. But given the chance to speak for themselves, the common
people obviously preferred to leave the unwelcome burden of defending the nation to the "leteren felers" who presumably had nothing
better to do than accept the king's bounty.

III

For the most part, of course, ordinary men and women in Hanoverian
England had few opportunities to speak for themselves, at least in the
sense of reaching a larger "national" audience. As a result, the militia's
supporters continued to make patriotic claims on their behalf, even though
such language increasingly functioned not as a way of appealing to the
common people of England and Wales, but as a kind of rhetorical screen
for masking the true extent of their opposition. As Charles Yorke wrote
to his father at the height of the rioting in 1757, "my newspaper (I observe)
studiously conceals from me every disorder which tends to affect the
credit of the Militia Bill."[53] Indeed, once the Crown started to embody
the county regiments two years later, it became almost impossible to
read anything but positive accounts of new corps. Where the county
leaders managed to raise the requisite number of officers and men, reg-
imental gatherings frequently took on the features of carefully staged
spectacles. What did not appear in print were the private reports of
fatigue in the ranks, of tensions with regular soldiers, of discontent over
being kept under canvas during harvest, and occasionally of opposition
among the enlisted men to marching beyond the borders of their home
counties.[54] Not surprisingly, when a serious mutiny by the Devonshire
militia at Plymouth Dock received no comment at all in the London
press, the militia's critics began to suspect "that some industry is used
to restrain the publication of such incidents."[55] "As the Militia seems to
be the Fashion of the Year," wrote a perceptive observer in 1760, "it is
but a common Degree of Complaisance in Government . . . not to
obstruct its Operation."[56]

   All this would seem to confirm Williams's insight about how invoking the "country" invariably carries implications detrimental for the very
society being invoked.[57] In the case of the militia reform of the Seven
Years' War, though, this insight can carry us only so far, for behind

the public screen of popularity, both Parliament and the magistrates charged with administering the new law proved only too happy to negotiate less onerous terms of service. One of the clearest indications of this willingness involved the proliferation from 1759 onward of clubs, societies, and charitable associations designed to shield their members from having to assume the cost of hiring a substitute in the event any of them were balloted. In some instances, these organizations consisted entirely of ordinary men like the Sussex shopkeeper, Thomas Turner, who entered into an agreement with his neighbors in 1762.[58] In other cases, local gentry and the wealthier members of the urban middle class undertook subscriptions to cover the costs of substitutes for the poor.[59] On still other occasions, such ventures were the work of commercial enterprises like the Colchester firm which maintained offices in the principal market towns of Essex and which promised subscribers that it would find substitutes in return for payments ranging from four shillings and sixpence for one-year's coverage to nine shillings for three years.[60] Whether organized for profit or charity, the cumulative effect of societies like this was to free those with families and trades from militia duty and turn the detested ballot into a form of voluntary service not all that different from the one that prevailed in the regular army.

Without question, appealing to an idealized notion of the country often worked to cloak political activities which had their origin in Parliament and the urban press in the authoritative mantle of England's rural past. For this reason, initiatives like Pitt's militia reform often carried real, if hidden, consequences for the rural countrymen who were supposed to participate in them. As the Militia Act of 1757 also demonstrated, though, the sheer variety of possible answers to the question "what is the country?" guaranteed that English patriotism remained susceptible to repeated revision and multiple interpretations. Notwithstanding the images dispersed by the Pittite press, the militia ended up confirming that for most of English society, patriotism remained more a public spectacle or artifact for mass consumption than a virtue to be sustained by direct and personal sacrifice. "Every one of us cannot shine *in deeds of arms*," observed the London philanthropist Jonas Hanway in 1760, "but we may demonstrate our inclinations to do so, by showing our respect for *military virtue*."[61] No doubt words like this struck the more enthusiastic of the militia's supporters as anathema. But for anyone who had experienced the ballot directly they must have rung true indeed.

130 ELIGA GOULD

NOTES

1 David Cressy, *Bonfires and Bells: National Memory and the Protestant Calendar in Elizabethan and Stuart England* (Berkeley, Calif., 1989); Linda Colley, *Britons: Forging the Nation, 1707–1837* (New Haven, Conn., 1992). See also Kathleen Wilson, *The Sense of the People: Politics, Culture and Imperialism in England, 1715–1785* (Cambridge, 1995).

2 Colley, *Britons*, p. 5. The work on social reform in Hanoverian England is vast, but see Donna T. Andrew, *Philanthropy and Police: London Charity in the Eighteenth Century* (Princeton, N.J., 1989); Joanna Innes, "Politics and Morals: The Reformation of Manners Movement in Later Eighteenth-Century England," in Eckhart Hellmuth, ed., *The Transformation of Political Culture: England and Germany in the Late Eighteenth Century* (Oxford, 1990), pp. 57–118; and Kathleen Wilson, "Urban Culture and Political Activism in Hanoverian England: The Example of Voluntary Hospitals," in Hellmuth, ed., *Transformation*, pp. 165–84

3 The multifaceted, often misleading influence that the "country" had on the way the English understood industrial society is, of course, the central argument in Williams's *Country and City*. The argument in this chapter also owes a substantial debt to Pierre Bourdieu, *Language and Symbolic Power*, ed. and intro. John B. Thompson, trans. Gino Raymond and Matthew Adamson (Cambridge, Mass., 1991), especially pp. 90–102 ("Did You Say 'Popular'?").

4 See my "To Strengthen the King's Hands: Dynastic Legitimacy, Militia Reform, and Ideas of National Unity in England, 1745–1760," *Historical Journal* 34 (1991): 329–48; Marie Peters, *Pitt and Popularity: The Patriot Minister and London Opinion during the Seven Years' War* (Oxford, 1980), pp. 67, 89, 106–7.

5 J. R. Western, *The English Militia in the Eighteenth Century: The Story of a Political Issue* (1965), pp. 17–18; Linda Colley, "The Reach of the State, the Appeal of the Nation: Mass Arming and Political Culture in the Napoleonic Wars," in Lawrence Stone, ed., *An Imperial State at War: Britain from 1689 to 1815* (1994), pp. 165–84, especially pp. 167–8.

6 Letter from G. Lane, York, October 1, 1757, PRO State Papers Domestic (hereafter SPD), 36/138, fols. 43–4.

7 Williams, *Country and City*, pp. 9–12.

8 The phrase comes from John Brewer, *The Sinews of Power: War, Money and the English State, 1688–1783* (New York, 1989).

9 Joyce Lee Malcolm, *To Keep and Bear Arms: The Origins of an Anglo-American Right* (Cambridge, Mass., 1994), pp. 114–22. See also J. G. A. Pocock, *The Machiavellian Moment: Florentine Political Thought and the Atlantic Republican Tradition* (Princeton, N.J., 1975), chapters 12–14.

10 [Shebbeare], "Letter II. On Liberty, Taxes, and the Application of Public Money," in *Three Letters to the People of England*, 6th edn. (1755; rpt. 1756), pp. 70, 71.

11 *The Voice of the People: A Collection of Addresses to His Majesty, and Instructions to Members of Parliament by their Constituents upon the Unsuccessful Management of the present War, both at Land and Sea; and the Establishment of a National Militia* (1756), p. ix.

12 Draft legislation, [1745–6], Papers of Francis Dashwood, Lord Dispencer, Bodleian Library, MSS D. D. Dashwood (Bucks) (hereafter Dashwood Papers), c.4/B8/2/11a. For the printed version of the bill, see *A Bill for the Better Regulation of the Militia in that part of Great Britain called England* ([1746]).

13 *An Enquiry into the Causes of our Late and Present National Calamities: And some Methods proposed to Remove them, and Prevent the like for the Future* ([1745/6]), p. 26.

14 *An Enquiry into the Causes of the Late Rebellion, and The proper Methods for preventing the like Misfortune for the future* (1746), p. 24.

15 Montagu, *Reflections on the Rise and Fall of the Antient Republicks. Adapted to the Present State of Great Britain* (1759), p. 380.

16 *The Folly and Danger of the Present Associations Demonstrated. With some proposals for rendering the Zeal for Liberty, which appears in all Ranks of people, of Real Use and Advantage to the Public. By a Citizen of Westminster* (1745), p. 18.

17 William Cobbett, ed., *The Parliamentary History of England, from the Earliest Period to the Year 1803*, 17 vols. (1806–1820), 8: 1244.

18 [Tucker], *The Important Question concerning Invasions, a Sea War, Raising the Militia and Paying Subsidies for Foreign Troops: Fairly and Impartially stated on both sides, and humbly referred to the Judgment of the Public* (1755), p. 24.

19 [Ongley], *An Essay on the Nature and Use of the Militia, with Remarks on the Bill offered to Parliament last session* (1757), p. iii.

20 G. J. Barker-Benfield, *The Culture of Sensibility: Sex and Society in Eighteenth-Century Britain* (Chicago, Ill., 1992), chapter 3; Laura Brown, Ends of *Empire: Women and Ideology in Early Eighteenth-Century English Literature* (Ithaca, N.Y., 1993).

21 *A Plan Address to the Farmers, Labourers, and Commonalty of the County of Norfolk* (1757), p. 16.

22 [Thomas Stona], *A Letter to the Norfolk Militia, upon the Proceedings of Ancient Nations when engaged in War . . . by a Dumpling Eater* (1759), see pp. 1–3.

23 *Motives for a Peace with England. Addressed to the French Ministry. By an Old Sea Officer. Translated from the French . . . Shewing the dangerous consequences of reviving the Antient Spirit of the British Nation, by a continuance of the present War* (1757), p. 4.

24 Letter to Pitt, October 28, 1757, PRO Chatham Papers, 30/8/77/2/214.

25 Townshend, "Dedication," in Sir William Windham, *A Plan of Discipline for the Use of the Norfolk Militia*, 3rd rev. edn. (1759; rpt. 1768), pp. ii–iii.

26 Young, *A Letter from a Militia-Man to his Colonel: Representing the Inconveniencies that may attend a Deviation from the Regular Established Exercise of the ARMY. Wrote with a Design to promote the Service of the MILITIA* (1760), p. 11.

27 The riots are treated extensively in Western, *English Militia*, pp. 290–302; and Ian Gilmour, *Riots, Risings, and Revolution: Governance and Violence in Eighteenth-Century England* (1992), pp. 295–300.

28 Letter from Charles Gore, September 5, 1757, PRO Chatham Papers 30/8/77/2, fols. 168–9, 172–3.

29 Letter from Sir John Chapman, Cockinhatch, September 6, 1757, ibid., fols. 178–9; Hardwicke to Newcastle, Wimple, September 7, 1757, BL Add. MSS 32,873, fols. 510–11; Hardwicke to Lord Royston, Wimple, September 9, 1757, BL Add. MSS 35,531, fols. 407–9.

30 Letter from Gabriel Hanger, Dryffield, November 6, 1757, SPD 36/138, fols. 117–18.

31 Letter from G. Lane, York, October 1, 1757, ibid., fols. 43–4.

32 See especially E. P. Thompson, "The Moral Economy of the English Crowd in the Eighteenth Century," *Past and Present* 50 (1971): 76–136, and *Customs in Common: Studies in Traditional Popular Culture* (New York, 1991).

33 Hardwicke to Royston, September 9, 1757, BL Add. MSS 35,351, fols. 407–9.

34 Duke of Ancaster to Newcastle, September 19, 1757, BL Add. MSS 32,874, fols. 157–8.

35 Nathaniel Cholmley to Newcastle, Hawsham, September 14, 1757, ibid., fols. 46–7.

36 Bedford to Pitt, Woburn Abbey, September 1, 1757, SPD 36/138, fols. 1–2.

37 Hardwicke to Charles Yorke, Wimple, September 8, 1757, BL Add. MSS 35,353, fols. 222–5.

38 Hardwicke to Newcastle, Wimple, September 11, 1757, BL Add. MSS 32,874, fols. 1–6.

39 See, for example, Hardwicke to Newcastle, Wimple, September 19, 1757, ibid., fols. 144–7.

40 *The Autobiography of Edward Gibbon*, ed. Dero A. Saunders (New York, 1961), p. 132.

41 Western, *English Militia*, pp. 140–5.

42 Letter from Lord Cowper, Colegreen, September 7, 1757, PRO Chatham Papers, 30/8/77, fols. 172–3. The strategy was not entirely successful, since riots occurred in parts of Hertfordshire the following year, encouraged at least in part by the "principal farmers" and the memory of magistrates' ineffectiveness the previous summer: see G. Jennings to Cowper, Newsells, September 7, 1758, ibid., fols. 227–8.

43 Western, *English Militia*, pp. 301–2.

44 Lawrence Monck, "Representation" to the Duke of Ancaster, Lincolnshire, September 9, 1757, BL Add. MSS 38,874, fols. 159–60. On the other hand, Lord Poulett reported in 1761 that the common people of Somerset had "so little Faith & Reliance . . . in the Promises of the Government" that they did not believe they could obtain any "legal Security for their Liberties from an express Act of Parliament" (letter dated November 2, 1761, SPD 41/32, fol. 18).

45 Newcastle to Hardwicke, September 10, 1757, BL Add. MSS 32,873, fols. 541–9.

46 Duke of Ancaster to Newcastle, September 19, 1757, BL Add. MSS 32,874, fols. 157–8; anon. letter to James Bateman and Samuel Dashwood, no date (included in Ancaster's letter), ibid., fols. 161–2.

47 David Hansfeld to Lord Rockingham, Halifax, September 24, 1757, ibid., fols. 274–5; letter from G. Lane, York, October 1, 1757, SPD 36/138, fols. 43–4; Lord Dupplin to Newcastle, Brodsworth, September 3, 1757, BL Add. MSS 32,873, fols. 444–7; J. S. Charlton to Newcastle, Staunton, August 27, 1757, ibid., fols. 311–12.

48 J[ohn] Railton, *Proposals to the Public; Especially Those in Power. Whose Spirits may be sincere enough, at all Events, by a brisk Militia, to save Great-Britain. Likewise to regain the important Island of Minorca, besides our late Possessions in America, and those famous Places that were lately lost, for Want of more disciplined Forces, in Germany* (1758), p. 13.

49 Royston to Hardwicke, Wrest, September 15, 1757, BL Add. MSS 35,351, fols. 415–16.

50 Lord Irwin to Newcastle, September 17, 1757, BL Add. MSS 32,874, fols. 121–2.

51 See, for example, George Townshend to Pitt, February 28, 1758, PRO Chatham Papers 30/8/64, fols. 151–2.

52 "To the Constables of the Parish of Hambledon," [1765–6?], Dashwood Papers, c.4/b82/2a.

53 Yorke to Hardwicke, September 15, 1757, BL Add. MSS 35,353, fols. 226–9.

54 William Beckford to Pitt, Camp near Winton, September 18 and October 5, 1759, Chatham Papers, 30/8/19/1, fols. 51–2, 53–4; Lord Clanricarde to Lord Holdernesse, Bath, June 10, 1759, SPD 36/142, fols. 64–5; Lord Shaftesbury to [Pitt], [May 29, 1759], Chatham Papers, 30/8/56/1, fols. 15–16; letter from Lord Cowper, Colegreen, July 27, 1759, SPD 41/30, fols. 157–9.

55 Hardwicke to Royston, September 1, 1759, BL Add. MSS 35,351, fols. 118–19. For more on the mutiny, see Duke of Bedford to Pitt, Woburn Abbey, September 2, 1757, Chatham Papers, 30/8/19/1, fols. 164–5.

56 *Reflections without Doors on What passes Within. Recommended to the Perusal of all Friends to the Militia: As Well as Those who wish to preserve Unanimity and Coalition between Administration and People, so necessary at this critical Conjuncture. By a Country Gentleman* (1760), pp. 9–10.

57 For Williams, this was even true of the Marxist theory which informed his own analysis: see *Country and City*, especially pp. 302–6.

58 *The Diary of Thomas Turner, 1754–1765*, ed. David Vaisey (Oxford, 1984), p. 251.

59 Western, *English Militia*, p. 252.

60 John William Burrows, *The Essex Militia*, volume 4 of *Essex Units in the War, 1914–1919*, Essex Territorial Army Association (Southend-on-Sea, 1929), p. 141.

61 Jonas Hanway, *An Account of the Society for the Encouragement of the British Troops, in Germany and North America* (1760), p. 20.

CHAPTER 9

Who's making the scene? Real people in eighteenth-century topographical prints

Richard Quaintance

From the Restoration through the reigns of the first three Georges, the shaping and reshaping of parkland surrounding country houses developed a complexity which, by 1800, Britons and Europeans alike would term "English." Successive styles by which wealth altered such spaces were normalized in concord with shifting political dominances, in ways broadly and familiarly distinguishable. The courts of Charles II and James II, returned from their exile in France, recalled horizon-pointing tree-avenues, terracings and sheets of water geometrically correct, so summoning attention to symmetrical control over earth, plants, and people through a quasi-Bourbon idiom. After 1689, reduction in scale and preference for trim evergreens bespoke new openness to the Dutch models left behind by William III at palaces like Het Loo. The Governor's Palace garden at Williamsburg, Virginia – as completed during the second decade of the eighteenth century – represented a late and colonial expression of that particular spatial expression of power. But in the 1720s, it was clear that under the Georges, stylistic initiatives in landscape design had been diffused and diversified among an oligarchy usually distant from the court in miles, taste, and ideology. Whether the wealth to improve a "place" were as old as that of the Howards of Henderskelfe in Yorkshire, or as new as that of the brewery heiress who married Marlborough's general, Richard Cobham, the vistas unfolding at Castle Howard, Stowe and other seats proceeded to offer individualized perceptions of social, political, and *country* space.

The pace and variety of these variations stimulated the minor industry of "place-visiting" which, by mid-century, embraced a clientele far beyond the place-owner's social circle. Among the by-products of this form of tourism, there appeared a striking change in the conventional engraved depiction of improved estates. Initiated by Europe's leading topographical draughtsman Jacques Rigaud when he was hired to portray Stowe, this new style of advertizing the pleasure of visiting a country seat would be copied within a generation by some of England's best engravers of landscaped views. Before Rigaud's work in and near London during the 1730s, of which some forty-five drawings and prints remain, the staffage of strollers depicted to give scale and perspective to any famous vista had lacked the dimension of interest to prompt print-collectors to imagine themselves among them. Beyond imparting a Watteauesque *politesse* of interaction to his fashionable staffage, Rigaud deployed recognizable personages – uncited in any caption – through-out his work. His eye for purchasers ready to be teased by a brush with "celebrity" thus bequeaths us a sequence of sketchy on-the-spot portraits of four trend-setting Whig proprietors, their families, and, in their entourages, the leading poet, the leading landscape-designer, and a leading castrato of the moment. Though unnoted from that time to this, the *parerga* of Rigaud's and his follower's prints – their ventures beyond topography toward genre and conversation-piece – render such prints rich documents in a development recently termed "a middle-class territorialization of the landscape."[1]

I

THE PEOPLE OF STOWE IN JACQUES RIGAUD'S ENGRAVINGS

In order to help its human figures approach their size in the original engraving, the detail given here in figure 9.1 offers only the right-hand three-fifths of the original wherein, for instance, the man in center fore-ground with his back to us stood two and a half inches high. Among the first things we notice is that figures near and far are as diversely interesting as the scenery around them. The pointing gestures of the man and woman right of center, if wooden, still seem pertinent to their conversation with the man seated on the wall, holding a staff (some sort of *major domo* or guide?). In the group at left a man in a bag-wig, and another wearing what almost seems to be his own hair, address their contrasting gestures to a man with a tricorn hat on – gestures clearly pertaining to some controversy about the plan in his lap and this ter-rain before us. Among others concerned in this conference, the gentle-man with a cane has kept his tricorn on too, and leans familiarly on the lady's chair-back: clearly a privileged member of the group domin-ated by that one man seated on a chair set out there for him, legs comfortably crossed, three-quarters turned away from us to compare his plan and their talk to what we see over his shoulder. Even the dogs interact. To complete our foreground, bustling up the stairs at right,

9.1 Rigaud, "View at the Entrance between the Pavillions" (detail),
engraved by Baron.

another tricorned man jingles his keys while behind him others peer
expectantly.

This detail is from the second of "Fifteen Perspective Views" of *Stowe
Gardens in Buckinghamshire, Belonging to the Right Honourable The Lord Viscount Cobham; Laid out by Mr Bridgman, Principal Gardener to their Majesties
King George I and II . . . Drawn on the Spot by Mons. Rigaud, and Engraved
by him and Mons. Bernard Baron*, as the work was partially entitled, in French
as well, upon its reissue. In 1739, at four guineas, it had proved over-
priced for its initial market, but by 1746, at two guineas, four London
booksellers hoped to reach the domestic and foreign tourist trade with
this reissue of the plates, abetted by a plan of Stowe Park.

Indeed the 1730s had seen the tourist industry focus on Stowe's layout, among all spots outside the capital, as the one most worth a visit.
By 1730 the route established for circling the landscaped terrain
around Stowe House departed from the head of those stairs where we
see visitors arriving in figure 9.1. Charles Bridgeman had arranged that
the first sight to greet them would be that same "Guglio" fountain which
William Congreve seems to feature in the fine poem he addressed in

1728 to his fellow-member of the Kit-Cat Club, Lord Cobham, Stowe's master. Marlborough's former general, Congreve writes, may shift aside grief for his recently dead "Chief," or vexation at the Walpole government's effete squandering of their victories' gains, by peaceably *disciplining*, instead, Stowe's

> latent Springs to lift their Heads,
> On watery Columns Capitals to rear,
> That mix their flowing Curls with upper Air.[2]

Verbal gestures like these lines help to gloss the visual gestures which the engravings show landscape making. Congreve's proposal to integrate a public persona for the proprietor with some manifestation in "his" landscaping typifies the estate-poems tumbling off the presses in these decades.[3]

Three years later, Pope's "Epistle to Burlington" enshrined landscape architecture among the arts. "One distinguish'd Line" of this critique "Of the Use of Riches" established Stowe as England's premier studio for mastering that art. Next, Gilbert West, one of Cobham's nephews and a likely participant in the planning of Stowe's iconography, won Pope's *imprimatur* for his 200-odd couplets guiding an actual or armchair visitor around its many sights. West broadens the conventional salute to the estate-owner, to cite Pope, Congreve, and Lord Lyttelton as famous visitors, and to "chat up" – after the anecdotal manner of a tour-guide – the mildly randy misbehavior of Stowe's Vicar, as well as the regretted death of a family friend for whose residence one of the pavilions had been designed.[4] The topographical poem thus proceeds to populate its landscape, and Stowe's, sketching for visitors a context of human histories a year before Rigaud arrived in 1733 to draw these vistas.

Before returning to the unusual auspices of his commission, let us carry this context of the public-relations record of Stowe's landscapes forward through the republication of Rigaud's prints in 1746. The verse and prints mentioned so far celebrated Cobham's patronage of the design-talents of Bridgeman and Sir John Vanbrugh. But what maintained Stowe's eminence as the flag-ship landscape for visitors was Cobham's readiness, right up to his death in 1749, to engage with and implement successively such remarkably different talents as those of William Kent and Capability Brown. With abundant energy he sponsored England's progressive revolutionizing of the very art that Pope's words had enshrined. George Clarke has already suggested that the man pictured in a chair in figure 9.1 represents this very alert Cobham.[5] How apt that, centered in this second of the suite of Stowe views, we should witness a conversation in which, as Cobham faces the less "finished" eastern sector of his gardens – which Kent after 1733 will lay out as the Elysian Fields, and Brown will crown with the Grecian Valley – another man gestures across his view toward the enormous westward complex just completed by Bridgeman (the left-hand two-fifths of this engraving missing from my detail). To prove that this gesturing man represents Bridgeman, or that this moment captures some historical turning-point in Cobham's planning, is impossible, and of course quite beyond the conventional functions of a suite of views like this one. What the human and non-human elements of this vista surely do commemorate is the array of styles – accomplished or potential – marshalled by Stowe to put people socially in touch with each other and artistically in contact with nature, distant and up-close, during the 1730s. Its foreground group represents the *kind* of conversation which made that array and contact happen.

Manuscript accounts by visitors and returnees through the 1730s and 1740s, *after* the moment depicted here, mark the excitement of Kent's and Brown's work on the *right* side of figure 9.1's vista. Signals from Stowe's emblematic architecture and sitings addressed far more explicitly than any other layout the national issues current in Robert Walpole's declining ministry. Samuel Richardson's 1742 revision of Daniel Defoe's *Tour* approximated the typical visitor's route around the grounds, anticipating the itch to copy or translate Latin inscriptions on statues or buildings, learn their height, catch all the fine views, and ponder a few issues of taste. Of twenty-four pages devoted to seven English gardens, Richardson's account of Stowe took sixteen. Hence it would have come as no surprise when, two years later Benton Seeley – a writing-master in nearby Buckingham – published the first guide-book to the gardens of a country seat, as a twenty-eight page pamphlet that was re-edited each year thereafter through 1749, and backed (in separate publication) by illustrations of thirty-nine architectural features of Stowe's landscape.[6] In 1748 William Gilpin launched his career anonymously with a sixty-page *Dialogue* vividly conducting us through Stowe's diverse aesthetic challenges.[7] From the 1720s through the 1740s the landscaping of this one estate thus drove the climaxing of Bridgeman's career, a rich phase of Kent's, and the start of Brown's. And Stowe led other estates in prompting the new "place"-visiting industry to develop its own resources of transport, food, lodgings, and of private and published self-reckoning and self-perpetuation – like those fifteen "Views."

During the thirteen years between Rigaud's drawings for these prints and their republication in 1746, then, Stowe's attractions had altered perhaps more dramatically than the fashions in dress the prints depicted, so even halving their asking price may not have quickened the trade. Dying in 1738, the landscape-designer Bridgeman was spared at least that disappointment, or beyond it his widow's struggle to recoup the £1,400 he had invested in Rigaud's visit. For another striking novelty about this suite of prints was their inception at the handshake of two professionals, rather than as a draughtsman's contract under aristocratic patronage. That reliable witness George Vertue confirms it was not Viscount Cobham but Mr. Bridgeman who commissioned this sumptuous depiction of a country seat, matched in Europe, then or since, only by the twenty-four views of Versailles which Rigaud had just published in Paris.[8]

Three motives may reasonably be ascribed to Bridgeman in undertaking this business risk. First, he knew that by 1733 Stowe represented the richest professional performance his particular genius might achieve, and wanted a published record of it made available to an appreciative public.[9] Second, he sensed that Cobham's preferences were shifting, and that – before Kent's more verbal wit and rococo shapes took over – Rigaud would be the man to catch the almost French ways that Bridgeman's turfed terracings and firm avenues of trees girded Stowe's space. Third, and returning us to those visitors in figure 9.1, Bridgeman had good reason to expect Rigaud would render fetchingly how well-dressed middle-class people enjoyed movement, interacted *en promenade*, and as one of them put it in 1763, "Enlivend the scene."[10]

The liveliest staffage in Rigaud's fifteen views of Stowe is found in the first of the engraved set. A pragmatic rationale for this is that his subject here presents, at 170 degrees, his widest-angled vista, of which my detail in figure 9.2 shows the middle 45 degrees. In order to display the broad distant stretch, from Stowe House at the upper right corner of my detail, leftwards past Vanbrugh's Rotunda and Brick Temple and across most of the rolling pasturage of Home Park – and to accommodate almost thrice as wide a span again (totalling sixteen named landscape features) at the sides of this center segment – the topographical draughtsman has committed himself to a broad foreground and middle distance that would be dull indeed if left featureless. Granted his limited resources in body-gesture and facial topography, Rigaud can

9.2 Rigaud, "View of such parts as are seen from the Building at the Head of the Lake" (detail), engraved by Baron.

nevertheless manage details of costume, and the spatial tranquilities which deliver to us those watery reflections in the lake. A *concert-champêtre* fore-grounded in a view of Meudon only months earlier included Rigaud's firmest allusion to Watteau, a girl leaning away from a man's embrace in the interaction Watteauistes term "the refusal theme" or "the faux pas."[11] With so much Stowe acreage to display in this opening vista, Rigaud's recycled foregrounding of musicians and audience, without the erotic by-play, is a practical solution.

But if the corpulence and stocking-clocks of the engraving's singer catch the eye, the fact that he replaces a lean, bespectacled conductor marking the beat with a rolled score in Rigaud's original drawing now at the Metropolitan Museum of Art,[12] must arouse suspicions that an actual singer is being portrayed. Indeed Antonio Maria Zanetti had drawn a portrait (figure 9.3) of a celebrated castrato of the day, Francesco Bernardi, nicknamed Senesino for his Siennese birthplace, so resembling this singer's body-type, dress and posture as to have certainly provided Rigaud or his engraver Baron with a model. Senesino had broken with Handel's management the month before Rigaud reached Stowe. So between 1733 and 1736 he was most likely to have been seen and heard here since he starred in the "Opera of the Nobility," patron-ized by Cobham and other aristocrats in open competition with royal patronage of Handel's troupe. Another Senesino patron during these years was Lord Burlington, who commissioned Rigaud to draw eight views of his Chiswick improvements; in the second of them the same large singer performs to other admirers, signaling the Whig oligarchy's independence of royal taste and munificence in musical affairs as in landscape architecture.[13]

Senesino's appearance in the Stowe staffage once granted, one begins to notice the re-entry of other figures here in other vistas. The tall if featureless youth pointing, just behind the violinist in figure 9.2, reappears in five other Stowe engravings.[14] In figure 9.4, aimed from the steps of Vanbrugh's Brick Temple back past the obelisk to the spot where figure 9.2 was drawn, he stands attentively over the couple seated like the pair in figure 9.1's foreground, the man now hatless, consider-ing a paper in his hand, while the lady, now wearing a necklace, eases her elbow behind his shoulder.

Such relaxed familial intimacy – seated couple, he with finger-curled hand casual on hip, she embroidering, foot on stool, lanky youth leaning on her chairback – recurs on the foregrounded portico overlooking the

9.3 Antonio Maria Zanetti, "A Stout Man." Brown ink and wash.

9.4 Rigaud, "View from the Brick Temple" (detail), engraved by Rigaud.

parterre and avenue down to that "Guglio" fountain with which we began (figure 9.5).[15] (The man approaching them, "chapeau bras" under elbow and plan in hand, represents Bridgeman, and reappears aptly in two other vistas.) This lady always has a nosegay at her breast, sometimes a tasseled cane, and both when she stands behind the bass-fiddle in the drawing on which figure 9.2 was based. The man usually hatted in the circle of hatless others, and his nosegayed partner – Lord and Lady Cobham – appear in eight of the fifteen views. The youth represents Cobham's nephew Richard Grenville, aged twenty-one in 1733 but to be known later as "Squire Gawkey," and to his wife as

9.5 Rigaud, "View of the Parterre from the Portico of the House" (detail).
Ink and wash.

"my dearest long man" (*DNB*). His participation in this suite of views opens a reassuring temporal vista down the decades ahead when as Earl Temple he will pace these scenes as the childless Cobhams' heir to Stowe.

The family group in figure 9.4 comprises Rigaud's closest approach to the composed frontality yet intergenerational momentariness of the conversation-piece that Philip Mercier and Hogarth were currently establishing in England. (To leave unchallenged such ensconced familial decorum, Rigaud's engraving canceled from his drawing a man urinating into the hedge at the left, and a seated man gesticulating toward him.) In a painted conversation-piece, commonly one, several, or even all of the family gaze back as if to say "We knew you'd be looking in on our property some day, indeed we paid the artist and sat here waiting for you, so have a good look." But when instead the *print-buyer's* leisure occasions the purchase, for such a glance to greet the viewer's might portend an intrusion on the landowner's privacy. No eyes meet ours from Rigaud's staffage, or that of his English followers.[16] This by-product and booster of the tourist industry manifests a style of tact which tempers, with a notion of accessibility, the adulation of the owner common to some portraits and estate poems.

A similar swerve distinguishes Rigaud's treatment of material characteristic of genre painting. Banished from these public spaces are the spidery beggars, vomiting drunkards, and ubiquitous urinators,[17] though more polite wit regarding family tourbehavior abides (figure 9.6), gently challenging patriarchal manners. The taming of this material for a public less clannish than that of West's poem on Stowe may be epitomized by other touches. When Conway Rand, Vicar of Stowe's chapel and target of West's waggery, appears in figure 9.7 and another print he greets visitors beside a woman who must be his wife, given their dignified posture and company; while his Fido sits patiently at his side in one, both prints show an identical spotted dog fleeing his back as if exorcized.[18] Rigaud has adjusted his product to a house-visiting clientele that would be genteel.

A different kind of distinction attaches to Rigaud's enterprise through another telltale switch – like that producing the Senesino "portrait" – between his drawing and engraving. Again like the Senesino, not social circumstance alone but physical resemblance as well confirms the identification. In one deep vista toward Vanbrugh's Rotunda, even the whirling statues of shepherds seem to lead visitors in a merry dance – a witty dialogue between art and reality perhaps typical of Rigaud (as in figure 9.7 when he stations Cobham in his most lordly demeanor before Gibbs's Temple of Fame encircled by busts of bygone British Worthies). Yet in Rigaud's preparatory drawing one man, conspicuously motionless on the foreground verge, listens to the conversation of an animated couple (figure 9.8). Thanks to details of Bridgeman's terracing behind them this drawing clarifies that the shorter man's eyes reach the level of the other man's chest: he must be under five feet tall. The shadow of a large tricorn obscures his face, but above his clenched hands his back shows a distinct s-curve. With the spine shaded as here, it is a curve slightly more marked than that of the most authentic surviving portrait of Alexander Pope from the side, William Hoare's red crayon drawing of perhaps eight summers later (figure 9.9).[19]

Pope's frequent "rambles" to Stowe in these years are well-documented, but what converts this ink-and-wash portraiture from likelihood to certainty is its suppression: Rigaud's engraving replaces him with a generic stripling. Whether that veto came from Pope's friends Bridgeman or Cobham, or from the poet himself is unknown. But from the inscription, almost certainly by Prince Hoare, son of the artist William, written *c.* 1790 on the back of that portrait which is figure 9.9, the reason why Rigaud's Pope went unpublished till now is clear enough:

9.6 Rigaud, "View of the Great Bason, from the Entrance of the Great Walk to the House" (detail), engraved by Rigaud.

9.7 Rigaud, "View from Gibbs's Building" (detail), engraved by Baron.

9.8 Rigaud, "View at the Queen's Statue" (detail). Ink and wash.

9.9 William Hoare, "Mr. Pope." Red Crayon.

This is the only Portrait that was ever drawn of Mr. Pope at Full-length. It was done without his knowledge, as he was deeply engaged in conversation with Mr. [Ralph] Allen in the Gallery at Prior Park; by Mr. Hoare who sat at the other end of the Gallery. Pope would never have forgiven the Painter had he known it. He was too sensible of the deformity of his Person to allow the whole of it to be represented. This Drawing is therefore exceedingly valuable as it is an Unique of this celebrated Poet.[20]

9.10 Rigaud, "View from Nelson's Seat" (detail), engraved by Baron.

Still almost true. Lady Burlington's late drawing of Pope, not quite a caricature, also displays his humpback with frank accuracy, while the poet is "deeply engaged" in cards.[21] That drawn by Rigaud, from mid-1733 or surely by mid-1734, is thus the earliest of the three surreptitious *ad vivum* portraits so far reported to show the pet's trunk from the side. Another by Rigaud might make a slightly less compelling fourth. In his Chiswick drawing mentioned above of Senesino near "the Temple by the Water," within earshot of the castrato and virtually dead-center in the foreground, a short hunchback lingers alone. The surmises of Jacques Carré and John Harris gain support when inspection of this less finished figure now at Chatsworth reveals the draughtsman's special attention to the profiled eye of the short man.[22] The woman seated, attended, holding sheet-music near Senesino, must represent Lady Burlington.

Changes between the original drawing and the published print direct us toward a targeted clientele for the set in one other instance, the "View from Nelson's Seat" (figure 9.10). As at Hampton Court Palace, and at eight royal French sites, Rigaud depicts himself in the foreground, with assistants, sketching the scene we observe over his head – a professional pledge that we may trust his accuracy. Beyond his seated figure, toying with her fan as she glances over her shoulder toward a tall man bowing her way, is the most intriguing woman at Stowe, uniquely dressed to kill. Her face framed by a fluttery narrow dark mantle tied at the throat, she wears a fashionable silk robe *à la française* (distinguished by its front and back pleats), with the widest hoops in sight.[23] Ignoring her, in the right foreground stroll a shorter man and woman, attended by a page, maid, and the usual frisky dog. This couple's features, nondescript in the drawing, are so worked up in the print that "They must be *some*one!" Since Baron finished this engraving after Rigaud returned to Paris in October 1734, it illustrates a continuing concern to pique the purchaser's curiosity about who these trend-setters were.

I propose no names, only a stratagem. What if no one in particular were intended this time? To recoup Bridgeman's investment required reaching, or creating, a public which owned no country house yet wanted to buy into the social space displayed here. Quite massively and persistently these fifteen prints entice us sociably to enter these scenes. While surely acknowledging the emblems of Cobham's public career, the dynamics of inheritance, the complex and spacious expression of his wife's wealth and his taste, this suite nevertheless introduces his family as engaged in leisurely, unmanagerial behavior requiring no special deference. In two views, though wheeled about in special three-wheeled chairs, they are spectators like us, not spectacle. Unlike the topographical poems, the guidebooks, or probably the guides' chatter, these images wordlessly invite us to interact with their cultivated spaces, and right on the level with these visitors improvise our own conversation with this bit of country. The narrative sequence of fifteen views – threaded by reappearing persons and landscape-features (the Rotunda nine times), whipping us around to face back along the axis just eyed, circling us about Bridgeman's spaces – partners us in a dance.

II

OTHER PEOPLE IN RIGAUD'S VISTAS

Among his *aide-mémoire* for the year 1732, the dependable documenter of London's engraving trade recorded:

The most remarkable Subject of painting that captivated the Minds of most People, persons of all ranks & conditions from the greatest Quality to the meanest, was the Story painted & designd by Mr. Hogarth of the Harlots Progress,

& the prints engravd by him & publishd . . . Whilst these plates were engraving he had in his Subscription between 14 or fifteen hundred. <by the printer I have been assured 1240 setts were printed> . . . all this without Courting or soliciting subscriptions.[24]

Vertue proceeds to associate the broad success of Hogarth's six-plate suite with the readily identifiable portraits it contained of Mother Needham, Colonel Charteris, Justice Gonson, and others abetting the Harlot's downward "Progress." Hence it seems likely that Bridgeman had good business reasons to encourage the "documentary" quasi-portraiture that Rigaud began to insinuate into his drawings at Stowe ten months after the Harlot's publication. But Rigaud had been doing this *paparazzo-parerga* for a dozen years; indeed around 1720 it may have boosted his leap from the provinces to the rue St. Jacques.

Rigaud's earliest surviving work reveals him, aged twenty-six, reaching through the role of military draughtsman toward that of history painter. From first-hand observation he inked a "Veüe de Toulon, et du Bombardement" of that port by artillery under the Duke of Savoy in August 1707. Not content to place the gunboats and batteries in his panorama with thirty-nine numbered key-features of the month-long siege, he adds shell-trajectories, cannon-smoke, and foregrounded cavalry and infantry charging those batteries *from* the city – the decisive counterattacks of 15 August which drove the invaders off. Then, when Europe's last bubonic plague struck his birthplace, Marseille, in 1720, Rigaud's popular and twice-pirated two prints chronicled, in the thick of grimly assembled generic circumstances, the good works of two actual heroes of the episode, Cardinal de Belzunce and the Chevalier de Roze. Since his growth in his craft received critical conditioning by such momentous actualities it was natural, by 1728 when he began to publish engravings of the royal gardens of France, that Rigaud should – still without verbal identification – portray among their visitors and entourages the dukes, princes, and their widowed mothers to whom each engraving was formally dedicated with family crest beneath. Celebrities are visually identifiable in his Tuilleries, Luxembourg, and St. Cloud gardens before he worked at Stowe, and at Chantilly later.[25] As in the Stowe engravings, enough bystanders make a fuss about the proprietor for us to spot him, but scores of others are preoccupied with their companions. Besides, as in many sets of non-topographical views he had published – scenes from the Bible or *l'Astrée*, the "progress" of Marseille's men-of-war from construction, launching, commissioning, to sinking in combat – vigorous narrative braiding marks his landscape suites: identical wheeled sedan-chairs bearing single passengers get paraded through five of his Versailles scenes. Since engravings like these are never far from drollery or *canard*, a dog may swim to retrieve a tourist's cane in the foreground of Versailles's bubbliest fountain display, the loafing or labor of real horses mocks the heroics of carved ones, or, at a royal wedding in St. James's Chapel which Rigaud enstaffaged and engraved for Kent, one foregrounded guest turns from the bridal couple to ogle women in the gallery with a spyglass.

Two other views Rigaud produced during his English visit (from February 1733 until October 1734, according to Vertue) deserve attention here. One broad vista embraces the south facade of Claremont in Surrey with Vanbrugh's early "Gothic" Belvedere beetling from the hilltop over it, and on the foreground verge, Claremont's master faces us commandingly (figure 9.11): Thomas Pelham-Holles, Duke of Newcastle.[26] During the very months of the excise crisis which cost Cobham his honors and thrust him into his most politicized landscaping, Rigaud could also work for this patron, who was as instrumental to the Walpole ministry as Cobham was critical of it. From his sixth Stowe view he even transferred to this drawing the motif of the groom rounding up horses. The youth in trimmed tricorn whom Newcastle eyes so steadily may represent his nephew both by blood and by marriage, Henry, ninth Earl of Lincoln, fourteen years old in the summer of 1734 and eventual heir of the childless Newcastle. Though this drawing was never engraved, Rigaud did engrave a strikingly similar vista toward Castle Hill in Devon, after John Wootton's painting of the house and Bridgemanic landscape of another Newcastle relative, but Cobham ally of 1733, Hugh Fortescue, first Earl of Clinton.[27] Its busy foreground figures include no visitors but both Clintons, an artist at work, and possibly the designer Bridgeman or the architect Roger Morris, whose work, completed in the early 1730s, the painting celebrates, along with the hilltop rotunda never built.

Why engrave another man's painting? Clearly Rigaud addressed his work to a public likely not to own a "place," but concerned to enter enviable places both social and geographic. Whether he drew and engraved the public spaces of Devonshire, London, Paris, or Provence, what drove his career and left him well-off at his death in 1754 was a clientele hanging on its household walls (or collecting in albums) his convincing windows on where they were not. Comparisons to his predecessors' work in two more respects can help clarify how enterprisingly he and his English followers constructed new relationships to country vistas, on the part of a public neither elite nor working-class.

First, he was not the first topographical engraver to station famous persons in center foreground without captioned notice: precedents could be cited in Jacques Callot, Wenceslaus Hollar, and Israel Silvestre.[28] Not the aristocracy but the well-to-do, would-be-polite citizenry of Nancy, London, or Paris would be the anticipated purchasers of their

9.11 Rigaud, "Claremont, with portrait of Thomas Holles Pelham, Duke of Newcastle" (detail). Ink and wash.

in-situ glimpses of the Duchess of Lorraine, the family of Charles I, the current resident of the Tuilleries. Yet we have seen at Stowe an easy accessibility to the rich and famous in their unbuttoned moments that had not been engraved before.

Secondly, his departures from conventions of the topographical prints by Johannes Kip, Leonard Knyff, and others dominating the trade from 1707 to 1728 have interesting social implications. Their bird's-eye views virtually *mapped* an entire property, maintaining a sharp focus on distant orchards within the domain, abruptly losing focus beyond it, to celebrate in detail the various productivity of the owner whose name and arms adorned the bottom margin. Rigaud brings us down to earth, makes distant objects harder to see, but, by associating us with "other" visitors, privileges leisurely interaction. Among the tiny figures earlier engravers included for scale, it is still easy to distinguish those who bowl from those who labor, while any of Rigaud's loungers might, judging by posture and dress, address any other. The Kip-Knyff terrain was equine-oriented: distant hunts or races, nearby manèges, approaching coaches, roads rutted to set off the utter smoothness of milord's lawns, canal, bowling-green, and vegetable plots. Rigaud's perspective has shifted from the landowner's to the visitor's.

III

UNNOTED NOTABLES IN OTHER TOPOGRAPHICAL PRINTS,
1746–1772

What traces of Rigaud's methods can we find in later English prints? A few examples follow.

In the center foreground of Nathaniel Parr's engraving of Kensington Palace in 1751, the year Prince Frederick died, stands a strikingly splendid sashed figure who might be the Prince, surrounded by the kind of attentions we have noted. In 1754 (republished in 1772) the decade's finest suite of engravings, by Thomas and Paul Sandby, revealed in four of eight views the Duke of Cumberland, as royal Ranger of Windsor Great Park, performing his supervisory or hospitable duties on his newly improved grounds called Virginia Water.[29] His heavy build was hard to mistake as he greeted his nephew and future sovereign George beside the man-made lake, comic treatment of the watching crowd precluding the semblance of a formal court occasion. Luke Sullivan's "View of the Terrace" (1759) at Oatlands Park sweeps far down to the water that the terrace overlooks. Yet the foreground is busy too, with some

9.12 John Donowell, "A View of the Grand Walk, Marylebone Gardens" (detail). Watercolor and pen over pencil.

ladies at their diversions and a separate cluster of four men, two seated, concerned with the plans in their hands: a reminiscence surely of the Bridgeman-Cobham conferences we have seen, with one of the men supposed to make us think of the ninth Earl of Lincoln.

A fourth example complicates the game of celebrity-spotting with possible commercial motives beyond the engraver's, and now the *rus* has moved *in urbe*. Figure 9.12 shows the center foreground of John Donowell's "View of the Grand Walk, Marylebone Gardens." Neither this drawing nor the fine engraving after it (1755) explain why the elderly couple are "worked up" so much more than the figures around them, and to the point where they are rather conspicuously old-fashioned. Two other gentlemen among the score in view wear swords, but lack his trimmed underjacket, full wig, darker clothes and brilliant shoebuckles: no other woman wears hoops so wide. The couple's features seem neither flattery nor caricature, just distinctively their own, as they gaze steadily over our shoulder. I believe they are William Bentinck, second Duke of Portland, and his lady Margaret Cavendish Harley. Of course they have nothing to do with the commercial venture which is Marylebone Gardens, but they are Lord and Lady of the Manor on which it has been a popular haunt for two decades. Apparently either the artist, the management, or some well-meaning friend thought their appearance here would focus interest upon this pleasure-garden. Their nameless presence owes something to the precedent Rigaud developed. Whatever the motives and whoever's they were, after the Duke's death in 1762 a pirated version of Donowell's print suppressed the couple just as conspicuously as they had first appeared.

Rigaud and the English engravers who followed his lead demystified place-making, leaving English ground visually more accessible to more people.

NOTES

1 Peter de Bolla, "Antipictorialism in the English Landscape Tradition: A Second Look at *The Country and the City*," in Christopher Prendergast ed., *Cultural Materialism: On Raymond Williams* (Minneapolis, Minn., 1995), pp. 173–87, this passage p. 186. De Bolla's concern to demote an elitist Claudian model foregrounds two prose descriptions of 1785.

2 Cited from George B. Clarke, ed., *Descriptions of Lord Cobham's Gardens at Stowe (1700–1750)* (Buckingham, 1990), pp. 25–6.

3 Robert A. Aubin, *Topographical poetry in XVIII-Century England* (New York, 1936), pp. 320–2, lists fifty-seven poems about specific estates written if not published during the 1730s, as against twelve for the 1720s, and twenty-eight for the 1740s. Marcia Pointon's indication how "Houses like Stowe were three-dimensional portraits of their owners" might have noted Rigaud's record of Bridgeman's landscaped celebration of Cobham's military career, in crenelated topiary, and storm-poles reasserting the ha-ha; see *Hanging the Head: Portraiture and Social Formation in Eighteenth-Century England* (New Haven, Conn., 1993), p. 20. Carole Fabricant uses printed material mainly twenty to ninety years later than Rigaud's work to evaluate landowners "display rituals;" see "The Literature of Domestic Tourism, and the Public Consumption of Private Property," in Felicity Nussbaum and Laura Brown, eds., *The New Eighteenth Century: Theory Politics English Literature* (New York, 1987), pp. 254–75, this passage p. 258.

4 For West's poem of 1732 and three Rigaud drawings for other Stowe engravings, see John Dixon Hunt and Peter Willis, eds., *The Genius of the Place: The English Landscape Garden 1620–1820* (Cambridge, Mass., 1988), pp. 215–27 and 138. West's episode of the pre-Boucher "Maid in the Swing," two local clergymen, and Stowe's "Private Grotto" named the Randibus, pp. 221–2, matches the macho-male innuendo of some of Stowe's garden structures and their interior decoration by that year.

5 See the descriptive note for "Plate Number 3" in the unpaginated facsimile republication of Rigaud's *Stowe Gardens in Buckinghamshire, Laid out by Mr Bridgeman, Delineated in a large Plan*, ed. George B. Clarke (1987).

6 Seeley, *A Description of the Gardens of Lord Viscount Cobham, at Stow in Buckinghamshire* (1744), rpt. in Clarke, *Descriptions*.

7 Gilpin, *Dialogue upon the Gardens of the Right Honourable Lord Viscount Cobham, at Stow in Buckinghamshire* (1748).

8 For details of this contract, the place of Stowe in Bridgeman's career, and fuller illustration of Rigaud's work there, see Peter Willis, "Jacques Rigaud's Drawings of Stowe in the Metropolitan Museum of Art," *Eighteenth-Century Studies* 6 (1972–3): 85–98; Willis, *Charles Bridgeman and the English Landscape Garden* (1977), pp. 113–27, and plates 127–45; and Clarke, ed., *Stowe Gardens*. A fairly complete listing of Jacques's and of J-B Rigaud's works appears in G. K. Nagler, *Neues allgemeiner Küntsler-Lexikon*, 2nd edn. (Linz, 1909), pp. 14, 489–92, but its biographical errors require correction by Emmanuel Bénézit, *Dictionnaire critique et documentaire des Peintres . . . et Graveurs*, rev. edn. (Paris, 1976), pp. 8, 763.

9 In 1736 he had Rigaud publish in Paris, likewise with bilingual captions, four superb views of royal domains over which Bridgeman exercised authority less creative, more stewardly: the parks at Greenwich, Hampton Court, and St. James. While bustling Thames and coach traffic on their margins authorizes the *rus in urbe* topos, one Rigaud view "from the River" was copied by a better-known *vedutist*: see Jane Dacey, "A Note on Canaletto's Views of Greenwich," *Burlington Magazine* 123 (1981): 485–7.

10 John Parnell, "An Account of the many fine Seats, of Noble: &c. I have seen," Folger Library MSS M.a.11, p. 139. This twenty-year-old law student, son of an Irish baronet, uses the same words of "the mowers or Haymakers" in "a common feild" of Southcote's Woburn Farm, ibid., p. 159.

11 Mary Vidal reads the transaction as impolite male aggression in her *Watteau's Painted Conversations: Art, Literature and Talk in Seventeenth- and Eighteenth-Century France* (New Haven, Conn., 1992), pp. 113–21.

12 See Willis, "Jacques Rigaud," figure 5, or Willis, *Bridgeman*, plate 133.

13 Never engraved, but illustrated in Willis, *Bridgeman*, Plate 57a; and in Jacques Carré, "Through French Eyes: Rigaud's Drawings of Chiswick," *Journal of Garden History* 2 (1982): 133–42, figure 2; and in John Harris, *The Palladian Revival: Lord Burlington, His Villa and Garden at Chiswick* (New Haven, Conn., 1994), plate 28. For a frontal close-up of Senesino singing, see William Hogarth's "Marriage a la Mode," plate 4. For Count Algarotti's contemporary copy of Zanetti's portrait, identified as "Senesino," see Edward Croft-Murray, *An Album of Eighteenth-Century Venetian Operatic Caricatures* (Toronto, 1980), p. 47.

14 In Willis, *Bridgeman*, these are plates 129, 130, 132, 137, 142 and possibly also 141; or see his "Jacques Rigaud," figures 2, 3, 4, 7, 8.

15 Thus six Rigaud images of Lord and Lady Cobham – at Willis, *Bridgeman*, Plates 129, 132, 133, 136, 137, 139, or the relevant prints – depict them self-absorbed, backs to us, or immersed like their visitors in the spectacle of their landscape, while only in plates 135 and 142 may we catch this pair embodying what E. P. Thompson calls "a studied and elaborate hegemonic style, a theatrical role" in the performance of hospitable routines; see *Customs in Common: Studies in Traditional Popular Culture* (New York, 1991), p. 46.

16 For perspective on the casual captionlessness of Rigaud's approach to conversation-piece material, see Ronald Paulson's suggestion that the etymology of conversation signals "its origin as a reaction against such forms of 'high art' as history painting . . . and idealized portraiture," *Emblem and Expression: Meaning in English Art of the Eighteenth Century* (1975), p. 121.

17 See an earlier generation of topographical prints, such as the anonymous cathedral views of Peterborough, Oxford, and Bath, in *Nouveau Theatre de la Grande Bretagne: ou Description Exacte des Villes, Eglises, Cathedrales . . . Tome Second* (1714), plates 14, 18, and 19. Public pissing persists in landscape vistas whether drawn in fun by William Kent – see the artist and his dog in Harris, *Palladian Revival*, frontispiece and plate 86 – or painted with royal staffage by Joseph Nicholls – "St. James's Park and the Mall," *c.* 1745 – so Rigaud's deletion seems deliberately audience-focused.

18 For the other print see Clarke, ed., *Stowe Gardens*, plate 14; Willis, "Jacques Rigaud," figure 3; Willis, *Bridgeman*, plate 130.

19 On Pope's crippling disease, and control of his published image, see Maynard Mack, *Alexander Pope: A Life* (New York, 1986), especially pp. 153–8, 660.

20 William K. Wimsatt, *The Portraits of Alexander Pope* (New Haven, Conn., 1965), p. 302, and see p. 300. Frank enough about Pope's deformity, Voltaire by 1731 had seen enough oil portraits which concealed it to testify: "The picture of the prime minister hangs over the chimney of his own closet, but I have seen that of Mr. Pope in twenty noblemen's houses," p. xvii, and see p. xxiv – currency which could only embolden Rigaud to sneak Pope thus into a more popular medium.

21 Reproduced in Mack, *Alexander Pope*, p. 157.

22 Both speculate that the figure might be Pope; see Carré, "Through French Eyes," p. 133, and Harris, *Palladian Revival*, p. 102.

23 She is not to be confused with the somber widow in mourning-veil accompanied by young Grenville on the parterre: see Willis, "Jacques Rigaud," figures 7 and 3; Willis, *Bridgeman*, plates 141 and 130; or Clarke, ed., *Stowe Gardens*, plates 9 and 14. As for male fashion, the frock-coats worn by Cobham and almost all visitors bespeak a country-house informality which would not be acceptable in London for another quarter-century. Sophie K. White has agreeably helped me with the social implications of Rigaud's dress code.

24 Vertue's emphases, my punctuation; Notebook A.f, Vertue III, *The Walpole Society* 22 (Oxford, 1934), p. 58.

25 Four of these French scenes are illustrated and others discussed in my "Unnamed Celebrities in Eighteenth-Century Gardens: Jacques Rigaud's Topographical Prints," *Cycnos* 11 (1994): 93–131. After the French Revolution, John Tinney catered to other sensitivities by issuing in London (1794) engravings after Rigaud's Versailles and Marli, captioned in English and French.

26 So identified by A. P. Oppé, *English Drawings of the Stuart and Georgian periods in the Collection of His Majesty at Windsor Castle* (1950), p. 84 and figure 95. A pendant Rigaud vista toward the Belvedere from the other side, with men and women bowling, is D.259/1890 at the Victoria and Albert Museum.

27 This Rigaud engraving is best consulted in Kenneth Woodbridge, "Landscaping at Castle Hill," *Country Life*, January 4, 1979, p. 18, figure 3; misattributed in Arline Meyer, *John Wooton 1682–1764: Landscapes and Sporting Art in Early Georgian England* (1984), pp. 81–2. Since Rigaud fully inscribed his first name on only two works, an essential guide is Charles Ginoux, "Jacques Rigaud, dessinateur et graveur marseillais, improprement prénomé Jean ou Jean-Baptiste (1681–1754)," *Réunion des Sociétés des Beaux-Arts des Départments* (Session 22) (Paris, 1898), pp. 726–40, illustrating Rigaud's Toulon "Bombardement."

28 See Callot, "The Palace Gardens at Nancy" (1625), Hollar "Richmond" (1638), and Silvestre, "Tuileries" (1668).

29 On Paul Sandby's affinities with Rigaud rather than with Italianate tradition, see Bruce Robertson, *The Art of Paul Sandby* (New Haven, Conn., 1985), pp. 10, 18.

CHAPTER 10

Imperial georgic, 1660–1789

Karen O'Brien

I

For Raymond Williams, georgic was both a set of literary conventions and a mode of social understanding; it belonged to his literary history of rhetorical contrasts between the country and the city, and it also embodied a particular ideological expression of the relations of agricultural production. In *The Country and the City*, Williams argued that the popularity of the georgic poetic mode in Britain coincided with the gradual implementation, in the late seventeenth and eighteenth centuries, of a new order of agrarian capitalism. Whereas earlier forms of pastoral dissolved into landscape, the human agents of agricultural production, georgic rendered laborers visible, albeit as mere instruments of aristocratic projects of rural improvement. For Williams georgic represented a modification, rather than a transformation, of the broadly pastoral paradigm within which he described the mediation of the social order through imaginative projects of the country: it maintained, and, to some extent, rendered more explicit, the "ideological separation between the processes of rural exploitation" and "the conspicuous expenditure of the city."[1]

Since the publication of Williams's study, a generation of critics has deepened our understanding of the structural positions of the country and the city in georgic, and their comparability with pastoral. It is now possible to see something of a paradigm shift in the transformation of the city from its status, in pastoral, as a reverse mirror image of the country to its position, in georgic, as the *destination* of rural production. The purpose of this essay is to develop this line of criticism by reassessing the nature and degree of "ideological separation" between country and city in georgic poetry, and to recover the discursive contexts within which their separation and similarity were imaginatively constructed. I will contend that British versions of the georgic mode presented readers

with a model of social self-understanding which allowed them to com-
prehend the country and the city as separate yet integrated spheres of
activity within an expanding British Empire. Unlike earlier versions of
pastoral and georgic, which tended to treat trade and agriculture as
discontinuous enterprises, later seventeenth- and eighteenth-century georgic subsumed the binary opposition of country and city within the larger
imaginative structure of universal, peaceful empire. It was georgic, more
than any other literary mode or genre, which assumed the burden of
securing the aesthetic and moral links between country, city, and empire.
It sought, at the same time, to preserve a hierarchical sense of the incom-
mensurability of different social arenas, as well as a pastoral sense of
the different geographical distributions of virtue. This was a difficult
balancing act, and this difficulty was, it will be argued, encountered
and foregrounded by poets as a problem of tone and register.

II

Genre is both a set of conventions and mode of social understanding,
but few genres or modes invite their readers to consider their recrea-
tions of the social domain as openly as georgic. The broadly pastoral
paradigm within which Raymond Williams described the mediation of
the social order through imaginative projections of rural life regrounded
the contrast between the country and the city. However, particular attention to georgic poetry in the early modern period reveals a somewhat
different manner of approach to the rural world; rather than emphasizing its contrast with the city, georgic imaginatively and morally secured
the links between the economic realms of country, city, and empire.

Critics have more often observed than explained the ascent of georgic
through the seventeenth- and eighteenth-century hierarchy of literary
genres, and the comparative decline of pastoral. The displacement of
pastoral by georgic modes and genres of English poetry, accelerated by
Dryden's 1697 translation of Virgil's *Georgics*, is one of the more conspicuous features of that period's literary history.[2] It is a feature which,
the critics of that period from Addison to Johnson would have us believe,
can be accounted for in literary historical terms – in terms, that is, of
fluctuations in taste and changing sources of influence. Addison's essay
on Virgil's *Georgics*, which formed the preface to Dryden's translation,
proposed to the next generation of poets and critics, not so much a revival
in formal didactic, as new adventures in voice and style. Johnson's report,
in the late eighteenth century, of the death of pastoral (a mode "easy,

vulgar, and therefore disgusting") may now seem premature in the light
of subsequent Romantic developments, but it, too, issued from a critical preference for the uneasy middle style of georgic.[3]

In our own age, some critics have been inclined to accept and
explore this stylistic explanation for the evolution of English georgic,
while others have looked for the cultural and economic factors discernible
in the shift from pastoral to georgic poetic modes.[4] Anthony Low has
written of a "georgic revolution" in seventeenth-century poetry, finding
evidence for the rise of a bourgeois literary outlook in the way that labor-
centered representations of the countryside steadily replaced the aristocratic contempt for agricultural work often implicit in pastoral. This
chapter argues for a very different "georgic revolution" in the seventeenth to eighteenth centuries by linking the rise of georgic and georgic-
descriptive kinds of poetry to a new and growing awareness of the
British Empire, and finds the agricultural landscape of these poems
imbued with a sense of spatial and economic continuity with the wider
imperial world. Yet such a link cannot be made through a simple decod-
ing of the social or political content of these poems, since georgic conventions were themselves a means of discursive approach to empire in
many non-literary writings. Moreover, Low's reading of poetry as a
straightforward "barometer [of] social history" underplays the stylistic
uneasiness of English georgic, and so misrepresents the nature of its
interaction with the social and political domain.[5]

The uneasy tonal oscillations between technical, middle, and mock-
heroic registers, which make those seventeenth- and eighteenth-century
formal georgics on cider-making, wool production or sugar-growing seem
so unpalatable today, are not merely incidental features of the English
georgic style. If anything, English georgics, from Dryden's translation
onward, tended to inflate the mock-heroic aspects of Virgil's style, and
to magnify the asymmetries, in the *Georgics*, between the passages of technical advice on farming, the miniature heroics of the animal kingdom,
and prophecies of the coming Augustan peace and empire.[6] Indeed,
Addison interpreted Virgil's *Georgics* as a work of unreconciled but art-
fully managed tonal and topical contradictions.[7] Later critics such as
Joseph Warton confirmed and elaborated Addison's reading of the *Georgics*
as a patchwork of farming advice alleviated by picturesque and patriotic set-pieces.[8] This thematic flexibility, bound up as it was with the
idea that, on the *scala Virgilii*, georgic was the preparation and, also,
the postponement of national epic, became central to late seventeenth-
and eighteenth-century literary articulations of empire. Georgic presented

poets with an adaptable middle style that could rise to national prophecy and rapture or descend to technical detail without breaching generic decorum. In an age suspicious of epic and romance, this adaptability proved highly attractive to poets wishing to communicate the elation of empire, the moral dangers which it could bring, and the mechanics of its implementation. Many poets viewed georgic, which, unlike pastoral, was written in the poet's own voice, as a personal act of homage to the source of an expanding British civilization.

Despite the presence and growing prevalence of georgic elements, many early seventeenth-century poems sustained a thematic separation between husbandry and the nation's engagement with the international economy through trade and territorial acquisition. Hesiod's *Works and Days*, which exerted some influence in this earlier period through Chapman's 1618 translation, combines farming tips and rotas with advice on sea trading. In general, however, the modified georgic ethos of country-house poetry tended to dissociate, for a variety of political reasons, the world of domestic rural pursuits from the world of trade. Herrick's poem "The Country Life. To the Honoured M. End. Porter" celebrates the economic and spiritual detachment of the poem's gentleman-husbandman addressee from imperial and trading activities:

> Thou never Plow'st the Oceans foame
> To seek, and bring rough Pepper home:
> Nor to the Eastern Ind dost rove
> To bring from thence the scorched Clove.[9]

Endymion Porter's friend Thomas May provided the first seventeenth-century translation of the *Georgics* in 1628, and this was followed, in 1649, by John Ogilby's rendition of the complete works of Virgil.[10] Although both translators were important sources for Dryden, their work, like other contemporary poems in the georgic mode, tended to attenuate rather than to emphasize Virgil's sense of interplay between husbandry and empire.

Dryden's 1697 heroic couplet translation precipitated a major reorientation of georgic toward imperial concerns. It reinforced, at every opportunity, the connections between the rhythms of country life and the renewal, after a time of war, of Roman imperial civilization even as it intensified the note of protest against the violent "Arms of Peace" of Octavian – the 1698 version amended this to "Arts of Peace" (4: 811). Dryden had been an enthusiastic literary supporter of Charles II's and James II's imperial ventures, and, in particular, in *Annus Mirabilis* (1667), of Charles's wars of imperial competition against the United Provinces.[11]

Now writing in opposition to William III, Dryden transformed Virgil's country world into a principled political retreat, an alternative realm from which to imagine and predict the restoration of a legitimate British monarchy and empire. As one might expect, the famous passage, toward the end of Book 2 of Virgil's poem, on the happiness of country life ("O fortunatos nimium . . . / Agricolas") bears the interpretive burden of this imaginative adjustment. Virgil's provincial farmers become, in Dryden's version, a single "Country King" who "his peaceful Realm enjoys" free from a distinctively 1690s assortment of urban and court vices (2: 660).

Dryden augments Virgil's desire for similar rural seclusion (the couplet "Or lead me to some solitary Place, / And cover my Retreat from Human Race," 2: 696–7 supplements Virgil, 2: 486–9), and contrasts an image of the political illegitimacy of the court with the idea of the original Roman Empire as the organic outgrowth of the Saturnian golden age:

> So *Remus* and his Brother God were bred:
> From whom th'austere *Etrurian* Virtue rose,
> And this rude life our homely Fathers chose.
> Old *Rome* from such a Race deriv'd her birth,
> (The Seat of Empire, and the conquer'd Earth:)
> Which now on sev'n high Hills triumphant reigns,
> And in that compass all the World contains.   (2: 778–84)

Dryden expands Virgil 2: 533–5, opening up, here as elsewhere in the translation, the national and imperial horizons of the poem.[12] Dryden's sense of England's potential yet politically compromised international greatness is communicated most forcibly in his translation of Virgil's celebrated praise of Italy in Book 2 (2: 187–246 translates 2: 136–76). Dryden raises the emotional pitch by speaking, with obvious, deflected patriotism for his own fairest isle, of "our happy climate," "our Land," and "our Cities," where Virgil derives a different kind of intensity from the imperative mood (2: 204, 207, 213). Virgil is more preoccupied with Italian unity than with the imperial extension of Rome, but Dryden adds a line that evokes the idea of an island seafaring nation: "Our twofold Seas, that washing either side, / A rich Recruit of Foreign Stores provide" (2: 217–18).[13] This image of an island trading nation is then corroborated and given a more explicitly English imperial context in the translation of Virgil's mock-heroic portrait of the life of bees in Book 4. Here Dryden metamorphoses Virgil's alternately internecine and servile bees into an unmistakably urban hive of "trading Citizens" (4: 20 translates 4: 16 "volantes"); their kings are "adventr'ous"

("Magnanimos . . . duces"), in the seventeenth-century sense of being given to financial or colonial ventures, and when they swarm, their princes lead out a "vent'rous Colony" to new bee territory (4: 4, 28 translates Virgil 4: 4, 21–2). The bees even appear, in lines added by Dryden, to have their own joint stock trading company: "The Bees have common Cities of their own: / And common Sons, beneath one Law they live, / And with one common Stock their Traffick drive" (4: 225–7). Despite their unRoman loyalty to a king, Virgil's bees are given the title of citizens ("Quirites"), a point not lost on the parliamentarian May whose attractive translation of this passage makes much of the idea of the hive as a voluntary commonwealth ("They all elect their king, / And little nobles . . ." translates Virgil 4: 201–2).[14] Addison's translation of the same book turns the hive into a 1688 kind of constitutional monarchy ("In well dispos'd Societies they Live, / And Laws and Statutes regulate their Hive").[15]

Despite his hostility to William's regime, Dryden's translation of the *Georgics* transformed seventeenth-century Virgilian conventions and topoi into a national kind of poetry,[16] and rapidly gave rise to a vogue for poems tracing the roots of the nation's imperial expansion and happiness to the daily grind in the countryside. This vogue coincided with a critical rediscovery of georgic as a means of articulating and creating a language of national self-awareness that belonged, in turn, to a wider public re-evaluation, in the late seventeenth to early eighteenth centuries, of the nature and function of empire.[17] Some of the reasons why the British imperial resonances in Dryden's *Georgics* sounded so deeply with younger poets and critics can be found in the economic and imperial debates of the period. Dryden's vision of agricultural labor at the heart of an expanding British civilization mirrored a changing perception in the 1690s of the sources of prosperity in the national and colonial economies. The tumultuous economic changes of the final decade of the seventeenth century, including the creation of the Bank of England and the national debt, and the shake-ups of the large East India, Royal Africa, and Hudson's Bay monopoly companies, led to vigorous new debates about all of the major tenets of traditional mercantilist economic theory. Mercantilists had for decades assumed that stocks of gold and silver were the measure of a nation's relative wealth. However, by the 1690s, Charles D'Avenant was among the many revisionist economic theorists beginning to argue that a nation's true capital was its labor force and the agriculture sustaining it: "the wealth of all nations arises from the labors and industry of the people; a right knowledge therefore of the numbers is necessary to those who will judge of a country's power and strength."[18] This idea was restated, through a suggestive bee simile, by the late seventeenth-century economist Humphrey Mackworth:

I propose Employment, and there is no doubt, that the Consumption of the People is not so much, as the Product of their Labours, which is the real Riches and Strength of the Nation; And the more the merrier, like Bees in a Hive, and better cheer too.[19]

This emphasis upon agricultural and manufacturing labor and production, rather than upon consumption, would become a notable feature of eighteenth-century georgic poems, such as those by Philips, Thomson, and Dyer.

III

Seventeenth-century commentators expressed pride in the fact that the British Empire was not, like the Dutch Empire, simply an affair of exports and trading bases, but a process of agricultural improvement overseas. Dryden detected and developed poetically this georgic inflection of contemporary public discussion of colonization and international trade.[20] He added a note to Book IV of the *Georgics* describing, in language which recalls debates about the dangers of depopulation caused by emigration to the colonies, what happens when a "Young Prince" bee of the hive wishes to lead out a swarm and form a new colony. The prince presents himself at court and asks for the bee equivalent of a colony charter:

and for three successive Mornings demands permission, to lead forth a Colony of that Years Bees. If his Petition be granted, which he seems to make by humble hummings; the Swarm arises under his Conduct: If the Answer be, *le Roy s'averisera*, that is, if the Old Monarch think it not convenient for the Publick good to part with so many of his Subjects; the Next Morning the Prince is found dead, before the Threshold of the Palace.[21]

The story would have reminded Dryden's readers of the process by which royal charters were obtained for the proprietary colonies in the Americas. Anthony Ashley Cooper (later Achitophel, the Earl of Shaftesbury), was among the lords proprietors granted a charter for the Carolina colony in 1663. Among Dryden's political allies, William Penn received a charter for Pennsylvania in 1681, and James II, as Duke of York and as king, took an active part in plantation schemes.

All of these ventures were publicized in pamphlets and circular letters which emphasized the benefits brought by good husbandry in the plantations to the population and wealth of the mother country. Farmers and laborers were encouraged to purchase or indenture themselves for land, and to go and live out their own georgic in the colonies. This is the tenor of William Penn's first promotional piece on behalf of Pennsylvania in which he defends plantations in terms of their high agricultural productivity, and the way in which "they have manifestly inrich'd, and so strengthned" the economy and population of England. He then places "Industrious Husbandmen and Day-laborers" at the top of his list of suitable emigrants to the new colony.[22] The georgic accent of later seventeenth-century promotional literature marks a change from the pastoral presentation of earlier colonial schemes which is to be found, for example, in Sir Walter Ralegh's advertisement for Guiana.[23]

This accent is also audible in the writings of the idealistic eighteenth-century colonial projector James Oglethorpe, who in the early 1730s set up a board of trustees for the chartering and settlement of Georgia. Oglethorpe's prospectuses for the new colony are imbued with a georgic ethos of independent agricultural labor. The colony was designed to outlaw slavery, deal peaceably with the natives, and to lease smallholdings to anyone of an industrious and frugal disposition, whatever their social status or religious persuasion.[24] Oglethorpe's venture was commended in a poem by Samuel Wesley, cousin of Charles and John, as a splendid new outpost of George II's empire of peace; natural abundance in the new land is seen as a "waste" and an invitation to colonial labor:

> See where beyond the spacious Ocean lies
> A wide waste Land, beneath the Southern Skies!
> Where kindly Suns for Ages roll'd in Vain,
> Nor e'er the Vintage saw, or rip'ning Grain;
> Where all things into wild Luxuriance ran,
> And burden'd Nature ask'd the Aid of Man.[25]

Despite the attractiveness of the scheme – Pope's friends were among those who supported it financially – Georgia soon went the way of all southern colonies toward large, slave-holding estates.[26]

The idea of a plantation as a private estate created and managed for the good of its inhabitants is residually present in *Paradise Lost* when Milton calls God the "sovereign planter."[27] Milton's poem is hostile to imperial adventures and exploits which he associates with Satan, but early eighteenth-century poets salvaged the idea of Adam's "nether empire neighbouring round" paradise and his gentlemanly labor in his "happy rural seat of various view" for a revised, morally redeemed type

of imperial georgic.[28] Most eighteenth-century poems in the georgic
mode were written in self-consciously Miltonic blank verse from which
descriptions of landscape and livestock gained easy redolence of the prelapsarian, benign empire of Milton's Adam. This infusion of Miltonic
style enabled poets to circumvent the political concerns of Dryden's
georgic, thereby creating a residually pastoral idiom for imperial georgic that was at once idealistic and admonitory.

John Philips, a Tory poet of the Pope and Bolingbroke circle, domest-
icates Virgil's praise of Italy and Italian grapes through the medium of
Miltonic verse and diction: "Autumn paints / *Ausonian* Hills with Grapes,
whilst *English* Plains / Blush with pomaceous Harvests, breathing
Sweets."[29] Philips provides instructions on cider-making interspersed with
reflections on the civil wars of the previous century, mythical stories,
and praise for patrons, all in the Addisonian georgic manner. Britain,
with its rural swains and harmless apples – "Tempting, not fatal, as the
Birth of that / Primaeval interdicted Plant that won / Fond Eve"[30] –
is imaginatively recreated as an expanding yet unspoilt paradise: the
industriousness of its people and the productivity of its lands are the
true and imminent source of its global empire. The poem ends with a
prospect of Queen Anne's trading empire flourishing under the "double
Cross" of the recent Anglo-Scottish Union.[31] Philips's closing panegyric
of the British trading empire resembles the apotheosis of the Thames
and the prophecy of a peaceful global trading order at the end of Pope's
Windsor-Forest (1713): "The Time shall come, when free as Seas or Wind
/ Unbounded *Thames* shall flow for all Mankind."[32] Yet the generic
orientation of Pope's poem toward pastoral rather than georgic, and
the mythic displacement (in imitation of Virgil's fourth eclogue) of the
modern British by an ideal, universal empire, allow him a greater degree
of moral ambivalence about questions of empire. John Gay's *Rural Sports:
A Georgic Inscribed to Mr. Pope*, which also appeared in 1713, offers no
pronouncements, ambivalent or otherwise, on the subject of empire,
preferring to celebrate "peaceful hours" spent on recreational pursuits
in the countryside.[33]

It was the Scottish poet, James Thomson, however, who would forge
the strongest connection between rural labor, commerce, patriotism, and
empire, thereby ensuring the triumph of a georgic rather than a pastoral mode of imperial vision in eighteenth-century poetry. In place of
Pope's pastoral empire of ease, Thomson imagined an empire won from
nature by industry and cultivation. The *Seasons* were initially published
in the late 1720s for the purpose of developing patriotic images and

rhetoric for the Whig opposition to Walpole.[34] They shared this political motivation with other oppositional georgics such as William
Somervile's *The Chace* (1735), a blank verse didactic poem which yokes
together hunting instructions and encomia on Britain's expanding
empire of trade.[35] Thomson's poem, however, acquired a more generally national and imperial flavor during the substantial processes of
revision which led to the final authorial edition of 1746. The sense of
empire embedded in Thomson's gentlemanly survey of cultivated agricultural lands is conveyed through a variety of, often contradictory, poetic
responses.[36] Initially, in his free adaptation of Virgil's praise of country
life at the end of "Autumn," Thomson heightens the contrast between
the joys of rural retirement and the turbulence of worldly ambition (lines
1235–373). He turns Virgil's conquerors, politicians, and adventurers ("hic
petit excidiis urbem – alio patriam quaerunt sub sole iacentem," 2: 505–12)
into aggressive, modern imperialists:

> Let others brave the Flood in Quest of Gain,
> And beat, for joyless Months, the gloomy Wave.
> Let such as deem it Glory to destroy
> Rush into blood, the Sack of Cities seek;
> Unpierc'd, exulting in the Widow's Wail,
> The Virgin's Shriek, and Infant's trembling Cry.
> Let some, far-distant from their native Soil,
> Urg'd on by Want or harden'd Avarice,
> Find other Lands beneath another Sun.
> Let This thro' Cities work his eager Way,
> By legal Outrage and establish'd Guile,
> The social Sense extinct.[37]

Despite the dramatization of rural life in this closing section of
"Autumn" as the moral opposite of imperial conquest and slavery,
Thomson elsewhere endeavors to strengthen the connection between
the countryside and Britain's commercial empire by means of georgic
set-pieces. A passage from the end of "Summer," greatly expanded
between 1727 and 1744, adapts Virgil's praise of Italy into a prospect
extending from Britain's "Hills, and Dales, and Woods, and Lawns, and
Spires" to the "rising Masts" of ships in urban ports, to the whole "Island
of bliss! amid the subject Seas . . . / At once the Wonder, Terror, and
Delight / Of distant Nations" (lines 1439, 1462, 1595–8).

Thomson reinforces this visual integration of rural activity and
commercial progress at a practical level by reminding readers about the
importance of agricultural produce to the imperial economy. "Spring"
exhorts "generous Britons" to "venerate the Plow" and:

                                As the Sea,
            Far thro' his azure turbulent Domain,
            Your Empire owns, and from a thousand Shores
            Wafts all the Pomp of Life into your Ports;
            So with superior Boon may your rich Soil,
            Exuberant, Nature's better Blessings pour
            O'er every Land, the naked Nations cloath,
            And be th'exhaustless Granary of a World!   (lines 70–7)

For Thomson, as for Philips, Miltonic blank verse and diction facilitate
a realignment between prelapsarian or redeemed nature and the
British peaceful way of empire. "Summer" embarks on a search for perspectives, over and above those created by Virgil and Milton, from which
to contemplate and regulate philosophically Britain's engagements
with the rest of the world. In 1744, Thomson added to *The Seasons* a
long, virtuoso prospect of the torrid zones of the earth where the sun
exercises "hot Dominion" like a despot over his subject (lines 629–897).
Under the sun's terrible regime, these lands have become both lux-
uriously profuse and economically unproductive: "What avails this
wondrous Waste of Wealth?" the poet asks, "This gay profusion of
luxurious Bliss? / This pomp of Nature?" (lines 860–2). We may recall
Samuel Wesley's description of unsettled Georgia as a "wide waste land,"
and Thomson's word "Waste" here similarly elides the idea of a waste-
land with economic waste. The tropics are "unseen and unenjoy'd"
places where the "seasons teem in vain" and fruits remain forever
"unplanted" (lines 849–50, 865). The "Waste of Wealth" in the tropics
is associated with their deprivation of trading contacts with the global
Pax Britannica. Although Thomson insists that the Muse is "no ruffian"
come, like Cortez, for plunder and conquest, but that she brings
"the softening Arts of Peace . . . / Kind equal rule, the Government of
Laws," he makes his imaginative approach to foreign lands by means
of inverted georgic (lines 875, 881). With their spontaneous natural luxury and undisciplined landscape, the tropics represent for Thomson the
opposite of the civil and imperial order of Britain described in georgic
passages elsewhere in *The Seasons*. There is fitting irony in the fact
that in 1744 Thomson, who would have heard as a boy about the
catastrophic waste of Scotland's wealth which occurred as a result
of the collapse of his country's tropical Darien colony in Central
America, was granted the sinecure of Surveyor-General of the Leeward
Islands.[38]

In Thomson, eighteenth-century poets found inspiration both for formal georgic and for poetry consisting of excursions on rural themes. Richard Savage combines expeditions across the globe with praise for British industry which "fells the monarch Oak; which borne away, / Shall with new Grace the distant Oceans sway."[39] Such outbursts of imperial feeling might now appear artistically redundant, but they indicate how close was the aesthetic association in this period between the georgic mode and imperial themes. Robert Dodsley's blank verse poem *Public Virtue* (1753) combines, in the usual manner, general description, agricultural advice, and imperial prospect. "This, this", Dodsley writes of sheep-shearing, is "the solid base on which the sons / Of Commerce build, exalted to the sky, / The structure of their grandeur, wealth, and power!"[40] Christopher Smart's early formal georgic, *The Hop-Garden*, published at the same time, also gives vent, with similarly unfortunate artistic results, to patriotic sentiment on the contribution of Kent to the British navy: "The lofty forest by thy sons prepar'd / Becomes the warlike navy, braves the floods, / And gives Sylvanus empire in the main."[41]

Among the most systematic and technically specific of the eighteenth-century georgics, John Dyer's *The Fleece* (1757) describes in detail the production of wool and the manufacture of textiles in Britain.[42] Dyer's technical register and his thematic preoccupation with the economic integration of agriculture, manufactures, and trade in Britain overwhelm the paradisal connotations of the Miltonic blank verse. For Dyer, as to a lesser extent for Thomson, the tendency of British land to generate surplus production and Edenic superabundance must be regulated by a virtuous process of export. Britain's trading and colonial empires are visually present throughout the poem, both as the export destination of woollen manufactures and as partners in the creation of wealth. The poem reflects accurately the growing importance, by mid-century, of trade with the Americas and India to the British economy, picturing American natives purchasing "woolly garments" in Virginia's markets, and predicting a time when Britain will "clothe the world."[43] A product of the Seven Years' War, *The Fleece* gives voice to a spirit of imperial competition with the French – "Rejoice, ye nations, and vindicate the sway / Ordain'd for common happiness" (4: 654–5). Nevertheless, the controlling myth of empire is not conquest but mutual cooperation for the sake of prosperity and peace; only peaceful trade and imperial collaboration can turn a fleece into a frock:

> For it suffices not, in flow'ry vales,
> Only to tend the flock, and shear soft wool:
> Gums must be stor'd of Guinea's arid coast;
> Mexican woods, and India's bright'ning salts;
> Fruits, herbage, sulphurs, minerals, to stain
> The fleece prepar'd.   (2: 565–70).

Richard Jago's blank verse georgic *Edge-Hill* (1767) conveys a similarly integrated sense of the rural, industrial, and imperial economies despite a routine opening pronouncement that he plans to sing only of "Britannia's rural Charms and tranquil scenes."[44] The poet's eye alights upon a sublime prospect of the coal and iron industries in Birmingham and Solihull before entertaining a brief vision of "native British Ore" sailing round the world in endless trade. The civilizing impact of industrialization, Jago uneasily insists, is guaranteed by the positive role of its output in the imperial system of peace.

Jago's assimilation of the industrial Midlands to a georgic idea of secondary productivity had few imitators. His vision of industry and agriculture as part of a single, global economic system does, however, provide an interesting exception to Williams's account of the myth of the industrial city as the post-lapsarian version of the country. The decline in the popularity and critical status of imperial georgic, during the final quarter of the eighteenth century, may, indeed, have reflected a growing sense of the city as a site of industrial production rather than as a trading entrepot. It may also be explained in terms of the demise of the reciprocal, fraternal model of inter-colonial relations which obtained for much of the century, but did not survive the American Revolutionary War. Before the War, georgic poets approached the empire as an imaginative framework which allowed them to articulate and reconcile the regional, class and, occasionally, gender conflicts inherent in their subject matter. Insofar as the empire absorbed surplus, luxury output, and so provided the economic rationale for virtuous, productive labor over and above the subsistence requirements of the nation, it could also function as a moral safety valve: national greatness could be celebrated without fear of the politically corrupting effects of national self-indulgence. After the American War, the loss of moral confidence in the integrative function of the empire became a georgic topic in its own right. This topic is, for instance, central to William Cowper's *The Task* (1785), the best-known poem of this period to combine georgic elements with reflections on the moral failings of the British Empire. The poem deliberately undertakes a revision of the imperial georgic by segregating, spatially and morally, the rural and imperial domains: in the georgic passages, Cowper emphasizes – often with mock-heroic afflatus – the economic unproductivity of the countryside, whereas the sections discussing the Empire are placed outside the generic frame of georgic.[45] Even so, a residually georgic perspective governs the poem as a whole since the spiritual function of the country, as a site of regeneration, is transitive rather than pastorally transcendent.

IV

Another way of approaching the question of the decline of georgic and its, ultimately problematic, reliance on the Empire as the moral underwriter of economic activity, is to examine the georgics written in the colonies themselves. Before the Revolutionary War, the imperial georgic mode was highly popular among North American poets. They readily embraced a form of poetry which gave dignity and legitimacy to their economic activities within a global system of peaceful exchange. One loyalist British colonist, for instance, who was forced to return to England during the war, described the lost colonial era in America as a georgic golden age. His *Carolina: or, The Planter* (written in 1776, printed 1790) gives detailed instructions on setting up and running a rice plantation, and explains how colonial produce is distributed by the British merchant navy: "By it the Planter's labours are convey'd / To climes remote – by it his toils are paid / With all the luxuries either Ind' bestows, / And all the arts ingenious Europe knows" (p. 25).

With examples like these in mind, it might be concluded that the transposition of metropolitan imperial georgic to the colonial contexts of North America and the West Indies was a straightforward affair, and that georgic had been an important impetus to the literary construction of colonial identity. Yet from the outset, local economic and cultural conditions strained the georgic mode to the limits of its flexibility, and laid bare the processes of economic exploitation occluded in British georgic. In particular, the fact of slavery in the Southern states and West Indies could not be digested by georgic poetry. Few, if any, poets were willing to defend slavery, and some argued for abolition, but its very presence broke the association between productive labor and civic virtue central to the tradition of imperial georgic. In turn, the phenomenon of colonial poets writing back to the center (and often using London printing houses) attuned some British readers at home to the latent bathos and thematic inconsistencies intrinsic to the georgic

mode in general. Colonial georgic, which made a virtue of literary derivat-
iveness and of economic dependence on Britain, held up an unacceptable
mirror image of the metropolitan vision of empire.

The beginnings of this, ultimately terminal, generic strain can be
seen in James Grainger's *The Sugar-Cane* (1764), a step-by-step, blank verse
guide to Caribbean sugar production. The place of sugar in the British
imperial economy, described at length, provides the moral rationale for
planter life. Yet commodity output does not, for Grainger, fully justify
the use of slavery – a practice which exercises and embarrasses him
throughout the poem. At various points, he resolves this dilemma by
setting aside the georgic imperative of labor in favor of a pastoral idea
of natural spontaneity: the sugar-cane itself defies seasonal rhythm
by growing all year round, and the land is abundantly productive even
without cultivation by slaves. However, Grainger's insistence upon the
exotic superabundance of the land ruptures the sense of spatial continuity between colony and mother country, isolating planter life from
the normative context of the British peaceful Empire. Toward the end
of the poem, Grainger attempts to recuperate georgic didacticism
when he gives advice on how to pick a good slave, but ends up courting
ethical as well as tonal bathos: "Let health and youth their every Sinew
firm; / Clear their Ample eye; their Tongues be red."[46] Although the
Critical Review declared that Grainger had discovered new and promising poetic territory ("he may not have entirely subdued the natural
rudeness of the soil, yet he certainly has opened a delightful track for
future cultivation"), the bathos of his poem was not lost on many of
his readers. Lines such as "Enough of composts, Muse; of soils, enough"
are reported to have reduced Joshua Reynolds and his friends to help-
less laughter.[47]

The aesthetic domestication of slave-cultivated landscapes proved more
feasible for colonial writers in prose texts, such as Edward Long's *History
of Jamaica* (1774), discussed by Elizabeth Bohls in the next chapter. For
West Indian colonial poets, in particular, an acute awareness of the problem of slavery, heightened by anti-slavery campaigns at home, rendered
unworkable the thematic reconciliation of dignified labor, agricultural
didactic, and imperial prospect required by the georgic mode. Faced
with the moral problem of slavery, many West Indian colonial poets
took the pastoral exit, and described instead an abundant, luxuriant,
and seasonless landscape with no trace of laboring people.[48] This
defensive generic reorientation of georgic back toward pastoral can be
seen in John Singleton's blank verse *General Description of the West-Indian*

Islands (1767), where the West Indies appear to defy the georgic logic of the seasons by yielding "Perpetual produce springing all the year."[49] Despite avowed debts to Grainger's georgic, Singleton's local descriptions are closely assimilated to pastoral: plantations are avoided or effaced, and technical details disappear into the footnotes. Nathaniel Tucker, author of *The Bermudian: A Poem* (1774), recalls the island of his childhood as a lost pastoral paradise, whilst the author of *Jamaica, A Poem* (1777) uses Thomsonian language to separate the pastoral luxuriance and "eternal green" of the "torrid zone" from the distortions of slave-driven agriculture (lines 54, 20).

Other West Indian colonial poets preferred to avoid, altogether, the tonal rupture entailed by references to slavery. Slaves are nowhere visible in George Heriot's *A Descriptive Poem, Written in the West Indies* (1781), which enumerates scientifically the characteristics and produce of the region in ways calculated to detach the "fertile Sugar-canes, / Whose grateful juice, mellifluous and strong / Contributes to the luxuries of life" (p. 28) from the conditions of production. The author of "The Antigua Planter" (1783) wonders aloud about the applicability of georgic to the West Indies as he recalls Virgil:

> sweetly sinking, in his Georgick strains,
> His muse sat brooding o'er the fertile plains.
> No golden years, nor plenteous crops, I sing;
> No harvests waving to the zephyrs vine;
> Far other scenes, ye muses, join your train,
> The dying negroe, and the drooping cane.[50]

Another veteran of the West Indies, Edward Rushton, abandons georgic altogether when poeticizing his memories of the brutality of the colonies in *West-Indian Eclogues* (1787), where oppressed and desperate slaves assume the role of Virgil's speaking shepherds. The Antiguan poet William Gilbert employed the same form in *The Hurricane: A Theosophical and Western Eclogue* (Bristol, 1796) to give an allegorical dimension to the story of a little European girl shipwrecked and rescued on the shores of a West Indian island paradise.

By mediating their representations of the West Indies through eclogue, and through pastoral-descriptive modes in general, colonial poets implied that, whatever the depredations of slavery, the real value of the colony was guaranteed by its landscape: the land was both anterior and surplus to forms of labor. However, by taking the literary initiative and by replacing the dominant mode of georgic with a new version of pastoral, colonial poets effectively renegotiated the aesthetic terms of their membership of the British Empire. Through pastoral, many of these poets presented the colonies to the metropolitan imagination as separate, remote *loci amoeni*, rather than as part of the continuous territories of the British Empire. The opposition between the country and the city, abridged by imperial georgic, was thus replayed in the later eighteenth century as the opposition between colonies and mother country, with ideological results similar to those described by Raymond Williams. As with georgic, the colonial transformation of pastoral had significant consequences for poetic practice in Britain in general. The London-based Irish poet Tom Moore recorded his brief official posting in Bermuda in a collection of poems, many of which are in the pastoral mode.[51] Other Romantic poets articulated their hostility to empire by appropriating the colonial ecologue to domestic purposes, including Thomas Chatterton in his anti-slavery *African Ecolgues* (1770), and Robert Southey in his four "Botany-Bay Eclogues" (1797). In both, colonial and British varieties of pastoral, the spatial discontinuity between center and periphery was foregrounded. This aesthetic separation was the inevitable corollary of changing imperial attitudes after the loss of the first British Empire, and the advent of the anti-slavery movement. But it also sprang from the internal logic of poetic tradition: Virgil's imperial georgic legacy had been taxed to its limit, and poets no longer felt exhilarated by seeing an empire in an ear of corn.

NOTES

1 Williams, *Country and City*, p. 46.
2 See Alastair Fowler, "Georgic and Pastoral: Laws of Genre in the Seventeenth Century," in Michael Leslie and Timothy Raylor, eds., *Culture and Cultivation in Early Modern Europe: Writing the Land* (Leicester, 1992), pp. 81–8, and *Kinds of Literature: An Introduction to the Theory of Genres and Modes* (Oxford, 1982); John Chalker, *The English Georgic: A Study in the Development of a Form* (1969). This chapter is indebted to the discussion of georgic, economics, and class in John Barrell, *English Literature in History, 1730–80: An Equal, Wide Survey* (1983).

Quotations from Dryden's translation of Virgil's *Georgics* (1697; rev. 1698) are from *The Works of John Dryden*, ed. H. T. Swedenborg *et. al.*, 21 vols. to date (Berkeley, Calif., 1956–), vols. 5–6. Quotations from Virgil are from *Opera*, ed. Carolus Ruaeus (1695), the text used by Dryden which differs slightly from modern editions. All references to Virgil's *Georgics*, including translations, are given parenthetically to book and line.

3 Samuel Johnson, *Lives of the Poets*, ed. G. B. Hill, 3 vols. (Oxford, 1905), I: 163.

4 In the second group are Anthony Low, *The Georgic Revolution* (Princeton, N.J., 1985); Turner, *Politics of Landscape*; and McRae, *God Speed*.

5 Low, *Georgic Revolution*, p. 12.

6 Chalker, *English Georgic*, pp. 40–2, and Barrell, *English Literature*, pp. 90–1 provide interesting reflections on the tonal embarrassments of English georgic. Examples of Dryden's deliberate raising of the military and political metaphors in Virgil to the level of mock-heroic can be seen in 1: 223–38 (translating Virgil 1: 150–9), 2: 501–9 (translating 2: 362–70), and 3: 339–74 (translating 2: 219–31) which draws serious political analogies from the battle of the bulls (whose power struggle resembles that of James II and William III).

7 "An Essay on the Georgics," cited in Dryden, *Works*, 5: 146.

8 "Reflections on Didactic Poetry," in *The Works of Virgil. In English Verse*, trans. Warton and Christopher Pitt, 4 vols. (1763), 1: 298.

9 Herrick, *Hesperides: or, the Works both Humane and Divine of Robert Herrick* (1648), lines 5–8; compare *Georgics*, 2: 461–6.

10 May, *Virgil's Georgics Englished* (1628); and Ogilby, *The Works of Publius Virgilius Maro* (1649, 1650, 1654). See Helene Maxwell Hooker, "Dryden's Georgics and English Predecessors," *Huntington Library Quarterly* 9 (1946): 273–310.

11 Dryden's poem on the death of Charles II, *Threnodia Augustalis* (1685) uses georgic imagery to praise his establishment of a peaceful political order after the Restoration: "The Royal Husbandman appear'd, / And Plough'd, and Sow'd, and Till'd" in *The Poems of John Dryden*, ed. James Kinsley, 4 vols. (Oxford, 1958), 1: 356–7.

12 Compare Abraham Cowley's translation of the same passage in "Of Agriculture" which looks back nostalgically to Roman farmers taking part in the running of the state and the empire. See *The Works of Mr Abraham Cowley* (1668), pp. 98–9.

13 An idea which Dryden may have derived from Knightly Chetwood's overtly imperial rendition of this passage in the Dryden-Tonson *Miscellany Poems* (1684), p. 314. Subsequent translators dropped the trading imagery: for example Joseph Trapp, *The Works of Virgil*, 3 vols. (1731), 2: 195 (in blank verse); Thomas Nevile, *The Georgics of Virgil* (Cambridge, 1767), 2: 179–80 (in couplets); William Mills, *The Georgics of Virgil* (1780), 2: 208–9 (in blank verse).

14 May, *Virgil's Georgics*, p. 121.

15 "A Translation of all Virgil's Fourth Georgick, Except the Story of Aristeus" in the Dryden-Tonson *Annual Miscellany: For the Year 1694*, p. 71. Compare Charles Sedley's pious version of these lines: "Under eternal Laws they wisely live, / Each knows his little Cell, and loves his Hive," "The Fourth Book of Virgil" (lines 173–4), in *Works*, 2 vols. (1722), 1: 129.

16 See Gerald MacLean, *Time's Witness: Historical Representation in English Poetry, 1603–1660* (Madison, Wisc., 1990), pp. 64–73.

17 On the appropriateness of georgic for celebrating Britain's naval and imperial power, see Thomas Tickell, "De Poesi Didactica," translated by J. L. Austin in Richard Eustace Tickell, *Thomas Tickell and the Eighteenth Century Poets* (1731), p. 209; and Joseph Trapp, *Praelectiones Poeticae* (1711, 1715), translated as *Lectures on Poetry read in the School of Natural Philosophy at Oxford* (1742) by William Clarke and William Bowyer (rpt. Bristol, 1994), p. 201.

18 D'Avenant, *Discourses on the Public Revenues* (1698) in Charles Whitworth, ed., *Political and Commercial Works*, 5 vols. (1771), 1: 138. See also Jacob Viner, *Studies in the Theory of International Trade* (1937); and Leonard Gomes, *Foreign Trade and the National Economy: Mercantilist and Classical Perspectives* (1987). The idea had earlier been developed by William Petty: "all things ought to be valued by two natural Denominations, which is Land and labor," *A Treatise of Taxes and Contributions* (1662), p. 26.

19 Mackworth, *England's Glory; or, The Great Improvement of Trade in General* (1694), pp. 20–1.

20 The best survey of the debates about colonization remains Klaus E. Knorr, *British Colonial Theories, 1570–1850* (1944). Some of the most import-ant pamphlets are collected in J. R. McCulloch, ed., *A Select Collection of Early English Tracts on Commerce* (1856; rpt. Cambridge, 1952).

21 Dryden's note to *Georgics* 4: 27, cited from *Works*, 4: 815.

22 Penn, *Some Account of the Province of Pennsylvania in America* (1681), pp. 2, 6.

23 Ralegh, *The Discoverie of the Large, Rich And Bewtiful Empyre of Guiana* (1596).

24 Oglethorpe, *A New and Accurate Account of the Provinces of South-Carolina and Georgia* (1733), pp. 33, 71–2.

25 Wesley, *Georgia, A Poem* (1736), pp. 5–6. See also Richard C. Boys, "General Oglethorpe and the Muses," *Georgia Historical Quarterly* 31 (1947): 32–46; and David Shields, *Oracles of Empire: Poetry, Politics, and Commerce in British America, 1690–1750* (Chicago, Ill., 1990).

26 Howard Erskine-Hill, *The Social Milieu of Alexander Pope: Lives, Example and the Poetic Response* (New Haven, Conn., 1975), p. 163.

27 *Paradise Lost*, cited from *The Poems of John Milton*, eds. John Carey and Alastair Fowler (1968), 4: 691.

28 Ibid., 4: 145, 247.

29 Philips, *Cyder: A Poem in Two Books* (1708), p. 52.

30 Ibid., p. 32.

31 Ibid., pp. 88–9.

32 *Windsor-Forest*, cited from *The Poems of Alexander Pope*, eds. John Butt, et. al., 11 vols. (1939–69), 1: 397–8.

33 Gay, *Poetry and Prose of John Gay*, eds. Vinton A. Dearing and Charles E. Beckwith, 2 vols. (Oxford, 1974), vol. 1, 1: 443.

34 On the oppositional context of *The Seasons*, see Christine Gerrard, *The Patriot Opposition to Walpole: Politics, Poetry and National Myth, 1725–1742* (Oxford, 1994).

35 Somervile, *The Chace: a Poem* (1735), 1: 21–31. On classically-derived hunting georgic, see Chalker, *English Georgic*, pp. 180–94.

36 On prospect and economic vision in Thomson's poem, see Barrell, *English Literature*, and "Being is Perceiving: James Thomson and John Clare," in *Poetry, Language and Politics* (Manchester, 1988), pp. 100–36.

37 "Autumn," lines 1278–89, cited from *The Seasons*, ed. James Sambrook (Oxford, 1981). Subsequent references to this edition of the 1746 text are given parenthetically.

38 See James Sambrook, *James Thomson, 1700–1748: A Life* (Oxford, 1991), p. 236.

39 Savage, *The Wanderer: a Poem* (1729), I: 279–80, cited from *The Poetical Works of Richard Savage*, ed. Clarence Tracy (Cambridge, 1962). See also *The Excursion* (1728) by Thomson's friend David Mallet.

40 Dodsley, *Public Virtue: A Poem in Three Books* (1753), 3: 309–11.

41 *The Hop-Garden*, cited from *The Poems of Christopher Smart*, eds. K. Williamson and M. Walsh, 4 vols. to date (Oxford, 1980–), 2: 282–4.

42 There has been a recent revival of interest in this once forgotten poem. See John Goodridge, *Rural Life in Eighteenth-Century English Poetry* (Cambridge, 1995), pp. 91–180; and Barrell, *English Literature*, pp. 90–104.

43 Dyer, *The Fleece: A Poem in Four Books* (1757), 4: 541, 668.

44 Jago, *Edge-Hill, or, The Rural Prospect Delineated and Moralized* (1767), I: 1. The poem appeared in its final enlarged version in *Poems, Moral and Descriptive. By the Late Richard Jago* (1784). See O. H. K. Spate, "The Muse of Mercantilism: Jago, Grainger and Dyer," in R. F. Brissenden, ed., *Studies in the Eighteenth Century* (Canberra, 1968), pp. 119–31.

45 See my "Still at Home: Cowper's New Domestic Empires," in Thomas Woodman, ed., *Early Romanticism* (forthcoming).

46 Grainger, *The Sugar-Cane* (1767), 4: 74–5.

47 See James Boswell, *The Life of Johnson LL. D.*, ed. G. B. Hill, revised L. F. Powell, 6 vols. (Oxford, 1934–50), 2: 433; *The Critical Review* 18 (1764), p. 277 (review possibly by Thomas Percy). On New World georgic, see Shields, *Oracles of Empire*, chapter 4.

48 The pastoral image of the West Indies can be found throughout the century; see, for example, *An Ode Pindarick on Barbadoes* ([1710]); and William Shervingham, *The Antigonian and Bostonian Beauties; A Poem* (Boston, Lincs., 1750).

49 Singleton, *A General Description of the West-Indian Islands, As Far as Relates to the British, Dutch and Danish Governments* (Barbados, 1767), lines 28–9.

50 "The Antigua Planter: or War and Famine" (written 1779), lines 19–24, cited from *Poems, on Subjects arising in England and the West Indies* (1783).

51 Moore, *Epistles, Odes, and other Poems* (1801).

CHAPTER II

The gentleman planter and the metropole:
Long's History of Jamaica (1774)

Elizabeth A. Bohls

Empire was the countryside writ large: an idyllic retreat, an escape, and an opportunity to make a fortune.

Simon Pugh[1]

It is possible and useful to trace the internal histories of landscape painting, landscape writing, landscape gardening and landscape architecture, but in any final analysis we must relate these histories to the common history of a land and its society.

Raymond Williams[2]

I

Raymond Williams's injunction has already ably guided a generation of writers on landscape aesthetics.[3] To implement it fully, I shall argue that we must consider Britain's historical identity since the seventeenth century as not just one land, but an imperial collection of landholdings throughout the globe.[4] North America, the Caribbean, India, Africa, the Pacific: the semiotics of the English landscape were extended to all these heterogeneous scenes.[5] To term the history of empire a "common history" in the postcolonial era entails an uncomfortable stretch, suggesting a nationalist slant in Williams's practice of cultural studies.[6] Indeed, landscape aesthetics, as I shall demonstrate through the example of Jamaica's colonial historian, Edward Long, belonged to a repertoire of discursive technologies set to advance the imperial project. Long's prominent use of the language of landscape aesthetics in his three-volume *History of Jamaica* (1774) helps him project the identity of a highly civilized British gentleman, only to conscript that persona in the defense of Jamaica's most glaring and contentious difference from its mother country: the institution of colonial slavery. Patriotically showcasing this outpost of the imperial countryside for metropolitan readers, Long's aesthetic vocabulary constructs it as an idyll in an attempt to make palatable the ugly foundation of West Indian fortunes. As we review his tactics, we will need to keep in view the constitutive disjunction in Long's colonial self-construction: both quintessentially English and, at the same time, anchored in a very un-English geographical and economic reality.

The geographer Stephen Daniels has remarked, "Imperial nationalists . . . have been intent to annex the homelands of others in their identity myths. They have projected on these lands and their inhabitants pictorial codes expressing both an affinity with the colonizing country and an estrangement from it."[7] At the time Long wrote, of course, Jamaica was no longer the ancestral homeland of anyone who lived there, its indigenous peoples having been wiped out nearly a century previously by violence and disease.[8] Taken from the Spanish in 1655, the island was shared by two deracinated groups – the British who were there more or less voluntarily, and their African slaves who were there wholly by force. Like its French, Spanish, and British Caribbean neighbors, Jamaica was the site of a process of creolization or cultural mixture: a process governed and warped, as Edward Brathwaite has argued, by the white colonists' colonial dependence, economic exploitation of their slaves, and racial separatism.[9] Long's *History*, and in particular its use of the verbal-pictorial code of landscape aesthetics, affords insight into the conflict or contradiction at the heart of the process of constructing Jamaican identity. The *History*, as we shall see, is deeply divided between affinity and estrangement, imperial nationalism and creole patriotism.

Besides his better-known role as the "father of English racism," Long was also a radical advocate of Jamaican political and economic self-sufficiency.[10] Born in Cornwall in 1734, fourth son of the planter Samuel Long of Longville, Jamaica, Long lived only twelve years on the island, from his father's death in 1757 until 1769, when bad health sent him back to England for good. His marriage to the heiress Mary Ballard connected him with the fabulously wealthy Beckford-Ballard-Palmer family group, which as of 1750 owned at least 44,670 acres of Jamaica (as of 1775 approximately 1 million acres were cultivated).[11] While there, Long, trained in the law, served as private secretary to the Lieutenant Governor and later as a judge in the Court of Vice-Admiralty.

The first avowed purpose of the *History* is to attract more white settlers to Jamaica, partly to strengthen the colony's defense against external and internal aggression (i. e., slave revolts) and minimize the cost to residents of maintaining the British garrison.[12] Amid the gathering threat of rebellion by the North American colonies, Long advises reducing Jamaica's dependence on trade with these in particular. To this immediate end, he proposes measures for economic diversification and more extensive use of home-grown products – measures that, in the longer run, could have led toward greater overall self-sufficiency for the island:

Corn, in abundance, we may have of our own growth, and lamp oil of our own manufacture, both far cheaper than we can buy of them. How strange, and inexcusable is it, that we should pay so much money every year for their horses, when those of our own breed are so incomparably more beautiful and serviceable! Great quantities of hoops, headings, and shingles might be provided in the island, were proper methods taken to encourage our own settlers. (1: 541)[13]

Local law, Long further asserts, should reflect local conditions (1: 72–3). Although advocating more imports from across the Atlantic, he also proposes measures that would weaken the ties between colony and metropole, justifying Brathwaite's portrayal of him as a creole patriot.

How could the language of landscape aesthetics help further Long's purpose of enhancing both Jamaica's growth and its local autonomy? An answer may be found by analyzing this discourse, which encompasses a set of characteristic topics and a vocabulary for talking about them.[14] Eighteenth-century landscape aesthetics encompassed a burgeoning tradition of estate gardening rooted in reactions to seventeenth-century French and Dutch imports. Somewhat later, it involved a closely related aesthetics of wild nature and scenic tourism, as well as writings on theoretical and applied aesthetics by a variety of authors including Shaftesbury, Addison, Pope, Hume, Hogarth, Burke, and later Reynolds, Gilpin, Uvedale Price, and Richard Payne Knight. Poetry, notably James Thomson's influential *The Seasons* (1726–46), contributed as well. The concerns of landscape aesthetics included, first and foremost, the relation between nature and art, infiltrated early on by the possibility that, as well as art imitating nature, nature (or our perception of it) could imitate art. As young male aristocrats returned from the Grand Tour with trunk-loads of paintings by Continental masters like Salvator Rosa and Claude Lorrain, these influenced both gardening practice and the conceptualization of wild nature, which came to be viewed as framed, composed "scenes" or "prospects," like paintings (hence the concept of the picturesque, defined as a scene suitable for painting). The appreciation of such scenes was guided by aesthetic categories, notably the beautiful and the sublime, and the principle of "Uniformity amid Variety."[15]

Beyond this evolving terminology, the fashionable theory and practice of landscape aesthetics was governed by the master concept of taste,
a powerful discursive marker of both class and gender.[16] The man of
taste had what it took to appreciate the beauty and sublimity of natural scenes. Whether by birth or through the education and exposure
that stemmed from his privilege, he believed himself to be among the
happy few with access to what Joseph Addison termed "the pleasures
of the imagination."[17] Taste both expressed and fostered the immense
sense of entitlement that pervades eighteenth-century writings on aesthetics: a consciousness of distinction from the majority who lacked
access to these rarefied sensations. The aesthetics of land, in particular, was infused with a proprietary tone. To see and describe land aesthetically was to exercise imaginative appropriation on the model of
the landed property that grounded the man of taste's class privilege.
Landownership went along with a stake in the symbolic turf of high
culture, whose essence was to be distinguished from the landless, taste-
less vulgar.

For Long, such a distinction had multiple uses. Firstly identifying himself, as a colonial gentleman planter, with the metropolitan elite had
political consequences. It supported his claim to possess the full rights
and privileges of a British citizen – rights that, in his constitutional argument, entitled Jamaican landowners to more self-government. I will be
concerned, however, with the cultural politics of the *History*: the ways
in which Long deploys landscape aesthetics in the service of a colonial
identity that carefully negotiates between the prestige of metropolitan
paradigms and the defense of local difference. To this end, Long
modifies and mixes established metropolitan modes of representing
land. To confer aesthetic value on the colonial plantation, he alloys
the pictorial discourse that would soon burgeon under the designation
"picturesque," and that tended to exclude traces of agricultural labor
from the represented landscape, with the established tradition of the
georgic, which dignifies and aestheticizes labor. Such admixture can be
found in metropolitan poetry as early as Pope's *Windsor Forest*, pointing
to the central tension between labor and leisure in imperial British
society that John Barrell has discussed, and on which Long gives us
a specifically colonial perspective.[18] Long also employs the cultural
capital of the man of taste to defend the distinction on which rested
the entire edifice of slavery: that of race. The *History*'s central argument
in favor of slavery depends on the fundamental distinction between
"civilized" Europeans and "savage" Africans – different species, as Long

would have it. I will conclude by exploring this aspect of Long's deployment of aesthetics in the service of early scientific racism.

II

Columbus, Long reports, landing in Jamaica in 1494, pronounced "the face of the country" the most beautiful he had yet seen, no mean compliment in comparison to Cuba and Hispaniola (1: 343). The ideologically powerful founding moment of European "discovery" is coupled with and confirmed by an authoritative aesthetic judgment: Columbus's aesthetic capacity – like Long's own – is offered as evidence of special entitlement to own the aesthetic object so appreciated. Throughout the *History*, Long capitalizes on taste to protect and enhance planter-owners' investment in the colonial plantation economy.

Much of the second volume of the *History* provides a parish-by-parish description of the island in which aesthetics serves the function it still serves with respect to the Caribbean: to advertise scenic appeal. Tourist travel to Jamaica was unlikely in 1774; besides a general enhancement of the colony's value in the eyes of metropolitan readers, Long's puff can be assumed to be addressed to the potential white settlers he is concerned to court. The language, however, is often comparable to that of contemporary travel accounts and tourist guidebooks. For example, the county of Cornwall in Jamaica offers an abundance of scenery that lends itself to aesthetic description:

the prospects are finely variegated, and, from some stations, are extended ... many miles: but one of the most pleasing scenes is, the spacious tract of open land, called Labor-in-vain Savannah, which appears partly of a vivid green, and partly of a russet color. One side of it is girt around with romantic hills and woods; the other, towards the South, is washed by the sea; the middle sweep is graced with scattered clumps of trees and under-wood; which objects all together combine in exhibiting a very picturesque and beautiful appearance. (2: 184–5)

Conceptualizing the countryside as a series of painting-like "prospects" or "scenes," Long calls viewpoints "stations," the term used by Thomas West just four years later in his influential *Guide to the Lakes* (1778), a founding text of the scenic tourism whose popularity would soar in the 1780s and 1790s. Such tourism – searching for natural scenes to be judged by criteria of style and composition – was already practiced in England by the time Long wrote. His descriptive language is general enough to apply to English scenes as well as Jamaican ones. It

11.1 Isaac Taylor, "A View of the White River Cascade," from Long,
History of Jamaica vol. 2 plate 9.

suggests a pictorial composition, summed up with the aestheticizing catch-all "picturesque and beautiful." The "clumps of trees" suggest the trade-mark belts and clumps of the garden designer Lancelot "Capability" Brown.[19] Underlying this allusion, of course, is the durable trope of the colony as garden, Edenic in its beauty and potential for exploitation.[20]

An earlier description, illustrated by one of Long's sixteen plates (figure 11.1), acknowledges local variation, though in a muted fashion. Here Long encounters one of the "sights" of the island, a 300-foot water-fall whose "grandeur" he honors with a two-page description. Declaring the scene "beyond the power of painting to express," Long quotes a dozen lines from his favorite poet Thomson before concluding:

to complete the picture, the bason is ornamented with two elegant trees of the palm kind, which spring like strait columns out of the water, placed by the hand of nature at such even distance from the banks on each side, that art could not have done the work with more attention to propriety and exact-ness. The whole, indeed, has been executed by nature in a taste that surpasses either description or imitation. The late Sir Charles P–e, within whose ter-ritory it lay, would not suffer the least alterations to be made to it . . . He preferred its natural beauties; and, in order to enjoy them, formed a club of gentlemen, and built a range of apartments on a pretty lawn just fronting the cascade. Here they had an annual meeting, which continued some weeks; during which, they took the diversion of shooting the ring-tail pidgeons, which in this part of the country are very numerous, and in great perfection at the proper season. If the lesser cascade [on the Rio Alto, described previously] is delicate and curious, this is grand and sublime. The former is contemplated with delight, and this with a pleasing and reverential wonder. The fall is said to exceed in grandeur that of Tivoli, or any other in Europe, though much inferior to that of Niagara. (2: 95)

Once again Jamaican nature rises to the stature of a work of art. The palm trees, a mark of local specificity and exotic difference from England, keep in step with European civilization by imitating classical columns. Flattering the taste in which nature has executed the scene, Long flatters his own and his reader's taste in being able to appreciate it as he delivers a lesson on the difference between the beautiful and the sublime. Cosmopolitan comparisons to Tivoli and Niagara draw the reader into a global system of aesthetic value that shadows and implicitly legitimates the global reach of British influence.

Most remarkable in this description is the way Long subordinates the natural sublimity of the falls to aristocratic ownership in the person of Sir Charles, who has the good taste not to tamper with nature, but instead forms a gentlemen's club and builds a shooting lodge to get maximum enjoyment from his cascade. Replicating the leisure activities of the English countryside in the island setting, Sir Charles translates into cultural practice the imperial drive to remake colonized territory in a metropolitan mold. And yet local differences, though Long does not foreground them, are quietly evident in the palms, the ringtail pigeons, and – in the plate – the slave carrying the tourists' parasol. This mixture between the aesthetic language and leisure customs, closely identified with metropolitan culture, and the unobtrusive yet obvious local content given to these familiar forms, signifies ambiguously. As he assimilates the Jamaican gentleman planter to the highest echelon of British society in the tasteful figure of Sir Charles, Long quietly asserts colonial difference – in preparation for the key difference, the institution of slavery, which the *History* sets out to defend. A model of colonial identity emerges that asserts colonial dignity through metropolitan cultural paradigms, while at the same time carefully reserving a domain of colonial difference or autonomy. This need to defend difference will emerge more distinctly when we examine the place of plantation labor, or its traces in the landscape, in Long's representation of the sugar plantation as country estate.

The figure of the English-style country gentleman does considerable ideological work in the History. Long's rhetorical persona is a true gentleman: a man of liberal education, wide-ranging knowledge, privileged leisure and, crucially, good taste. Landownership anchored the gentleman's privileged status, and its display centered in the country house, that centerpiece of British culture. Celebrated in literature from Jonson to Pope, Fielding, and Austen, the country estate enjoyed a heyday during the eighteenth century.[21] Its symbolic value was measured on an aesthetic scale, as we learn from studying the widespread and competitive practice of estate "improvement," or landscape gardening. The expensive but socially rewarding practice of creating pleasing scenes out of the raw material of one's patrimonial estate (with the help of a master planner like Capability Brown or Humphry Repton) helped change the face of the English countryside, abetted by the continuing "Agricultural Revolution" and the enclosure movement.[22] The 1750s and 1760s saw the creation of several of England's most celebrated landscape gardens, including Stourhead, Hagley Park, and the Leasowes.[23] Much of this activity, such as William Beckford's lavish improvements to his estate at Fonthill, was funded by colonial profits.[24]

Williams's discussion of the "morality of improvement," which he sees driving the eighteenth-century transformation of the English countryside, is useful in separating "two meanings of improvement, which were historically linked but in practice so often contradictory . . . the improvement of soil, stock, yields, in a working agriculture" and that "of houses, parks, artificial landscapes, which absorbed so much of the actually increasing wealth."[25] The contradiction to which Williams refers is, in part, a moral one: the taste displayed by the "improved" house and grounds implied good character in their owner, a trope familiar in literature from Pope's *Epistle to Burlington* to Austen's *Pride and Prejudice*. But such moral elevation is not very compatible with the practices of engrossing, rack-renting, and enclosure whose profits often financed expensive "improvements" – nor, in the colonial case, with slavery, in the opinion of growing numbers of Britons.[26]

Long's rhetoric leans heavily on the moral overtones that this tradition gave to the aesthetic value of the country estate. He calls the planter "Mr. F–n" of Clarendon Parish, for example, a gentleman "worthy of being esteemed among the first ornaments of this country," conflating

the aesthetic connotations of "ornament" with the moral aura of
"esteem." Mr. F–n's mansion

commands [an] extensive prospect . . . The beauties of nature that are displayed
here are innumerable. In one place is seen a long, wavy surface, adorned with
the lively verdure of canes, interspersed with wind-mills and other buildings.
In another are beheld several charming lawns of pasture-land, dotted with cattle
and sheep, and watered with rivulets. In a third are Negroe villages, where
(far from poverty and discontent) peace and plenty hold their reign; a crested
ridge of fertile hills, which separates this parish from those contiguous on the
North and East, distantly terminates the lanscape. (2: 64)

Long positions the reader with the owner, in "command" of the mansion's aesthetic and practical value, looking outward. He composes the
view in vaguely pictorial terms, "wavy" alluding to Hogarth's serpen-
tine "line of beauty," a staple of mid-century garden design, and
bounds it with a hilly horizon line. As in the description of the water-
fall, locally specific details like windmills, used to power cane-crushing
machinery, and slave quarters vary the aesthetic pattern derived from
a European countryside.

    These local specificities are also visual evidence of the working planta-
tion economy. We do not see here the dichotomy that Williams finds:
"A working country is hardly ever a landscape."[27] Williams chronicles
the ideologically driven segregation in the British countryside between
agricultural production and the consumption of land, aesthetically,
as landscape. Prospects from "improved" mansions, he writes, were
artificially emptied of the traces of labor, "inconvenient barns and mills
cleared away," following the impulse Williams documents in his discussion
of Jonson's country-house poem, "To Penshurst" (1616), in which the
"magical extraction of the curse of labour is . . . achieved by a simple
extraction of the existence of labourers."[28] This feature of gardening
practice corresponds to developments in theoretical aesthetics familiar
from Kant's version in his *Critique of Judgement* (1790): the emerging
paradigm of disinterested aesthetic contemplation, which calls on the
viewer to divest himself of practical vested interest in what he regards.
A useful or profitable object does not qualify as an aesthetic object.[29]

    But Long's description of Mr. F–n's prospect does not invoke this
metropolitan paradigm. Although he aestheticizes the sugar plantation,
he does not try to conceal its barns and mills. Instead we see him, here
and elsewhere in the *History*, attempting to combine a pictorialized or
aestheticized view of the Jamaican landscape with another discourse
about land that possessed considerable power in Britain during the first

two-thirds of the eighteenth century: the georgic, capable of aesthetically recuperating the traces of labor. Georgic poems from John Philips's
Cider (1708) to John Dyer's *The Fleece* (1757) drew on the Virgilian tradition to dignify agricultural production and "imaginatively and morally
secured the links between the economic realms of country, city, and
empire" in ways that Karen O'Brien has explored in the previous
chapter. Poems such as James Grainger's *The Sugar-Cane* (1764) and John
Singleton's *A General Description of the West-Indian Islands* (1767) use the
georgic tradition as a frame for asserting the importance of colonial
production.[30] The essence of the georgic mode is to dignify labor and
secure its moral and aesthetic place in the building of a nation or empire.
John Murdoch calls georgic "*the* characteristic eighteenth-century cultural mode," closely linked to the country house and landed estate – the
value system contrasting agricultural self-sufficiency with extravagant,
parasitical urban life. Eighteenth-century georgic after Thomson was,
as O'Brien points out, inseparable from imperial ideology, and georgic
conventions were invoked by nonliterary as well as literary works treat-
ing of empire. Long is working within a well-established tradition when
he invokes the georgic ethos of hard work and improvement to defend
the Jamaican colonists' contribution to the British nation.[31]

To do so, of course, he must obscure the less salutary features of the
labor system the planters operated: thus his heavy-handed editorializ-
ing about the "Negroe villages." He also needs to fudge a bit, as John
Barrell sees metropolitan georgic doing, as to who actually performs
the labor and who gets credit for labor through activities of management or ownership alone.[32] Aestheticizing the traces of labor into so
many ornaments to Mr. F–n's prospect, Long undertakes to fuse a
pictorial discourse of prospects and scenes with a georgic celebration
of agriculture – a fusion adapted to his colonial setting and rhetorical
purpose. The segregation of scenery from labor that Williams discovers in his metropolitan frame will not work, it seems, in the colonial context. Here even landscape aesthetics must feed directly into the
colony's material justification for existence, its productive contribution
to Britain's imperial wealth. Instead of isolating aesthetic pleasure from
its economic basis, Long's rhetoric seeks to transmute value from the
economic worth that justified the sugar island's existence in the imperial
system to an aesthetic value that accumulated cultural capital for the
gentleman colonist. That cultural capital, in turn, as we will see, he
applied to a more explicit and far-reaching justification of the sugar
plantation's economic basis in the institution of slavery.

Such aestheticizing is even more evident in an earlier scenic description. Discussing the beneficial effects of the Jamaican climate, Long attributes the "lively flow of spirits" experienced by arriving Europeans partly to the beauty of the landscape, which fosters "liveliness of imagination and temper. The cane-pieces too . . . enliven every where the view with tints unspeakably beautiful." He carefully describes the "tint" of the cane at each stage of its growth, and continues: "Last of all appear the busy slaves, like reapers, armed with bills instead of sickles to cut the ripened stems; and teams of oxen in the field, to bring the treasure home; whilst the laborers chear their toil with rude songs, or whistle in wild chorus their unpolished melody" (1: 363). Again, Long's description does not ignore the traces of labor, but sanitizes and beautifies them. He presents the slaves as "rude" and "wild," alluding to their African origin, but above all as cheerful, likening them to English reapers familiar to readers from what Murdoch calls "the quintessentially Georgic poem" of the British eighteenth century[33] (and a favorite of Long's, quoted throughout the *History*): Thomson's *Seasons*, where the "meadows glow, and rise unquelled / Against the mower's scythe."[34] Turning slaves into happy reapers and canes into treasure, Long struggles to assimilate the grueling proto-industrial routine of the colonial plantation to the Utopian idyll that had long been prominent in discourse about the Americas.

Long is far from alone in applying aesthetic terms to celebrate colonial agricultural production. The impulse appears as early as Charles Leslie's *New History of Jamaica* (1740): cultivated valleys "please no less" than wild ones, and "produce the richest Plants in the Universe; as, the Sugar-Cane, the Ginger, and others, which are better to their owners than a share in the mines of Potusi."[35] But no one aestheticizes the sugar plantation more enthusiastically than William Beckford (a cousin of the novelist of the same name) in his *Descriptive Account of the Island of Jamaica* (1790).[36] He follows a discussion of how to cultivate sugar, "this rich and singular exotic," with a pictorialized description of the plant itself: "A field of canes, when standing, in the month of November, when it is in arrow (or full bloom), is one of the most beautiful productions that the pen or pencil can possibly describe."[37] Beckford's aestheticizing, like Long's, culminates with an impassioned defense of slavery.[38]

We have seen Long's *History* use landscape description to enhance colonial prestige in several related, if not always compatible, ways. He adapts powerful metropolitan modes of representing land and its "improvement," both agricultural and aesthetic, to serve colonial purposes. Justifying Jamaica's importance to the empire, he simultaneously defends the local differences that support the colony's need for autonomy, especially with respect to its biggest difference from the metropole, the institution of slavery. Long's conflation of pictorial or aesthetic with georgic representation in his Jamaican landscapes serves these rhetorical ends in a manner not available through either mode alone. The *History* attempts to negotiate a delicate balance between a servile deployment of metropolitan paradigms and a feisty defense of local West Indian needs. Deep ambivalence between imperial boosterism and local patriotism, adherence to the center and the creation of a creole identity, is evident in Long's use of aesthetic discourse throughout his three volumes.

III

Long puts the fund of prestige that this deployment of aesthetics accumulates to its most concentrated use in the middle of the second volume, in a long chapter entitled "Thoughts on the Negroes of Africa in general." Here he defends slavery by vilifying Africans as "a brutish, ignorant, idle, crafty, treacherous, bloody, thievish, mistrustful, and superstitious people" (2: 354). He mounts his most sustained display of erudition in a long argument purporting to demonstrate that Africans are a different species from whites, citing Buffon, Linnaeus, Hume, and a wide variety of travel writers in support of his claim that Africans are more like orangutans than like Europeans. He is especially fascinated by reports of sex between African women and orangutans.

But the most striking feature of this diatribe, in view of Long's conspicuous display of his own cultivation, is the way he denies to Africans precisely these "civilized" features. They lack everything Europeans value most about themselves: "genius," "civility and science," "moral sensations," "self-discipline," and the ability to appreciate beauty. "Their houses are miserable cabbins. They conceive no pleasure from the most beautiful parts of their country, preferring the more sterile" (2: 353). Long contrasts the African character with the good taste he has been flaunting up to this point in the *History*, the crowning ornament of his gentlemanly accomplishments. The gentleman planter's identity is defined against the comprehensive negation that is the African character. The contrast between the planters' elegant mansions and the Africans' "miserable cabbins" enlists taste to justify colonial slavery. We glimpse the instability of colonial discourse in the peculiar mimesis or mirroring

– to paraphrase Michael Taussig – between the brutality slaveholders like Long attributed to Africans, and the brutality they themselves carried out in the name of civilization, meaning business.[39]

I need not dwell on Long's self-serving racism. What I do want to highlight is this chapter's structural position at the heart of the *History*. The contents of its three volumes are ordered to present an implicit structural argument echoing the explicit polemic in the chapter on "Negroes": the contrast between civilized Europeans and uncivilizable Africans. Long situates this polemic between two discourses, aesthetics and what we would now call science, both of whose cultural authority is vested in the supposed disinterestedness or objectivity of their gaze.[40] The first half of the second volume is taken up with the parish-by-parish survey-travelogue discussed above, larded with scenic descriptions like those quoted. Much of its second half discusses the "Inhabitants of the Island," including the long chapter "Thoughts on the Negroes of Africa" (2: 351–84). After canvassing related topics, such as slave insurrections and "the Jamaica *Negroe-Code*," Long steps back from the aggressive engagement of his assault on the humanity of those whose labor drove colonial agribusiness; the rest of the volume discusses health and medicine on the island.

The third volume is devoted to meteorology and natural history – climate, tides, storms, and means of protecting people and property from them, as well as a "*Catalogue* of foreign Plants, which might be introduced." Long's assault on the African character takes on greater weight, for sympathetic readers, by being sandwiched between demonstrations of the gentleman planter's aesthetic sensibility and his scientific knowledge, which collude to assert his title to his colonial property, emphatically including his slaves.

Long's heavy use of aesthetic discourse as part of his extended argument defending colonial slavery has much to tell us, first, about the sheer prestige that aesthetics, specifically landscape aesthetics, had attained by 1774 among Britain's elite. The extensive use of aesthetics in this history of empire (as in other colonial and neocolonial discourse, from Addison and Pope to the contemporary US publication *National Geographic*)[41] makes evident the potential of aesthetics, with its fundamental structure of distinction and exclusion, to advance imperial projects. Taste distinguishes the "polite" imagination from the impolite, the civilized from the uncivilizable; this central feature of aesthetics colludes in sustaining the fundamental divisions among individuals and groups that are indispensable to imperial ideology.

Furthermore, Long's use of aesthetics entails interesting questions about aesthetics' origins and development. Mary Louise Pratt has suggested that we seek the origins of Romanticism not necessarily at home, but perhaps in the imperial "contact zones" of the Americas, the Pacific, and elsewhere.[42] Her suggestion should be generally applied to the prestigious discipline of aesthetics, fundamental to metropolitan high culture. Long, as we have seen, makes use of established metropolitan modes – the pictorial and the georgic – for the aesthetic representation of land. Mixing these conventions is by no means unprecedented in metropolitan writing, as we have seen. Might the targeted modification that serves Long's creole ends in the *History of Jamaica* nonetheless make a distinctive contribution to the development of aesthetic paradigms? His example suggests we ought perhaps to seek explanations for this development neither exclusively at the center nor on the periphery, but in the interaction between the two: the complex negotiations, cultural as well as political and economic, that constituted and held – or sometimes did not hold – the ties between each European power and its colonial possessions.[43]

Such intricate processes of negotiation, in which geography and imaginary identity intersect or, just as often, diverge, yield in Long's case that peculiar hybrid, the colonial gentleman planter. Patterned on the English country gentleman and borrowing his prestige, yet emphatically distinguished from the former by the local specificity of that peculiar institution, the sugar plantation, the gentleman planter's identity as imagined by Long's *History* is essentially disjunctive, and to that extent, essentially unstable. It depends on a central paradox: imposing metropolitan sameness on the very different place that is the colony for the purpose of defending that place's indispensable local difference, the institution of slavery.

NOTES

I am grateful to the editors and to Elizabeth Heckendorn Cook for valuable criticisms of draft versions of this chapter.

1 Simon Pugh, "Introduction," *Reading Landscape: Country–City–Capital* (Manchester, 1990), p. 5; and see Williams, *Country and City*, p. 281: "The lands of the Empire were an idyllic retreat, an escape from debt or shame, or an opportunity for making a fortune."

2 Williams, *Country and City*, p. 120.

3 In addition to works by John Barrell that are contemporary to Williams, see: Turner, *Politics of Landscape*; Ann Bermingham, *Landscape and Ideology:*

The English Rustic Tradition 1740–1860 (Berkeley, Calif., 1989); Carole Fabricant, "The Aesthetics and Politics of Landscape in the Eighteenth Century," in Ralph Cohen, ed., *Studies in Eighteenth-Century British Art and Aesthetics* (Berkeley, Calif., 1985); Alan Liu, *Wordsworth: The Sense of History* (Stanford, Calif., 1989); Stephen Daniels, *Fields of Vision: Landscape Imagery in England and the United States* (Princeton, N.J., 1993); and the essays in Stephen Copley and Peter Garside, eds., *The Politics of the Picturesque: Literature, Landscape and Aesthetics since 1770* (Cambridge, 1994).

4 Williams was clearly aware of Britain's identity as an empire, which he discusses at length and perceptively in chapter 24 of *Country and City*. What that book does not do is to assess the specific relevance of empire to representations of country and city in the earlier period with which I am concerned.

5 See, for example: Bernard Smith, *European Vision and the South Pacific*, 2nd edn. (New Haven, Conn., 1985); Mary Louise Pratt, *Imperial Eyes: Travel Writing and Transculturation* (New York, 1992); and J. M. Coetzee, *White Writing: On the Culture of Letters in South Africa* (New Haven, Conn., 1988). James Turner also relates landscape ideology to colonial theories and poetic depictions of colonies in the seventeenth century; see *Politics of Landscape*, pp. 132–5, 140, 153–4.

6 See Paul Gilroy's brief but illuminating discussion of nationalism or "ethnic absolutism" in cultural studies, *The Black Atlantic: Modernity and Double Consciousness* (Cambridge, Mass., 1993), pp. 5–15.

7 Daniels, *Fields*, p. 5.

8 In *Colonial Encounters: Europe and the Native Caribbean, 1492–1797* (1992), Peter Hulme summarizes the history of the Indians of the Caribbean island colonies, culminating in the final defeat and deportation to Honduras of the Black Caribs of St. Vincent in 1796; see chapter 6.

9 Brathwaite, *The Development of Creole Society in Jamaica* (Oxford, 1971), pp. 100, 307.

10 Peter Fryer, *Staying Power: The History of Black People in Britain* (Atlantic Highlands, N.J., 1984), p. 70; and see Brathwaite, *Development*, pp. 73–5, 80–1.

11 Richard B. Sheridan, "Planter and Historian: The Career of William Beckford of Jamaica and England, 1744–1799," *Jamaican Historical Review* 4 (1964): 36–58.

12 Long, *History of Jamaica. Or, General Survey of the Antient and Modern State of that Island: With Reflections on its Situation, Settlements, Inhabitants, Climate, products, Commerce, Laws, and Government*, 3 vols. (1774), I: 69. Subsequent references are given parenthetically.

13 Quoted in Brathwaite, *Development*, p. 80.

14 For a definition of "discourse" as used here, see my *Women Travel Writers and the Language of Aesthetics 1716–1818* (Cambridge, 1995), pp. 5–6.

15 Edward Malins, *English Landscaping and Literature 1660–1840* (1966), pp. 80, 85.

16 See my *Women Travel Writers*, introduction and chapter 3.

17 Addison, *The Spectator*, ed. Donald Bond, 5 vols. (Oxford, 1965), 3: 535–82, nos. 411–21.

18 See Barrell's discussion of the mixture of georgic with pastoral (which is similar to what I call pictorial discourse in its exclusion of labor from the landscape) in works by Thomson and Dyer, *English Literature in History, 1730–1780: An Equal, Wide Survey* (New York, 1983), pp. 51–109. And see Karen O'Brien's essay in this volume on the "residually pastoral idiom" found in imperial georgic and the way many West Indian colonial poets, such as Singleton, re-orient georgic back toward pastoral as a way of dodging confrontation with the issue of slave labor.

19 Malins, *English Landscaping*, pp. 99–100, 107.

20 See, for example, William Smith, *Natural History of Nevis and the Rest of the English Leeward Charibee Islands in America* (1745), pp. 34, 37, alluding to Milton (though see p. 243). Long himself invokes Milton's paradise at 2: 222. Annette Kolodny, in *The Lay of the Land: Metaphor as Experience and History in American Life and Letters* (Chapel Hill, N. C., 1975), chapters 1 and 2, presents the North American counterpart.

21 See Williams, *Country and City*, chapters 6, 7, and 11, on these figures; Mark Girouard, *Life in the English Country House* (New Haven, Conn., 1978) on country houses, especially chapters 1 and 7.

22 See Bermingham, *Landscape*, on the relation between these. In terms of Robert C. Allen's distinction discussed in the Introduction to this volume, I am referring to the "agricultural revolution" of the landlords rather than that of the yeomen; this latter was primarily a seventeenth-century development as Eric Kerridge makes clear in *The Agricultural Revolution* (1967), p. 21.

23 Malins, *English Landscaping*, pp. 49–79.

24 See Sheridan, "Planter," p. 41.

25 Williams, *Country and City*, pp. 115–16; see also pp. 60–7 and *passim*. For arguments that the two kinds of improvement are actually compatible, see Peter Womack, *Improvement and Romance: Constructing the Myth of the Highlands* (1989); and Stephen Daniels and Charles Watkins, "Picturesque Landscaping and Estate Management: Uvedale Price and Nathaniel Kent at Foxley," in Copley and Garside, eds., *Politics*, pp. 13–41.

26 See Richard B. Sheridan, *Sugar and Slavery: An Economic History of the British West Indies, 1623–1775* (Barbados, Jamaica, Trinidad and Tobago, 1974), pp. 481–6, for a summary of anti-slavery activity up to 1775.

27 Williams, *Country and City*, p. 120.

28 Ibid., pp. 125, 32. See also Don Wayne, *Penshurst: The Semiotics of Place and the Poetics of History* (Madison, Wisc., 1984), pp. 126–7.

29 See my *Women Travel Writers*, pp. 68–73, 95–6. The influential writings of William Gilpin, continuing in this line, elaborate a doctrine of picturesque landscape that would erase laborers as well as the traces of cultivation; however, these were not published until after Long's *History*.

30 See O'Brien, "Imperial georgic," pp. 174–5. On the history of the English georgic see John Chalker, *The English Georgic: A Study in the Development of a Form* (Baltimore, Md., 1969). For my purposes I will define georgic, as Anthony Low suggests, as a literary mode rather than, strictly speaking, a genre: "an informing spirit, an attitude toward life, and a set of themes

and images" rather than, necessarily, a poem in imitation of Virgil. See Low, *The Georgic Revolution* (Princeton, N.J., 1985), p. 7.

31 John Murdoch, "The Landscape of Labor: Transformations of the Georgic," in Kenneth R. Johnston, Gilbert Chaitin, Karen Hanson, and Herbert Marks, eds., *Romantic Revolutions: Criticism and Theory* (Bloomington, Ind., 1990), pp. 176–93, this passage p. 189. And see John Barrell's Afterword to this volume.

32 Barrell, *The Dark Side of the Landscape: The Rural Poor in English Painting 1730–1840* (Cambridge, 1980), pp. 42–8.

33 Murdoch, "Landscape," p. 189.

34 "Summer," lines 1452–3; quoted from *The Seasons and the Castle of Indolence,* ed. James Sambrook (Oxford, 1972).

35 Leslie, *New History of Jamaica* (1740), p. 20

36 For details on the life and writings of this William Beckford, see Sheridan, "Planter."

37 Beckford, *Descriptive Account of the Island of Jamaica,* 2 vols. (1790), i: 46, 50–1.

38 The Scottish traveler Janet Schaw similarly aestheticizes the West Indian plantation; see my *Women Travel Writers,* chapter 2.

39 Taussig, *Shamanism, Colonialism and the Wild Man: A Study in Terror and Healing* (Chicago, Ill., 1986), p. 134.

40 Long's opus is a discursive and generic hybrid; it does not contain a very high proportion of "history" in the sense of a narrative of the colony's short past. The bulk of its three volumes contains a rather heterogeneous collection of information on the present state of the colony, drawing on a wide range of discourses including law, political economy, statistics, natural history, meteorology, medicine, surveying and topography, agriculture, civil engineering, travel writing, and what we would call ethnography (albeit of a polemical kind) on Africa. The *History of Jamaica* seems to emerge from a tradition of American and West Indian colony histories including such works as Robert Beverley's *History and Present State of Virginia* (1705), Thomas Prince's *Chronological History of New-England* (1736), and Thomas Hutchinson's *History of the Colony of Massachusetts Bay* (1764–1828). I am grateful to Karen O'Brien for these references.

41 See Laura Brown, *Ends of Empire: Women and Ideology in Early Eighteenth-Century Literature* (Ithaca, N.Y., 1993), pp. 103–34 on Addison and Pope; and David Spurr, *The Rhetoric of Empire: Colonial Discourse in Journalism, Travel Writing and Imperial Administration* (Durham, N.C., 1993), pp. 43–60, on more recent forms of aestheticization.

42 Pratt, *Imperial Eyes,* pp. 137–8.

43 We may look for this kind of two-way influence between colony and metropole in other areas of European culture as well. For example, Sidney Mintz, *Sweetness and Power: The Place of Sugar in Modern History* (New York, 1985), pp. 46–52, suggests that a form of industrial labor discipline existed on the colonial sugar plantation before it was found in Europe.

CHAPTER 12

Crown forests and female georgic:
Frances Burney and the reconstruction of Britishness

Elizabeth Heckendorn Cook

I

In July 1789, George III was judged to be substantially recovered from his first extended period of mental alienation. His convalescence would be completed by a pleasant tour through the New Forest in Hampshire followed by a stay in the seaside resort of Weymouth. George, his queen, three of the six princesses, and the requisite attendants made up the official traveling entourage.[1] The king's party stayed for nearly a week in Lyndhurst at the center of the New Forest, walking, riding, and enjoying the attentions of the bucolic residents – "the sunburnt daughters of labour" and their swains, as the *Hampshire Chronicle* described the country people who jammed the roads throughout the tour to see the royal family.[2] One of the attendants traveling with the royal family was Frances Burney, the queen's second keeper of the robes, and she described their visit at some length in her journal. The visit would be invoked once more, in Burney's last novel *The Wanderer*, published twenty-five years later in 1814, by which time George III had been shut away after his relapse in 1811. In *The Wanderer*, a series of newly coherent "British" identities – the heroine's, but also the nation's, and, as I will argue, the author's – is brought into being around a revised model of kingship that is established amid a crown forest. No longer a warlord or a Nimrod, in Burney's novel the monarch becomes something more like a royal gentleman-proprietor, the benignly paternalist landlord of even the most remote corners of his kingdom.

What are we to make of these various representations and recapitulations of a royal visit to a crown forest? As a particular kind of aesthetic, economic, and political space, the Crown forest unites nature and culture, terms that were themselves experiencing intensified pressure at the end of the century.[3] As such, it is a special case of a particular land-use category we might call the "acculturated landscape," a mediating space that functions to "naturalize" such properly cultural constructions as class affiliations, codes of gender, or national identity. My questions in this chapter are about the signifying potential of such an event and such a space in the summer of 1789, and about how that potential had been reconfigured by the time Burney rewrote the royal visit in the second decade of the nineteenth century. More speculatively, I am asking how various accounts of such an event and such a space might be deployed in the interests of very different cultural and political programs.

George's 1789 visit to the New Forest and Burney's refraction of that visit in *The Wanderer* twenty-five years later are both linked and distinguished by the kind of cultural work that is assigned to natural landscape in each case. Both accounts are deliberate revisions of previous visits to the New Forest: the king's tour reworks the bloody and oppressive royal history traditionally associated with this terrain, in part by constructing a domesticated subjectivity organized around the image of the male monarch. Burney's novel, I argue, rewrites the work done by George's visit for a different purpose: to make a place in the cultural landscape for a certain kind of female subjectivity. Both offer narratives of reconciliation and restoration – genealogical, professional, and national – mediated by the symbolic terrain of the crown forest.

II
DOMESTICATING MONARCHY

At the turn of the eighteenth century, the British countryside had become, in newly intense ways, the grounds simultaneously of private property and of public pleasure and knowledge. The landscape and its plants and animals could now be read – and represented – in multiple and sometimes contradictory ways: as objects of aesthetic apprehension; as income-producing property; and as the terrain of scientific investigation. While these ways of thinking about nature had existed for centuries, in these decades both broad cultural tendencies and specific events worked to reorganize these discourses of the landscape and to configure them differently in relation to each other, intensifying disparities between already conflicting modes of representation. This irreducibly plural and sometime paradoxical status of the landscape in general was complicated or intensified in the case of those specific pieces of British terrain designated crown forests. Carole Fabricant has argued that by the mid-eighteenth century the natural world had become the arena in which codes of gender and class were negotiated, consolidated, and contested; the crown forest, by virtue of its identification with monarchical prerogative, was also a space for the consolidation and contestation of national identity.[4] Thus crown forests and their literary and graphic representations constitute a fascinating test case for what Linda Colley calls "the invention of Britishness" during the long eighteenth century.[5] This chapter proposes that in 1789 George and his propagandists used the crown forest as a theater to stage and consolidate his image as a truly British monarch.

Colley describes the rise of a "new patriotic cult of the monarchy" in the second half of the reign of George III.[6] The first two Hanoverians, she suggests, saw themselves as Whig-identified politicians rather than as national symbols. In contrast, George III sought to package himself as a British icon, and, for a range of reasons, was increasingly successful at doing so from the 1780s on. A crucial part of this repackaging involved an appeal to domestication as a national principle, in two distinct senses. The first of these defines "domestic" in opposition to "foreign": for the refurbishing of Windsor Castle, George ordered a series of wall paintings "glorifying Britain's real and mythic history"; for the new construction at Kew, he chose an architectural style, Gothic revival, that made a similar appeal to a glorious and very specifically British past. The second of these senses has to do with "domestic" in opposition to "public" or "political": over and over again, George and his family were represented very precisely as members of a family.[7]

George III's reinvention of monarchy as domestic, as familial rather than dynastic, frames the cultural work done by his 1789 visit to the New Forest.[8] Throughout the early modern period, the cultural significance of the royal forests underwent a dramatic if gradual transition in conjunction with the transformations of models of monarchy. The feudal incarnation of the king-in-the-forest as Nimrod, lord and hunter of beasts and men, was replaced by the rather more prosaic figure of the royal silviculturalist.[9] The Farmer-King – Cincinnatus updated via an Enlightenment ethos of capitalized improvement – was icon and inspiration for the full range of eighteenth-century literature, from bucolic and topographic poetry to agricultural and silvicultural treatises to local natural histories to, as I will argue here, the novel. The image became indelibly associated with George III, whose agrarian interests earned him the ambiguous nickname "Farmer George."

THE CROWN FOREST: THEATER, TREE FARM, NO-MAN'S LAND

What exactly was a crown forest, and how did its definition change across
the early modern period? According to the 1717 edition of John Manwood's 1592 *Treatise of the Laws of the Forest*:

A forest is a certain territory of woody grounds and fruitful pastures, privileged for wild beasts and fowls of forest, chase, and warren, to rest and abide
there in the safe protection of the king, for his delight and pleasure . . . For
the preservation and continuance of which said place, together with the vert
and venison, there are particular officers, laws, and privileges belonging to the
same, requisite for that purpose, and proper only to a forest, and to no other
place.[10]

Those who held land, resided, or worked within the boundaries of crown
forests were subject to a highly elaborated body of law specific to the
forests that governed property and hunting rights. These laws were
remarkably detailed, covering not only obvious resources like timber,
nuts, and fruit but also waste branches and twigs; not only such charismatic game animals as deer and boar but also rabbits and squirrels.
Forest law was enforced by an elaborately articulated corps of forest
officials: agisters, bowbearers, huntsmen, justices, keepers, rangers,
regarders, verderers, verminers, and wardens, and woodwards. Such a
proliferation of regulators suggests the importance of the most minute
aspects of the forest, not only as economic resources but also as features
of a symbolic terrain shaped by a feudal understanding of kingship.[11]

With the seventeenth-century consolidation of the field of silviculture, a new way of reading the crown forest began to emerge, one
indebted to the discourse of political economy. The naval losses of the
Seven Years' War and the rupture with the North American colonies
intensified longstanding concerns over British timber supplies. The gradual transformation of the crown forest from theater of royal charisma
into tree farm for the British navy meant that timber increasingly came
to be seen as a commodity, a valuable economic resource, to be farmed
according to the capital-intensive practices of agrarian improvement.

The influence of political economics is everywhere evident in the seventeen Reports of the Commissioners on the Woods, Forests, and Land
Revenues of the Crown, issued from 1787 to 1793. The immediate occasion for the Commission's appointment by Parliament was the perception of a serious lack of naval timber. According to the Third Report,
the Commissioners of the Navy were getting only 2,000 of their yearly

requirement of 25,000 loads of timber from the crown forests, the rest being purchased on the open market at great expense.[12] This expense could be minimized if the crown forests were rationally administered according to sound silvicultural practices. The Commissioners initially considered blanket privatization: many of the crown forests could be officially "disafforested," converted to the highest bidder. This would reduce the hemorrhaging overhead expenses associated with the idiosyncratic administrative apparatuses of the Forests (hunting lodges, other official residences and salaries, perquisites and common rights, etc.). Private timber entrepreneurs, running efficient and cost-effective tree farms, could sell timber to the British Navy at a better price.

However, the Commissioners' final recommendation rejected privatization as a general solution. Because of the complexity of its multiple significations across a range of cultural registers, the crown forest is a key site in which to observe what we might call the delamination of various codes or discourses used to represent the natural world that, as Robert Markley's chapter in this volume makes clear, had begun accelerating during the seventeenth century. In the Commissioners' reports, national prestige, silviculture, and free-market capitalism prove radically incompatible: the Commissioners acknowledged that when it came to growing the mature oaks needed for shipbuilding, no invisible hand would arrange supply and demand according to the infallible laws of the market. In fact, free-market mechanisms would actually work to decrease the naval timber supply:

an Addition to the Demand for Naval Timber does not produce a proportional Supply from private Property; and the Reason is obvious: An Oak must grow an Hundred Years, or more, before it comes to Maturity; but the Profits arising from Tillage or Pasture are more certain and immediate, and perhaps as great: It cannot, therefore, be expected that many private Individuals will lay out Money on the Expectation of Advantages which they themselves can have no Chance to enjoy: Commerce and Industry seek for, and are supported by, speedy Returns of Gain, however small; and the more generally the Commercial Spirit shall prevail in the Country, the less Probability is there that planting of Woods, for the Advantage of Posterity, will be preferred to the immediate Profits of Agriculture.[13]

The industrious "Commercial Spirit" seeking "speedy Returns of Gain" cannot be expected to wait a hundred years for a hardwood plantation to mature, and for this reason the state would have to stay in the lumber business. The Commissioners eventually recommended that the Crown Forests should in most cases be preserved, with all their "improvident and often ill-defined Grants" and "the confused Mixture of Rights created by them," even though, as in some Hobbesian nightmare, "the Whole is a perpetual Struggle of jarring Interests, in which no Party can improve his own Share without hurting that of another."[14]

Paradoxically, then, despite their anachronistic idiosyncrasies and economic counterproductivity, crown forests were essential to the Commissioners' up-to-date vision of a commercial-imperial Great Britain. As I will argue, George III's visit to the New Forest, itself conditioned by both official and unofficial motives, suggests his grasp of this complicated mixture of the crown forests' discursive contexts. His daily agenda during the visit seems designed to insist on the double-lobed meaning of the *private* as a concept that links the family and the market, domesticity and property rights, and this very connection is the key to George's revision of a national identity of property-owners.

IV

AT HOME IN THE FOREST

Among British crown forests, the New Forest had always been something of a special case.[15] First of all, there is the irony implicit in its name. This forest is "new" only in relative terms, for it was established by William I, whereas the other crown forests supposedly antedate historical record. The story of its founding is tied to a national mythology of the Norman Yoke: to establish his new game preserve, William is said to have ordered some two dozen existing villages and churches across thirty miles to be razed.[16] Pope's *Windsor-Forest* (1713) takes up this material in its survey of the dismal state of the British forests from William I to William III, epitomized by the New Forest's history of Nimrodian tyranny and nativist revenge. Obviously, the triumphant complicity between British merchants and nature herself that produces the political and commercial empire celebrated in Pope's poem could not be staged on soil so saturated with the blood of both royal prey and royal hunters, and thus the New Forest is displaced by Windsor's pastoral retreats and groves under the reigning Protestant Stuart.[17]

Although several crown forests were sold after the Restoration as a fund-raising measure, the New Forest retained both its official status and its reputation as a refuge for wildness through the eighteenth and well into the nineteenth century. In 1781 an anonymous writer described residents of the Hampshire forests as an "idle, useless and disorderly set of people" who stole the materials for the very shacks they lived in.

Charles Vancouver, writing in 1813, referred to the royal forests of Hampshire collectively as "that nest and conservatory of sloth, idleness and misery."[18] The sense of the New Forest's "otherness" is most strikingly articulated in Robert Mudie's 1838 survey, which draws its terms of comparison from the South Sea voyages: "The district of the New Forest is one of the most peculiar . . . in England. It forms, as it were, a country apart," resembling "one of those larger islands in the Pacific, which have their margins settled by people insofar civilized, and carrying trade, while the interior is in a state of nature."[19] The connection Mudie imagines between a relatively primitive island on the far side of the globe and this woodland in the heart of Hampshire is based on the Forest's peculiarly bloody, even accursed history: among the "subjects which are almost certain to be suggested by even a simple allusion to the New Forest" is "the vengeance inflicted by heaven upon the country" in the figure of William the Conqueror.

Given the vexed relations between the crown and the New Forest thematized in both popular and high-cultural mythologizations, George III's 1789 tour of the New Forest had to stage a relation between monarch and landscape different from that described in Manwood's *Treatise*, Pope's *Windsor-Forest*, the Forest Commission reports, and the county surveys. The ceremonies built into George's visit did indeed gesture toward the older feudal relation between monarch and forest. In her journal entries about the visit, Burney records that the royal family stayed in a hunting lodge that had belonged to Charles II, the last king to visit the New Forest. Here George participated in an elaborate, self-consciously archaizing ceremony designed to commemorate feudal land-tenure customs. He was officially welcomed to the Forest by its traditional officers: the Warden, verderers, huntsmen, and foresters, the latter dressed in new green outfits, "each with a bugle-horn."[20] The chief local landholder presented to the king the two white greyhounds by right of which gift the freehold had originally been established centuries ago; Burney remarks with pleasure that the dogs were "peculiarly decorated."[21] In this spectacularization of feudalism, the costumes of both humans and dogs invoke the king-in-the-forest as Nimrod, conqueror and hunter.

However, other scenes from the visit form a striking contrast with this appeal to the past. Consider the journals' reports of the royal family vacation. In this context, newspapers are themselves tropes of modernity, and therefore appropriate sites for the (re)construction of the king's image. Accounts of the royal family's evening walks and the accompanying manifestations of the inhabitants' loyal devotion suggest the conscious invention of a new relation between the landscape and its owner. In these scenes, widely disseminated to the British reading public through the provincial and metropolitan press, George is presented not as the feudal hunting-king but as a benevolently paternalistic landlord who enjoys the rustic pleasures of the Forest among his tenants. One article describes how George gave five guineas to an old man who showed him the local picturesque sights; meanwhile, the queen found a deserving widow and mother of six whose parish allowance she doubled.[22] Striking the same domesticating note as the newspapers, Burney records that to give the populace pleasure, the royal family dined with their windows open on their first evening in Lyndhurst. Unfortunately, the enthusiastic crowd trampled down "all the paling, and much of the hedges, and some of the windows" despite being "perfectly civil and well-behaved,"[23] so thereafter the curtains had to be closed, but the point about George's domestic harmony had presumably been made.

In these accounts, the royal family – represented explicitly as a family – are shown as very much "at home" in the New Forest. Their performance of gentrified domesticity, combining picturesque tourism with paternalist charity, was thoroughly effective: the *Hampshire Chronicle* noted fulsomely that "the princesses are looked up to and almost worshipped as rural deities for their beauty, elegance of manners, condescension, and goodness."[24] This domestication of the New Forest exorcizes the tyrannical shadow of William the Norman Bastard and clears the ground for a further reconciliation of alienated national elements.

V

A "FEMALE ROBINSON CRUSOE"

If, as I argue, the visit to the New Forest plays a part in George III's reinvention of monarchy, what happens when it is restaged in Burney's *Wanderer*? This question is particularly pressing since, by the mid-1790s when Burney began drafting *The Wanderer*, the image of the prosperous and paternalistically benevolent Farmer George had already been questioned, as John Barrell documents in his Afterword to this volume. While critics have been drawn to the relatively brief episode at Stonehenge, reading that as the novel's narrative and hermeneutic crux, I find the georgic sequences in Books 8 and 9 of central importance to a broader political and cultural program.[25] Burney's New Forest sequence represents a deliberate engagement with the eighteenth-century georgic tradition, not its displacement in favor of a new "Romantic" mode.[26] Although *The Wanderer* describes itself as the story of a "female Robinson Crusoe" (p. 873), of a woman forced to support herself through her own labor in a world hostile to working women, it is not a story about, or one that calls for, women's emancipation from patriarchy through equal access to the means of economic self-determination, for the novel's all-pervasive fantasy is that of a return to patriarchal protection.[27]

Before the novel opens, Juliet has been compelled to marry a loathsome Jacobin minor official, an "agent of the inhuman Robespierre" (p. 739), to save the life of her guardian, a benevolent and aged bishop. To avoid consummating the marriage, she flees France for England *incognita*. There she is harried and hunted from shelter to shelter by her nominal husband and his agents. At the opening of Book 8, a near-discovery forces Juliet to flee from the London millinery shop she and her childhood friend have opened to support themselves. She scrambles into a coach without asking its destination and eventually finds herself in the New Forest, adopting a rural working-woman's attire as camouflage.

Initially, the forest seems to promise to soothe and even redeem Juliet's anguish by excluding the social order altogether. Burney rehearses a physico-theological reading of the natural world, nature as God's lesson plan, that sets up this exclusion. Juliet, she writes:

mounted a hillock to take a general survey of the spot, and thought all paradise was opened to her view . . . Here, for the first time, she ceased to sigh for social intercourse; she had no void, no want; her mind was sufficient to itself; Nature, Reflection, and Heaven seemed her own! Oh, Gracious Providence! she cried, supreme in goodness as in power! What lesson can all the eloquence of rhetoric, science, erudition, or philosophy produce, to restore tranquillity to the troubled, to preserve it in the wise, to make it cheerful to the innocent, – like the simple view of beautiful nature? (p. 676)

The urban-Gothic atmosphere of pursuit is effaced by the sublimity of the Forest's natural scenery, which seems to carry Juliet temporarily beyond the constraints of socially mediated identity.

This natural pedagogy is soon challenged by what the Forest actually teaches about British society. On the one hand, the novel gestures briefly toward an emancipatory reading of the lives of women in the New Forest: Juliet has entered an alternative economy, one driven primarily by the labor of rural women as freelance traders and travelers. Unlike middle-class urbanites, these women are not suspicious of Juliet's enforced isolation and mobility: "Free from the niceties of custom in higher life, and unembarrassed by the perplexities of discriminating scruples, the good women, often lonely travellers themselves, saw nothing in such a situation to excite distrust" (p. 660). On the other hand, this toleration of increased female mobility does not of itself guarantee pastoral harmony. Juliet learns repeatedly that the "mercenary . . . spirit" of the rest of the world has also "found entrance in a spot which seemed fitted to the virtuous innocence of our yet untainted first parents; or to the guileless hospitality of the poet's golden age" (p. 678). In this economic sense, the Forest proves to have been always already part of the society Juliet thought she was leaving behind when she entered it.

At other moments, Burney emphasizes the distance between the indigenes of the Forest and the cultivated observer, offering a sort of proto-ethnographic account of its human residents, who almost seem to belong to a different species. In Salisbury, on the outskirts of the Forest, Juliet finds that she can barely communicate with the children of a New Forest woman. They respond to her urgings

rather as if they did not understand, than as if they resisted her counsel . . . The children were not able to give any account of who they were that was intelligible; not of whence they came, save that it was from a great, great way off . . . To Juliet scarcely a word of their narrations was intelligible; but to the ears of their mother, accustomed to their dialect . . . these prattling details were as potent in eloquence, as the most polished orations of Cicero or Demosthenes, are to those of the classical scholar. (pp. 656–8)

This account of linguistic distance suggests something like the ethnographer's ironic relation to a group of "primitive" subjects. Juliet is in what we might think of as an *internal* "contact zone," adapting Mary Louise Pratt's term for "the space of colonial encounters."[28] The sense of alienation expressed here anticipates Mudie's 1838 comparison of the new Forest to a remote Pacific island, an appropriately "other" and exotic terrain for the female Robinson Crusoe.

Inside the Forest, Juliet must carefully negotiate relations with the natives, for the local customs are as opaque to her as the local dialect. Looking for a place to sleep, she comes upon a "small hut" where her money buys a night's bed and board. She is surprised by the refinement of the Mixon family's meal: the food "required not either air or exercise to give it zest; it consisted of scraps of pheasant and partridge, which the children called *chicky biddy*; and slices of such fine-grained mutton, that she could with difficulty persuade herself that she was not eating venison" (p. 679). Again, the ethnographic precision with which the children's food vocabulary is noted signals the manifold remotenesses of the territory Juliet has now entered, and Burney plainly suggests that the alienation is both linguistic and ethical: although this family lives in the very heart of Hampshire, they are outside the moral borders of Great Britain. This ethical otherness is brought home to Juliet that very night, when the husband sneaks out of the hut and returns with a mysterious sack. After he passes through the room in which Juliet is feigning sleep, she sees that "the passage from door to door was traced with bloody spots" (p. 682). Juliet is convinced that the bag contains the corpse of some unfortunate traveler, and she resolves to report the crime, even though this will mean exposing herself to her own pursuers.

However, no one Juliet subsequently encounters in the Forest shows much interest in this incident, which reinforces her anxious sense that she is beyond British law. Only later is the issue clarified, while Juliet is staying with Dame Fairfield, the mother of the children she met in Salisbury. When she tells her hostess the tale of the bloody bundle, the woman breaks down in tears, admitting her husband had been out with Nat Mixon that night. Juliet at first assumes he too is guilty of murder, but after some mutual confusion, she at last understands that what is in question is not the robbery and murder of travelers but a simple case of poaching. Dame Fairfield cries, " 'Why sure, and sure, there be no daunger to nobody in our Forest!' . . . [She] then confessed, that her husband and Nat Mixon were deer-stealers" (p. 714). In this princess-and-the-pea retrospect on Juliet's stay with the Mixon family, her (implicitly aristocratic) palate is vindicated: after all, she had not been deceived about the Mixon family's exceptionally delicate "mutton"; it really was venison, that noble and forbidden game.[29]

As these accounts of moral and gustatory confusion suggest, the New Forest initially figures in *The Wanderer* as in many ways a world apart from the rest of British society. However, this sense of distance and aliena-tion is reversed in the rest of the scene between Dame Fairfield and Juliet by their mutual invocation of the notion of private property as the principle that grounds and orders the New Forest, just as it does the rest of Great Britain. Juliet is pleased that she need not report her hostess's husband for murder, but she nonetheless insists on the wrong-ness of stealing, especially "the heinousness of a breach of trust" (p. 715) involved in stealing one's landlord's property. Dame Fairfield admits that the "deer were as much the King's Majesty's as the Forest" (p. 715) itself, and for this reason she never lets her children eat the illegal game her husband brings home: "it might strangle us down our throats; for it be all his King's Majesty's; and I do no' know why we should take hisn goods, when a do never come to take none of ours! for we be never mislested, night nor day" (p. 717). Her pious allusion to private property counters the idea that the Forest is a moral No-Man's Land filled with squatters, thieves, and murderers, the rejects of the rest of the nation. Instead, it is the property of the Crown, and the king its benevolent and watchful landlord. Her implicitly Lockean notion of subjectivity defines human beings as such according to their possession of private property; in this sense, king and subject differ only in degree, not kind, and are intimately linked by an economy of mutual obligations.

Before the New Forest sequence closes, then, the apparent social rupture articulated as a geographical and ethical distance between the Forest and the rest of British society is repaired by a description of the mutual affection between Britain's royal family and the people they rule that recapitulates what Burney observed during the 1789 tour and that echoes the domesticizing rhetoric of the *Hampshire Chronicle*'s reports. Dame Fairfield gushes about the king:

And a do deserve well of us all; for a be as good a gentlemon as ever broke bread! which we did all see, when a was in these parts; as well as his good lady, the Queen, who had a smile for the lowest of us, God bless un! and all their pretty ones! for they were made up of good nature and charity; and had no more pride than the new-born baby. And we did all love 'em, when they were in these parts, so as the like never was seen before. (p. 717)

In the context of Burney's novel, the New Forest episode represents the protagonist's encounter with a georgic world of labor that displays the fundamental virtue and industriousness of ordinary British men and, more particularly, British women, and furthermore affirms property rights as the key to a coherent and unified "British" identity. This display works to make plausible the denouement of Burney's plot: Juliet's enlightened reconstruction of her own social identity as the daughter of an aristocratic British family.

VI

THE CROWN FOREST AND FEMALE GEORGIC

We may be tempted to propose that in writing this story of a female Robinson Crusoe Burney was making a potentially revolutionary claim about women's narrative possibilities, even perhaps about the future of actual women in British society, a claim bringing together the discourses of literary georgic, landscape aesthetics, natural history, and property law.[30] Indeed, Burney's gendered inflection of the georgic mode in *The Wanderer* is an important – and implicitly feminist – gesture. When the female Robinson Crusoe explores her identity among the working men and women of the New Forest, she recovers georgic as a narrative framework for women's lives, and opens up new narrative terrain for women writers.

Read in the light of *The Wanderer*'s conclusion, however, this recovery is relativized and made ambiguous. For only by marking the New Forest as the property of the benevolent Farmer George, and *Father* George – that is, as a doubly patriarchal terrain – does Burney obtain a place for her heroine within it. In the end, the borders of the new narrative landscape opened up by Burney's last novel are everywhere signposted by a paternalist authority that alone guarantees genealogical and national identity. This reading revises Margaret Doody's comment that "the novelist produces no propaganda for, or even references to, the pathos of suffering monarch . . . There is no King Louis's head haunting the pages of *The Wanderer*."[31] The pathos of suffering monarchy is indeed represented, but indirectly: not by Louis's severed head, but by George's mental alienation. Burney's defensive filial response to that pathos, as I have argued here, shapes the conclusion of this text.

Such an ambivalent resolution of her heroine's "FEMALE DIFFICULTIES" is likely to be staged only by a writer who, far from rejecting the embrace of the Father, definitively identifies herself as a daughter.[32] I have argued that *The Wanderer* contains a double narrative of reconciliation: that of the novel's heroine, restored to her aristocratic family, and that of Burney's nation, exhausted by two decades of war abroad and troubles at home. The novel also mediates Burney's own reconciliation with her readers, including as chief among these her father. *The Wanderer*'s dedication to Charles Burney, who lived just long enough to see its publication, has a powerfully epitaphic quality. If in 1814 it was accurate to call Burney "the most eminent living [British] novelist," it is also crucial to note that she "had not published a novel in eighteen years," and also that she had been living abroad from 1802 to 1812.[33] *The Wanderer*'s ambiguous georgic fantasy addresses the conflicts, deferrals, and displacements that lay behind its publication. Although internal and external evidence suggests that the novel was drafted during the later 1790s, Burney continued to work on it in France in the always troubled, sometimes terrifying post-revolutionary climate of the first dozen years of the century.[34] In this context, Burney's nostalgic staging of George's act of self-reconstruction and national consolidation suggests the desire to reconcile her own multiple identities as author, British national, spouse, and daughter. The series of newly coherent and properly British identities written into being in *The Wanderer* are organized around and guaranteed by a revision of royal identity that looks back a quarter of a century: no longer Nimrod the hunter, a charismatic figure of conquest and violence, the king-in-the-forest becomes the gentleman-landlord, a gentrified "Farmer George" whose benevolent attentions extend even beyond the most remote corners of his kingdom to those of his subjects, like Burney herself, in exile.

At the opening of the nineteenth century, then, the *crown forest* sustains a range of suggestive readings of national identity. In the domestications of the New Forest practiced by George III and Frances Burney, this terrain is no longer the feudal theater of monarchical charisma and prerogative, nor yet merely a political economist's neutral repository of marketable resources. Instead, as these various accounts of a royal visit demonstrate, the crown forest served as a screen on which to project images of a new society, dramas of reconciliation and transformation, and fantasies of personal, professional, and political identity.

NOTES

1 *Hampshire Chronicle, or Southampton, Winchester, and Portsmouth Mercury*, June 29, 1789.
2 Ibid., July 20, 1789.
3 See Raymond Williams, *Keywords: A Vocabulary of Culture and Society* (1976; rev. edn. New York, 1983), entries on "culture" and "nature," pp. 87–93, 219–24.
4 Fabricant, "The Literature of Domestic Tourism and the Public Consumption of Private Property" in Felicity Nussbaum and Laura Brown, eds., *The New Eighteenth Century: Theory Politics English Literature* (New York, 1987), pp. 254–75.
5 Colley, *Britons: Forging the Nation 1707–1837* (New Haven, Conn., 1992), p. 1.
6 Ibid., p. 210.
7 On George's building projects, see ibid., pp. 214–15; on George's public relations, see ibid., pp. 201, 203.
8 For this opposition, see Simon Schama, "The Domestication of Majesty," *The Journal of Interdisciplinary History* 17: 1 (Summer, 1989): 155–83.
9 On feudal crown forests, see Robert Pogue Harrison, *Forests: The Shadow of Civilization* (Chicago, Ill., 1992), chapter 2. See also Simon Schama, *Landscape and Memory* (New York, 1995), pp. 135–84; and Stephen Daniels, "The Political Iconography of Woodland in later Georgian England" in Denis Cosgrove and Stephen Daniels, eds., *The Iconography of Landscape: Essays on the Symbolic*

Representation, Design and Use of Past Environments (Cambridge, 1988), pp. 43–82. Keith Thomas's *Man and the Natural World: A History of the Modern Sensibility* (New York, 1983) surveys English early modern attitudes toward trees and forests.

10 Cited in Harrison, *Forests*, p. 143.
11 See E. P. Thompson's account of Walpole's purchase of the rangership of Richmond Park in *Whigs and Hunters*, p. 181.
12 *House of Commons Sessional Papers*, 145 vols. (1975), 76: 101.
13 Ibid., 76: 101.
14 Ibid., 76: 102.
15 On the history of the crown forests, see R. K. G. Grant, *The Royal Forests of England* (Stroud, 1991) and Charles Young, *The Royal Forests of Medieval England* ([n. p.], 1979).
16 Historians now agree that this figure is exaggerated, but its very persistence suggests lasting popular discontent around the crown forests. See Young, *Royal Forests*, pp. 7–8.
17 Windsor Castle itself represents an absorption of several traumatic moments in English history in that it stands on the reputed site of both the Arthurian round table and William I's castle, but the point remains that Pope's poem doesn't find a way to absorb and recast the New Forest, as Burney's novel does.
18 Anon., *Observations on a Pamphlet entitled an Enquiry into the Advantages and Disadvantages, Resulting from Bills of Enclosure* (Shrewsbury, 1781), cited in Neeson, *Commoners*, p. 33. Vancouver, *General View of the Agriculture of Hants* (1813), cited in Thompson, *Whigs and Hunters*, p. 121.
19 Mudie, *Hampshire*, 3 vols. (1838), 2: 217, 218.
20 *Diary and Letters of Mme D'Arblay, 1778–1840*, ed. Charlotte Barrett, 6 vols. (1905), 4: 290.
21 Ibid., 4: 290.
22 *Hampshire Chronicle*, July 6, 1789.
23 Diary and Letters, 4: 291.
24 *Hampshire Chronicle*, July 20, 1789.
25 On the resonance of georgic from the seventeenth through the nineteenth centuries, see Kevis Goodman, *Passionate Work: Wordsworth's Georgics of the Feelings and the Emergence of English Romanticism* (forthcoming, Stanford University Press). I am greatly indebted to Professor Goodman for our discussions of georgic as literary genre and cultural category.
26 On the Stonehenge episode, see Julia Epstein, *The Iron Pen: Frances Burney and the Politics of Women's Writing* (Madison, Wisc., 1989), pp. 179–80, 186; and Claudia Johnson, *Equivocal Beings: Politics, Gender, and Sentimentality in the 1790s* (Chicago, Ill., 1995), pp. 186–87. See also Margaret Anne Doody, *Frances Burney: The Life in the Works* (New Brunswick, N.J., 1988), and her "Introduction" to *The Wanderer; Or, Female Difficulties*, ed. Margaret Anne Doody, Robert. L. Mack, Peter Sabor (Oxford, 1991), pp. xxxvi–vii. Subsequent citations to this edition are given parenthetically.

27 On the economic registers of Burney's writing, see James Thompson, *Models of Value: Eighteenth-Century Political Economy and the Novel* (Durham, N.C., 1996); and Catherine Gallagher, *Nobody's Story: The Vanishing Acts of Women Writers in the Marketplace, 1670–1820* (Berkeley, Calif., 1994).

28 Pratt, *Imperial Eyes: Travel Writing and Transculturation* (New York, 1992), p. 6. My notion of an "internal"contact zone is indebted to Michael Hechter, *Internal Colonialism: The Celtic Fringe in British National Development 1536–1966* (Berkeley, Calif., 1975)

29 On venison, see Thompson, *Whigs and Hunters*, pp. 158–61; and Douglas Hay, "Poaching and the Game Laws on Cannock Chase," in Douglas Hay, Peter Linebaugh, John G. Rule, E. P. Thompson, and Cal Winslow, eds., *Albion's Fatal Tree: Crime and Society in Eighteenth-Century England* (New York, 1975), pp. 189–253, especially p. 246.

30 This reading of *The Wanderer* modifies Kurt Heinzelman's claim that the georgic as a literary mode disappears in the late eighteenth century. Burney's novel suggests that instead, like Juliet herself returning to her native land in blackface, georgic stays around in disguise or translation, now surveying the arts of women's labor. See his "Roman Georgic in the Georgian Age: A Theory of Romantic Genre," *Texas Studies in Literature and Language* 33: 2 (1991): 182–214.

31 Doody, "Introduction," *The Wanderer*, p. xiv.

32 The quoted phrase is, of course, the novel's subtitle. On Burney's relations with her father, see Patricia Meyer Spacks, *Imagining the Self: Autobiography and Novel in Eighteenth-Century England* (Cambridge, Mass., 1976); and Kristina Straub, *Divided Fictions: Fanny Burney and Feminine Strategy* (Lexington, Ky., 1987). See also Gallagher, *Nobody's Story*, pp. 211–18; and Johnson, *Equivocal Beings*, pp. 142, 174.

33 Johnson, *Equivocal Beings*, p. 186.

34 See the Dedication's account of the writing of *The Wanderer*, p. 4.

CHAPTER 13

"Wild outcasts of society": the transit of the Gypsies in Romantic period poetry

Anne F. Janowitz

This chapter considers the imagery of Gypsies in the poetry of rurality toward the end of the period of transition from customary to waged economic regimes. Well before the mid nineteenth-century burst of interest in Gypsy life as a lens for focusing images of domestic exoticism, evinced in the works of George Borrow such as *Lavengro* (1851) and *Romany Rye* (1857), one finds many representations of groups of Gypsy travelers within the rhetoric of place. These include both representations of Gypsies as thieves and outsiders, and the empathetic evocation of Gypsy life as emblematic of rural poverty and hardship.[1] The more popular "Romantic" Gypsy figuring freedom and independence comes into prominence later in the nineteenth century, under the auspices of an urban and anthropological intellectual project, while poetry written during the Romantic period is quite harsh and bitter in presenting Gypsy-travelers.

In speculating on the meanings of the Gypsy, it may be of some interest to pair this rural domestic alien with its urban mirror figure, the Jew. And the figure of the Jew, which in earlier centuries and then again in the twentieth century is most often linked to the city, and to the working of finance rather than agricultural economy, occupies an interesting place in the iconography of the late eighteenth- and early nineteenth-century countryside. Unlike the Gypsy *band*, the Jew is imaged in isolation, either as an itinerant peddler or, more mysteriously, as a version of the legend of the Wandering Jew.[2] Interestingly, it is at least in part by way of absorption into the literary image of the Jew as wandering exile, and within the production of a racialist language in the mid-nineteenth century, linked to anthropological investigation, that a simultaneously sentimental and racist image of the Gypsy was formulated.

While Gypsy and Wandering Jew share strangeness and geographical mobility, what distinguishes them is the valence of their relationship to history and identity, which may be why they appear so often in poetry of the late eighteenth and early nineteenth centuries: poetry which, defined as Romantic, takes self-hood in time as a constitutive theme. In poems by William Wordsworth and by John Clare, the Gypsy is rarely imaged as an isolate, but collectively as a "wild brood," or as a member of the "vagabond tribe," and often this figure is female and maternal, available as someone recognizable albeit alien. The Jew, on the other hand, is known by his isolation, and masculine inwardness, and this image delineates inwardness as a condition of modernity, while the Gypsy figures community as a condition of the past. If the Jew is the repository of the feeling of historicity as an abstraction, the Gypsy often appears as the concrete bearer of the canny and superseded knowledge of native plebeian society. The paradox of Gypsy and Jew is that the Jew represents history, but conveys solitude and some kind of essential inwardness – the Wandering Jew is the early nineteenth-century rural *flaneur* – while the Gypsy, apparently without history, becomes the screen onto which the English native is reinscribed as an alien.

In brief, the Gypsy images various and competing structures of feeling about traditional, customary society, and the losses and gains involved in the movement into voluntaristic individualism, while the Wandering Jew focuses the aspirations and anxieties of the individuated, often isolated, subject of the modern regime.[3] As the bearer of rural, customary knowledge, and on a seasonal route across England and into the suburbs of London, the Gypsy band delivers the country into the city. The Jew had been banished and has returned, while Gypsy life parallels rural customary life, and so the Romany company appears even more houseless in an age when agricultural customary society is giving way to its waged form. The Gypsy is a figure who, living off the commons and waste in an age of enclosure, returns as a quasi-fantastical double to the English cottager. Although actual Jewish peddlers and the traveling Gypsy crews might be barely distinguishable from the large numbers of other persons displaced through parish exclusion, enclosure, failed harvests, and the ravaging press gang, their importance as images in poetry resides in the way they support the imagining of identity in a transitional world; one poised between customary and waged labor. The exchange between metropolitan and rural cultures that both Gypsies and Jews exemplify is grounded in historical processes at work since the mid-sixteenth century.

An exemplary moment occurs in Wordsworth's "The Female Vagrant," one of the poems in the first edition of *Lyrical Ballads* (1798), a volume dedicated to giving voice to patterns of rural life. Born into the life of a rural cottager, the Female Vagrant finds enclosure and displacement fragmenting her family, sending them from their place as traditional cottager laborers in the "old hereditary nook" out into the "free" waged labor of the provincial town and then to America, where they suffer deprivation and death.[4] Returning home to a world which now refuses to recognize or shelter her, the Female Vagrant manages her fate by adopting the role, first of Gypsy and then of Jew, finding identity itself to be both native and strange. The chaos of war unmoors identity, and the Female Vagrant finds herself traveling in the welcoming company of a Gypsy clan, and then isolates herself as a version of the solitary Wandering Jew. Among the Gypsies, the Female Vagrant is invited to become one of what appears to be a traditional and horizontal community where "all belonged to all, and each was chief." But she finds a canker of dissimulation at the core of the group, for these are Gypsy-thieves, and she takes on the "self-accused" penitent figure of Ahasuerus, the Wandering Jew, because she has, she says, "my inner self abused," invoking the morality of inwardness.[5] I take her choice of solitary identity to be emblematic of a critical Romantic period encounter between a view of identity as socially constructed and ensuing from rank location, and a view of identity as notionally prior to social choices and engagements: namely, a dialectic between identity as socially produced and as voluntaristic.[6]

When the Female Vagrant opts for the identity she can *choose*, she elects to move out from the customary world and into the world of individuation and individual sufferings. Even though the Gypsy crew welcomes the Female Vagrant, she remains separate from them, because her identity has been forged out of her personal experience of being displaced from cottager culture. As a solitary, however, and like the many Wandering Jews who figure in Romantic period poems, she becomes a candidate for Romantic transcendence.

The figure of the Gypsy is always replete with the particular social content of the rural commoner turning into something else: like the deracinated commoner on the road, the Gypsy's is a "Hard-faring race! / They pick their fuel out of every hedge, / Which, kindled with dry leaves, just saves unquenched the spark of life."[7] On the other hand, the anti-Semitic stereotype of the Jewish peddler is peculiarly shadowed by the sanitized presence of the Wandering Jew in many poetical locations.[8] The Jew, much more quickly than the Gypsy, becomes a generalized and abstracted image of consciousness in isolation. So it transpires that the notion of the Wandering Jew and that of the Wanderer, *tout court*, merge into the figuring of the essential modern self.

I

The vivid figure of the gypsy on the common or in a nook of woods or waste brings together the outlandish and the familiar. In the early nineteenth century, the exoticism of tribes of "Egyptian" nomads wandering the English countryside coincides with the more domestic cunning of beggar and thief, and with the residual canniness of the medieval "cunning man" and "wise woman" of the rural commons.[9] In poems by Wordsworth, Clare, Horace Smith, George Crabbe, and Samuel Rogers, Gypsies appear frequently, and are presented under a double aspect. Most obviously, they operate on the periphery of society. As economic agents, Gypsies are imaged as a "pilfering race," contriving "midnight theft to hatch."[10] Though one might expect to counterpoise agricultural commoners as sedentary, against Gypsies as nomadic, the reality of life in the period made the two rather more interchangeable, with Gypsies following a seasonal route of temporary agricultural work, and displaced agricultural laborers en route to the city for a part of the year as well.[11]

Socially, they appear to live without the sense of shame of sanctioned society: "I looked reproof – they saw – but neither hung his head," Wordsworth moralizes over two Gypsy youths; while Crabbe is repelled by a Gypsy girl, whose "light laugh and roguish leer express'd / The vice implanted in her youthful breast."[12]

The Gypsy motif in these examples serves as an anxious negative type for the laboring poor, commoners whose customary practices of access to the fruits and game of the commons and wastes have now been legislated into the theft of goods from enclosed and privatized lands. But running athwart the (negative) Gypsy image, and coexisting with it in the same poems, are versions of the Gypsy as a noble exotic, either a "fit person for a Queen / To lead those ancient Amazon files," or a prescient "Sibyl," whose "Eastern manners, garb, and face / Appear a strange chimera," disturbing the familiarity of the landscape with admonitions of other worlds and ages.[13] This twofold image of the Gypsy explains Gypsy cunning as both deceit and wisdom, and the imputed Gypsy identity may be thought of as a version of the return of the repressed under the sign of the uncanny: the native peasantry, with its customary knowledge, returning as an exotic foreign "tribe."[14]

The presentation of Gypsies offers an alternatively comforting and frightening picture: the clan is presented as firstly, contemporary thieves and vagabonds who embody an unmasterable version of the past and, secondly, apparently foreign and exotic presences who harbor a resolvable familiar and domestic identity of rural community life. The centrality of the female Gypsy in these poems is noteworthy. Many critics have noted the peculiar status of women in the landscape in Romantic period poetry, where the assimilation of femininity to nature often renders women silent epiphenomena of the landscape.[15] But the plebeian female of the Romantic Gypsy poem has a strong prescient presence, and controls her environment. Samuel Rogers observes the Gypsy as a witch: "Her moving lips, her caldron brimming o'er."[16] In Crabbe's "Lover's Journey," the young Gypsy woman conveys sexual power; in Clare, the Gypsy crone is the locus of an, albeit circumscribed, social power.

Matriarch or sibyl, the female Gypsy brings together past and future, canny knowledge of herbs and remedies, and uncanny knowledge of the future. The Gypsy crone is an androgyne spellbinder. In Walter Scott's *Guy Mannering*, the Gypsy Meg Merillies, in a voice in which the high notes were "too shrill for a man," and "the low seemed too deep for a woman," sings of a "canny moment" as a "lucky fit," and chants a wise woman's herbalist charm: "Trefoil, vervain, John's-wort, dill / Hinders witches of their will."[17] The female herbalist is as domestic as she is foreign, however, for her foremother is the medieval cunning woman who maintained a long hold on popular medicine and magic, and who worked on the commons as the practitioner of customary medicine and herb gathering.

Keith Thomas argues that in medieval England, cunning was a mode of community protection: "the most common [magical function performed by cunning men and wise women was] the detection of theft and the recovery of stolen goods."[18] Well into the nineteenth century, the magical agrarian practice of detection remained an increasingly illegal practice, though the cunning woman was still to be found throughout rural England, as Robert Southey noted in his *Letters from England* (1807).[19] The work of the cunning man and the wise woman before the seventeenth century was often that of divining where lost or stolen property might be.[20] The merging of the illegality of theft itself with the manner of detecting it may explain part of the close proximity in popular images of the Gypsy as thief and as fortune-teller: "Great skill have they in palmistry, and more / To conjure clean away the gold they touch."[21]

It is true that Gypsy fortune-tellers were long associated with their foreign origin, but there is a rural domestic language of fortune-telling as well. All these native plebeian activities were driven underground in the processes of secularization, reappearing in places and in times of instability and transition. The large numbers of early Renaissance statutes against itinerant fortune-tellers, drafted by the Church in its mastery of the rural population, gives us a hint of how the Gypsy came to take on the representational value of residual customary activities, activities which, as we move into the modern period, become increasingly associated with backward rural communities.

And the Gypsy *was*, from early on, an active figure in the taxonomy of persons in English rurality, figuring prominently in periods in which there have been highly orchestrated crackdowns on vagrancy. This remains true today, and was true between 1560 and 1640, a period of economic transition, when a large amount of legislation was introduced to tie the poor to a place. As A. L. Beier has argued: "Vagrancy legislation . . . reflected a new kind of poverty after 1300, that of 'masterless men;' persons no longer having manorial ties, but who were now subject to the buffeting of the market economy."[22] The Gypsy has the peculiar status in the countryside of being ever-present and ever-exotic. As the rituals of subsistence and the practices of customary knowledge diminish, the poetic image of the Gypsy encapsulates this passing as both nativity and outlandishness at once, providing a striking image for an agrarian proletariat which has become different to itself in the alienation of its labor.

John Clare's poetry of place harbors those resisting the regime of the "free" wage.[23] Clare's voice mediates the sociality of customary culture and the singularity of the voluntaristic lyric subject. We recognize him as the poet of enclosure who not only speaks about displacement, but was himself displaced from the commons and, through his derangement and incarceration, displaced from the sociality of the commonality. So it is not surprising that the image and the practice of Gypsies turn up often in his writing, nor that his Gypsy-poetic aims to demystify their exoticism. In his numerous Gypsy poems written before 1822, Clare's focus on the Gypsy band is part of his criticism of enclosure, an attack upon the rationalization of the logic of agricultural custom and familiar knowledge. This rationalization accomplishes the disenchantment of that traditional world: "Each little tyrant with his little sign / Shows where man claims earth glows no more divine."[24]

In "The Gipsey's Camp," written 1819–20, Clare rewrites a passage from Samuel Rogers's 1792 *Pleasures of Memory* in order to localize the common places of Rogers's literary walking-poem.[25] While Rogers's poetic anecdote of meeting a Gypsy fortune-teller offers a piece of picturesque scenery, Clare situates the anecdote in the concretion and physical reality of poverty. Clare recalls the "tawny smoaked flesh & tatterd rags / Uncooth brimd hat & weather beaten cloak" that these "real effigies of midnight hags" are wearing; and their camp is set up to "Keep off the bothering bustle of the wind / & give the best retreat." Clare's youthful speaker has common sense, not like the naïf of Rogers's tale, and when he doubts the truth of the Gypsy's fortune, "She furious stampt her shooless foot aground / Wipd by her sut black hair wi clenching fist / While thro her yellow teeth the spittle hist.".[26] This is a moment when the picturesque doubles back onto itself into the comic grotesque, alive with righteous indignation.

It is interesting and sad that in Clare's late Gypsy poems, written from the Northampton Asylum, the image of the Gypsy is, for the most part, linked to the fantasy of freedom.[27] "The Camp," "The Gipsy Lass," and "The Bonny Gipsey," all written in this later period, employ the rhetoric of confinement and freedom. In "The Bonny Gipsey" the female is given youth and beauty, and what had been "swarthy" in Clare's realist mode becomes, "Tanned with the summer sunshine she's like the berry brown."[28]

Most moving of Clare's late Gypsy poems is "The Gipsy Camp," a bitter yet understated poem that begins with an image of a local boy who has rushed from home into the woods to gather 'brakes'; then "thinks upon the fire and hurries back."[29] He is contrasted to the Gypsy who has no home to run back to, and who instead sets up his solitary fire within a putative domesticity of nature. But the entire setting is an alienated one and produces an anti-domestic vision – the meat cooking is "stinking mutton"; " 'Tis thus they live – a picture to the place, / A quiet, pilfering, unprotected race."[30] The act of theft, of "pilfering," is linked to the quiet of the tribe and its vulnerability. Customary practice has become legal theft, and the Gypsy is caught in an image of that transition.

In his autobiography, Clare analyzes the Gypsy mystique back into its elements of commoners' knowledge:

I had often heard of the mistic language & black arts which the gipseys possesd but on familiar acquaintance with them I found that their mystic language was nothing more than things calld by slang names like village provincialisms & that no two tribes spoke the same dialect exactly their black arts were nothing more of witchcraft than the knowledge of village gossips & the petty deceptions played off on believing ignorance.[31]

While he may sound somewhat flip here, in another passage in the memoir, Clare condemns what to our ears is the uncanny adumbration of the Nazi genocide of the Gypsies. Clare transcribes the speech of "an ignorant iron-hearted Justice of the Peace" who has just passed sentence on some Gypsies: " 'This atrocious tribe of wandering vagabonds ought to be made outlaws in every civilized kingdom & exterminated from the face of the earth.' "[32]

Although Clare easily identifies himself and the Gypsies as commoners, Wordsworth has a more uneasy relation to the Gypsies he encounters on his walking tours. In "Gipsies" the circularity of Gypsy life – the disposition of the camp itself, the circular non-productivity of the members, the circular link of generations – is set up in contrast to the progressive and linear works of poet, planets, and time: "Yet are they here? – the same unbroken knot / Of human Beings, in the self-same spot! / Men, Women, Children, yea the frame / Of the whole Spectacle the same!"[33] The punitive last lines of the poem – "The silent Heavens have goings on; / The stars have tasks – but these have none" – quietly make the contrast between modes of activity which are repetitive and those which are linear and productive, the distinctive temporalities of custom and reason.

In his 1820 revision of the poem, Wordsworth elaborates a patronizing disclaimer: "In scorn I speak not; – they are what their birth / And breeding suffers them to be; / Wild outcasts of society."[34] Wordsworth's negative identification *with* the Gypsies is transmuted into a philanthropic racial regard *for* them – they are doomed to remain outcasts because of their birth and breeding. While Clare's contemporaneous poems demystify the distance between Gypsies and commoners, Wordsworth's formulation reinforces it, and adumbrates the language of race, articulating the contradictory notion that Gypsies are both feral, beyond the reaches of society, and also, "outcasts," rejected by society.

Clare's poems tease out the homely from within the apparently alien, recovering the canny from the uncanny; Wordsworth's "Gipsies" finds something frightening and obstinate about the stasis of the Gypsy camp. This is the sublime of immobility, and the reiteration of "sameness" again and again in the opening lines of the poem opens up a breach of alterity within the apparently obvious laziness of the Gypsy group. "Oh better wrong and strife / Better vain deeds or evil than such a life!"[35] The Gypsies' immobility summons up within Wordsworth the dread lurking within the homely.

Gypsies perplex Wordsworth, and through them we can read as well some of his conflicts about traditional culture, which had itself been a central theme of *Lyrical Ballads*: invoked in the enumeration of local rights in "Goody Blake" and "Simon Lee"; the loss entailed in the shift from traditional to waged labor in "The Last of the Flock"; and the dispersal of persons out of communities into isolated existences in "The Female Vagrant." And the overarching rhetoric within which Wordsworth's customary lyricism is deployed is the most customary form of knowledge: the languages of magic, superstition, and madness.

The poem "Beggars" is an interesting site for Wordsworth's Gypsy anxiety. In the first version of the poem, composed 13 and 14 March 1802, and first printed in the first volume of *Poems, in Two Volumes*, the text opens with the figure of an androgynous begging Gypsy woman: "She had a tall man's height, or more; / No bonnet screen'd her from the heat." There is something strangely disingenuous about Wordsworth's next declaration:

> In all my walks, through field or town,
> Such Figure had I never seen;
> Her face was of Egyptian brown:
> Fit person was she for a Queen,
> To head those ancient Amazonian files:
> Or ruling Bandit's Wife, among the Grecian Isles.[36]

While it is certain that the Gypsy figured often in the English countryside, and that Wordsworth would indeed have seen versions of Gypsy women, he wants to distance himself and the environment from her alterity. Whatever she is, she cannot be native, and Wordsworth attempts to send the Gypsy woman back to where she came, albeit by an elevated poetic language. The narrator then meets up with two youths, who also demand a handout from him. The prescient Gypsy children assert that their mother is dead. But the narrator retorts, "Not half an hour ago / Your Mother has had alms of mine." / "That cannot be," one answer'd, "She is dead." / "Nay but I gave her pence, and she will buy you bread." They insist: "She has been dead, Sir, many a day." / "Sweet Boys, you're telling me a lie; / It was your mother, as I say – ."[37]

This poem produces a strange reversal of the norms of Wordsworth's more famous and earlier poem in *Lyrical Ballads*, "We are Seven." In that lyrical ballad, Wordsworth makes it clear that the rationalist narrator has ignored, to his spiritual detriment, the complex culture of commoners to which the "cottage child" belongs, and so he cannot make sense of the logic of her arithmetic when she insists that there are no geographical boundaries among her two dead siblings, the two who have gone "to sea," and the two who dwell at Conway. They have all been physically removed, by illness, lack of work, and the power of the press gang or the bounty, but they remain socially and narratively linked to the community of their cottage family.[38]

But in "Beggars," which reproduces that conversation in a more egotistical tone, neither poet nor narrator clarifies the status of the Gypsy woman. All that is certain is that there is tension around the figure of the Gypsy, in which, again, the homely harbors its opposite, and the beggar boys may be the familiars of the ghostly exotic Egyptian Queen, or of an Amazon. The insouciance of the speaker is undermined by the unnatural status of these apparitions in the landscape, at once domestic and familiar – the two healthy youths – and frightening and sublime – the Gypsy woman, "Haughty as if her eye had seen / Its own light to a distance thrown."[39] She is on the cusp of becoming less a Gypsy and more a Wanderer, but Wordsworth turns away from her before that happens, and in fact, deleted an early line which had begun by identifying her as a "wanderer."[40]

II

This temporary overlap between Wordsworth's Gypsy woman as "Egyptian," and as "Wanderer" returns us to the relationship between Gypsy and Jew in the imagined rural landscape. Gypsy and Jewish peddlers play fairly similar economic roles at the beginning of the nineteenth century. Just as the Gypsy travels from country to city in the seasonal round of itinerancy, the Jew moves from city to country, displaying the goods of the city, and bearing the impress of a foreignness compounded of both the alienness of city life itself and a more global indication of the links between England and the wider world.

The awkward companionability of the figure of the Gypsy and the Jew in Romantic-period literature mirrors a remnant of legendary narrative, in which both Gypsy and Jew function as Christian scapegoats, and prefigures the fruits of nineteenth-century racialism.[41] So, though by the end of the eighteenth century, the Wandering Jew and the Gypsy band face in opposite directions in terms of cultural and literary meaning, their histories are intertwined at the level of mythic narrative.

The Gypsy migrations of earlier centuries had brought them from India through Persia and into Byzantium, where the legend of an Egyptian origin was developed. As the Gypsies migrated further into Eastern and then Western Europe, they often carried with them copies of safe-conducts, which registered that the Gypsies were wandering as penitents for sins committed against the Holy Family.[42] As Holy Roman Emperor, Sigismund of Hungary issued letters to Gypsy groups allowing them safe passage on penitential terms; by 1422, they had acquired putatively papal letters as well, which gave them a seven-year order to wander "to and fro about the world without ever sleeping in a bed."[43]

The legend of the Wandering Jew, which also comes from the exigencies of a migratory period, and from within a Christian culture of pilgrimages, is clearly homologous to the Gypsy pilgrim tale. Hyam Maccoby and G. K. Anderson, who compiled the greatest number of versions of the legend, concur that the myth begins in the thirteenth century in the story of the Roman Cartaphilus, Pilate's doorkeeper, who was said to have harassed Jesus on his way to Calvary.[44] Jesus then doomed him to live until the last judgment. By the seventeenth century, the Roman had become a Jew, and he had been altered to be not only eternal but migratory.[45]

In England in the early medieval period, before their putative banishment, Jews were regarded as urban and corrupt, and were associated with the financial doings of the Court circles. It was the influx of Ashkenazi Jews from the 1770s to the end of the century which produced the stereotype of the Jewish peddler.[46] These immigrants arrived poor in English ports, and importantly, they arrived without many of the traditional ties which sustained the Gypsies in their continued life in England. The decline of corporatism, which had characterized Jewish life in Europe, left Jews in England as both strangers and without community ties to compensate for that strangeness.[47] The large amount of propaganda which, with their readmission, described a massive infiltration of Jews on the model of an invading army, links their presence in cities with the viruses of the cities themselves.[48]

Arriving in Georgian England, Ashkenazi Jews soon found an economic niche to fill once they moved out from port cities, particularly from London, to sell wares in the rural districts as their families had done in Germany before them.[49] But in the course of the nineteenth century, as roadways and other distributive links between city and countryside improved, these functions for both Jewish peddlers and Gypsies declined. The Jewish peddler returned to and was reabsorbed into the city, while the Gypsy group adapted, within the boundaries of a near to subsistence standard of living, to new conditions.

Frank Felsenstein has made the link between Jewish peddler and the literary figure of the Wandering Jew, and has made it clear that the Romantic image is a mirror to the anti-Semitic stereotype of popular culture in the period.[50] But it is striking that such a separating off of negative and positive images takes place in the figure of the Jew in the beginning of the century, while it is not until much later in the nineteenth century that something similar happens to the image of the Gypsy. And so the Gypsy remains a full sign of social particularity, while the Jew is emptied out of particular meaning, and comes to carry, in many Romantic-period texts, the abstract meaning of self-hood in general. Howard Weinbrot has recently studied the feature of philo-semitism in eighteenth-century British intellectual culture, and it is reasonable to speculate that as a residue from the positive literary value of Hebraism, there developed a negative value of Judaism, leading to differential values of the language of the Old Testament, and that of the eighteenth-century Yiddish of the Shtetl, associated with the figure of the Jewish peddler.[51]

In his discussion of what he takes to be the ambivalence of Romanticism to anti-Semitism, William Galperin makes the point that the intentional democratic internationalist language of Romanticism, "with [its] special commitment to the significance and autonomy of individual human beings," refuses the historic position of anti-Semitism.[52] And the work of many of the poems which treat of the Wandering Jew in the Romantic period elevates the solitary wanderer to a universalist position, and an imagined site of identification.

In the 1800 edition of *Lyrical Ballads*, Wordsworth included a "Song for the Wandering Jew." Without any narrative scaffolding, this is a ballad in the individualist lyric mode: a pure picture of the doubly separated consciousness of the modern individual. The degree of separation between self and the natural world is magnified in the poem's examples of those creatures which, apparently homeless themselves, are nonetheless at home everywhere. The "torrents" which rush down from the mountain, the chamois which runs alone across rocks, and even the sea-horse which "Own[s] no dear domestic cave" still "slumbers without motion / On the calm and silent wave."[53] Unlike Wordsworth's encounters with the Gypsies, in which he distances himself from them, and makes them even more bizarre than they would have been in the landscape of the 1790s, the Jew figures as a paradoxically alienated point of identification – less alien than not, and a place where narrator and stranger are coextensive and distinct: the Wanderer is "in" not "of" the speaker's "soul."[54]

Shelley returns often to the legend. In his juvenile portrayal of "The Wandering Jew; or the Victim of the Eternal Avenger," he insists in the

"Preface" that "the subject of the following Poem is an imaginary personage," participating in this severing of self and circumstance.[55] In *Queen Mab*, Shelley's Ahasuerus breaks from God and is heroic in the absolute of self-making and self-identity: his is the purest form of voluntaristic selfhood:

> Thus have I stood – through a wild waste of years
> Struggling with whirlwinds of mad agony,
> Yet peaceful, and serene, and self-enshrined,
> Mocking my powerless tyrant's horrible curse
> With stubborn and unalterable will.[56]

In the 1822 *Hellas*, Shelley presents a version of the Wandering Jew who is the emblem of the complete transcendence and autonomy of individual identity, abstracted from time and space: "What has Thought / To do with time, or place or circumstance?"[57] Shelley here melts away the alien mark of the Wandering Jew and discovers the bodiless abstract form of identity as a universal capacity of consciousness.

So, the landscape in which the Wandering Jew moves is not the embodied, appetitive, and domestic landscape in which Clare's and Wordsworth's Gypsies eke out their lives. Rather it is the supra-national landscape of transcendence, where the self encounters what is not self in a location emptied of persons. The Wandering Jew is not only solitary, he wanders in a geography which is fantastically unpopulated. Though figured as the living principle of continuity over both time and space – the Wandering Jew lives forever and journeys everywhere – he moves in poetry in a non-representational space. The landscape has been bifurcated into one which is the terrain of embodied and laboring peoples, and one which is the transcendent terrain of individual consciousness.

But this counterposition of the embodied, social Gypsy and the transcendent, individual Jew is not just a mirror image, the people without history versus the people of history, the nomad and the exile; for they also figure as versions of each other. By the middle of the nineteenth century, Gypsies were modelled enough on Jews to be seen as being in need of Christian conversion.

In the nineteenth century, discussions of the Gypsies as an historical people begin to emerge in the culture of both racialization and of historicity. First is the foregrounding of the Gypsy language, which is assimilated to interests in Sanskrit and William Jones's work on India, and so part of the larger phenomenon of Romantic orientalism: the Gypsy is reconsidered as an oriental in the landscape, a displacement in space.[58] The mysterious origin of the Gypsies becomes a source of interest: "Whether from India's burning plains / Or wild Bohemia's domains . . . / Or whether ye are Egypt's sons . . . / Arabs of Europe! Gipsy race!"[59] Alternatively understood as Egyptian or Indian in origin, the Gypsies become a religious and/or a linguistic object.

As the Gypsy is elevated into an exemplar of history itself, the quest to separate out the authentic from the malingering Gypsy takes off, and the "true Romany" is then distinguished from vagrants and dossers and drunks, and, perhaps most politically obvious, the Irish tinker, who is located at the bottom of the pyramid of Gypsy authenticity.[60] This separating makes room for a transcendent, and increasingly, solitary, version of the Gypsy, a partner to the transcendent consciousness of the Jew. For example, Matthew Arnold both identifies with and distinguishes himself from a Gypsy child who may have "known too much – or else forgotten all," reaching inward "with eyes that sought thine eyes thou didst converse, / And that soul-searching vision fell on me."[61] At the same time, the empirical Gypsy and Jew are being degraded and re-formulated into a version which will become fodder for racialism to become racism.

The racialization and historicization of the Gypsy opened a space as well for the Evangelical missionary movement to assimilate the Gypsy to the Jew as a wandering tribe in need of conversion in order to hasten general redemption.[62]

In 1837, Arthur Penryhn Stanley, at Balliol College, Oxford, won a poetry prize for his "The Gipsies," in which he describes the Gypsy and Jew as parallel wandering tribes, and as admonitory to Christian nations:

> Remnant of Ages – from thy glory cast –
> Dread link between the present and the past –
> One only race of all thy great compeers
> Still moves with thee along this vale of tears;
> Egypt's lorn people, outcast Israel![63]

In 1830, Samuel Roberts, who had long been a defender of the Gypsies, and had seen them on the model of victims rather than sinners, published a pamphlet called *Parallel Miracles; or, the Jews and the Gypsies*. His argument aims to show "that while the [Jews] remain a byeword and a reproach in the *cities* of all countries, the [Gypsies] . . . the descendants of the ancient Egyptians . . . continue, as predicted by the prophets, dispersed and despised in the open fields of the same, till the time appointed for the restoration of both to their own land."[64]

Whereas much anti-Gypsy argument was, echoing Wordsworth's case, that they were unproductive, Roberts reverses this argument and romanticizes the Gypsy: "The Gypsies are by far more intelligent and civilized than the depraved part of the lower ranks in the large towns ... See the mechanics at their work, or at the workhouse, surly and dissatisfied with themselves, their condition, their employers ... dirty, offensive, unhealthy, and miserable."[65] It is the industrial worker who is now described as cunning and feral, but the effect is no longer uncanny. Against the background of urban alienated labor, the Gypsy now appears as whole and integrated within an idealized community.

In the 1890s, Arthur Symons, *flaneur* and frequent contributor to the journal of the Gypsy-Lore Society, will define this essentially urban fantasy of the Gypsy, unmoored from the rough and tumble of the changing English countryside, as "the last romance left in the world. [The Gypsy] does what we dream."[66] Paradoxically, this romanticized Gypsy image of the later nineteenth century emerges as a literary by-product of the rise of anthropological Gypsy-lorists, who aimed to create a genealogy of the "authentic" Gypsy, distinct from the larger social texture of displaced and vagrant persons, a genealogy dependent upon categories of racial and linguistic separateness.[67] The irony is that in attempting to protect the "pure" Gypsy from repressive legislation and racist attitudes, and to preserve the cultural materials of the British Gypsy nomads, the Gypsiologists of the *Journal of the GypsyLore Society* relied on and reinforced a newly-developing racialist discourse, Symons describing the Gypsies as the "last free race."

The later nineteenth-century literary image of the Gypsy eases the alien into the benign, the disturbance of the sublime into an anodyne picturesque, and disperses the confusing memories of native instability into an exotic retrogressive nostalgia. Of course, its excrescence was the racism which marks all Europe.

NOTES

1 See Katie Trumpener, "The Time of the Gypsies: A 'People without History,'" in the Narratives of the West," *Critical Inquiry* 18: 4 (1992): 843–84; Angus Fraser, "Authors' Gypsies," *Antiquarian Book* 20 (1993): 10–18; and Peter Garside, "Picturesque Figure and Landscape: Meg Merrilies and the Gypsies," in Stephen Copley and Peter Garside, eds., *The Politics of the Picturesque: Literature, Landscape, and Aesthetics since 1770* (Cambridge, 1994), pp. 145–74.

2 George K. Anderson, *The Legend of the Wandering Jew* (Providence, R.I., 1965) enumerates the catalogue of Wandering Jews in Romantic literature. See

also Hyam Maccoby, "The Wandering Jew as Sacred Executioner," in Galit Hasan-Roken and Alan Dundes, eds., *The Wandering Jew: Essays in the Interpretation of a Christian Legend* (Bloomington, Ind., 1986), pp. 236–59; Frank Felsenstein, *Anti-Semitic Stereotypes: A Paradigm of Otherness in English Popular Culture, 1660–1830* (Baltimore, Md., 1995); and Bryan Cheyette, *Constructions of 'The Jew' in English Literature and Society: Racial Representations, 1875–1945* (Cambridge, 1993).

3 See E. P. Thompson, *Customs in Common: Studies in Traditional Popular Culture* (1993); Peter Linebaugh, *The London Hanged: Crime and Society in the Eighteenth Century* (1991); Neeson, *Commoners*; and Deborah Valenze, *The First Industrial Women* (Oxford, 1995).

4 R. L. Brett and A. R. Jones, eds., *Lyrical Ballads* (1963), pp. 44–5.

5 Ibid., lines 221, 254, 258.

6 See Charles Taylor, *Sources of the Self: The Making of the Modern Identity* (Cambridge, Mass., 1990); Alastair MacIntyre, *After Virtue: A Study in Moral Theory* (1981); Ruth L. Smith and Deborah M. Valenze, "Mutuality and Marginality: Liberal Moral Theory and Working-Class Women in Nineteenth-Century England," *Signs* 13: 2 (1988): 277–98.

7 William Cowper, *The Task, A Poem in Six Books* (1785), p. 30.

8 Felsenstein, *Stereotypes*, pp. 58–89.

9 For cunning and popular magic, see Keith Thomas, *Religion and the Decline of Magic: Studies in Popular Beliefs in Sixteenth- and Seventeenth-Century England* (1971), "Cunning Men and Popular Magic," chapter 7, pp. 252–300. And see Angus Fraser, *The Gypsies* (Oxford, 1995), p. 112.

10 Clare, "The Gipsy Camp," in *The Later Poems of John Clare 1837–1864*, eds. Eric Robinson and David Powell, 2 vols. (Oxford, 1995), 1: 29.

11 David Mayall, *Gypsy-Travellers in Nineteenth-Century Society* (Cambridge, 1988), pp. 1, 3. See also John Barrell, *The Birth of Pandora and the Division of Knowledge* (1992), p. 114.

12 Wordsworth, "Beggars," in *Poems, in Two Volumes, 1800–1807*, ed. Jared Curtis (Ithaca, N.Y., 1983), pp. 113–16; Crabbe, "The Lovers' Journey," in *The Complete Poetical Works*, eds. Norma Dalrymple-Champneys and Arthur Pollard, 3 vols. (Oxford, 1988), 2: 136.

13 Wordsworth, *Poems, in Two*, p. 114; Samuel Rogers, *The Pleasures of Memory; Pt. 1, 1792* (1865), p. 16; Horace Smith, "The Gipsies," *Miscellaneous Poems*, 2 vols. (1846), 1: 203.

14 Gilbert White, *The Natural History of Selborne*, ed. Richard Mabey (1977), p. 179.

15 See, among others, Margaret Homans, *Women Writers and Romantic Identity: Dorothy Wordsworth, Emily Brontë, and Emily Dickinson* (Princeton, N.J., 1980); Meena Alexander, *Women in Romanticism: Mary Wollstonecraft, Dorothy Wordsworth, Mary Shelley* (1989); Anne K. Mellor, ed., *Feminism and Romanticism* (Bloomington, Ind., 1988).

16 Rogers, *Pleasures of Memory*, p. 16.

17 Scott, *Guy Mannering* (1987), ed. J. Campbell, pp. 30–1.

18 Thomas, *Religion*, p. 253.

19 Southey, *Letters from England* (1951), ed. Jack Simmons, p. 295.

20 Thomas, *Religion*, p. 253.

21 Cowper, *Task*, 1: 30.

22 Beier, *Masterless Men*, p. 12.

23 Neeson cites Clare frequently when discussing displaced commoners; see *Commoners*, pp. 3, 5–6, 11, 12, 41, 52, 59.

24 Clare, "The Mores," in *Poems of the Middle Period: 1822–1837*, eds. Eric Robinson, et al., 2 vols. (Oxford, 1996), 2: 349. For Clare and enclosures, see Barrell, *Idea of Landscape*.

25 See Rogers, *Pleasures*, pp. 16–17.

26 Clare, "The Gipsey's Camp," in *The Early Poems: 1804–1822*, eds. Eric Robinson and David Powell, 2 vols. (Oxford, 1989), 1: 119–20.

27 Clare, "The Camp," "The Gipsey Lass," "The Bonny Gipsey," in *Later Poems*, 1: 457–8, 634–5; 2: 866–7.

28 Ibid., 2: 867.

29 Ibid., 1: 29.

30 On Clare's Gypsy poems in relation to heteroglossia see James McKusick, "Beyond the Visionary Company: John Clare's Resistance to Romanticism," in Hugh Haughton, Adam Phillips, and Geoffrey Summerfield, eds., *John Clare in Context* (Cambridge, 1994), pp. 221–37.

31 Clare, *The Prose of John Clare*, eds. J. W. and Anne Tibble (1951), p. 35.

32 Ibid., p. 35.

33 Wordsworth, "Gipsies," in *Poems, in Two*, pp. 211–12. See David Simpson's enlightening interpretation of "Gipsies" as dealing with Wordsworth's anxieties about poetic production in *Wordsworth's Historical Imagination* (1987), pp. 52–81. Simpson also discusses "Beggars" and "Sequel to the Foregoing," ibid., pp. 175–7.

34 Wordsworth, "Gipsies," in *Poems, In Two*, p. 212.

35 Ibid., p. 211.

36 Ibid., pp. 113–14.

37 Ibid., p. 115.

38 See *Lyrical Ballads*, pp. 66–8.

39 Wordsworth, *Poems, In Two*, p. 114 (1827 addition).

40 Ibid., p. 113.

41 Mayall, *Gypsy-Travellers*, shows how the racialization of Gypsies takes place in England in the course of the nineteenth century out of more varied earlier notions of the Gypsy; see chapter 4, "Romany or traveller – definitions and stereotypes," pp. 71–93.

42 Ibid., pp. 48, 79.

43 Ibid., p. 74.

44 Maccoby, "Wandering Jew," p. 237; Anderson, *Legend*.

45 Maccoby, "Wandering Jew," p. 237.

46 Todd Endleman, *The Jews of Georgian England, 1714–1830* (Philadelphia, Pa., 1979), p. 168.

47 Ibid., p. 70.
48 Felsenstein, *Stereotypes*, p. 47.
49 Endleman, *Jews*, p. 179.
50 Felsenstein, *Stereotypes*, pp. 58–89.
51 Weinbrot, *Britannia's Issue: The Rise of British Literature from Dryden to Ossian* (Cambridge, 1993), pp. 403–75.
52 Galperin, "Romanticism and/or Anti-Semitism," in Bryan Cheyette, ed., *Between 'Race' and 'Culture': Representations of 'the Jew' in English and American Literature* (Stanford, Calif., 1996), pp. 16–26.
53 Wordsworth, *Lyrical Ballads*, pp. 173–4.
54 Ibid., p. 174.
55 *Shelley: The Poems*, eds. Geoffrey Matthews and Kelvin Everest (1989), I: 41.
56 Ibid., I: 341–2.
57 *Shelley: Poetical Works*, ed. Thomas Hutchinson (Oxford, 1968), p. 471.
58 Garside, "Picturesque," p. 162.
59 Smith, *Poems*, I: 203.
60 Mayall, *Gypsy-Travellers*, pp. 78–9.
61 Arnold, "To a Gypsy Child by the Sea-Shore," in *Poems*, ed. Kenneth Allott (1965), pp. 22–6.
62 See Mayall, *Gypsy-Travellers*, pp. 97–129.
63 Stanley, *The Gipsies: A Prize Poem* (Oxford, 1837), p. 13.
64 Roberts, *Parallel Miracles; or, the Jews and the Gypsies* (1830), p. i.
65 Ibid., p. 76.
66 Symons, *Journal of the Gypsy Lore Society* n. 1 (1907): 294–9, this passage pp. 295–6.
67 David Mayall, "The Making of British Gypsy Identities, *c.* 1500–1980," *Immigrants and Minorities* 1 (1992): 21–41, especially p. 30.

CHAPTER 14

Afterword: moving stories, still lives

John Barrell

I

The editors of this book have represented it chiefly as a series of essays toward a history of the production of capitalist space in Britain, and have suggested that this afterword might like to reflect on some related aspect of space and identity. This is where I began my career, in the mid 1960s, but I have not been there for many years now, and I am as much embarrassed as flattered by the editors' belief that I might have something worth saying about a topic which, since I left it, has become one of the organizing concepts of a wide range of work in almost every discipline in the humanities. I can find no better way to begin than by going back to the beginning; by offering some reflections on my first attempt to address this topic, in a book about John Clare.

The Idea of Landscape and the Sense of Place attempted to examine the confrontation between two constructions of rural space. In the green corner was the local, stationary, circular sense of place associated with the pre-enclosure, open-field parish – specifically, John Clare's Helpston. In the red corner were the national, mobile, linear ideas of landscape differently exemplified in the eighteenth-century prospect view, and in the objectives of the agricultural improvers, members of an emerging rural professional class, seeking to produce homogeneous landscapes imagined as so many linked units in a national economy. The result was entirely predictable, for the fight had been staged many times elsewhere. Clare, punch-drunk, was forcibly retired to an institution for the insane, while the forces of modern capitalism looked for new fields to conquer, aided and abetted by an aesthetics of landscape in which the priorities of commerce were barely, if at all, disguised.

The book was intended not as a short story, in John Brewer's phrase, but as a chapter in the grand narrative of the triumphal march of capitalism. If I were writing it now, I would tell it differently: the narrative

231

has lost much of its grandeur for me, and whenever I have revisited
this terrain, I have, in common with every other tourist, found it much
more uneven, much less well sign-posted than before. The conflicts and
uncertain alliances within the culture of capitalism itself; between pastoral and georgic, between regional and national identity, between a
literature of sentiment and a science of political economy, between the
picturesque and the maximization of profits from agricultural land,
between the safety of home and the adventures of Empire; above all
the recognition that these opposing notions, discourses, ideologies are
to be discovered not simply in different economic classes or in the different identities of male and female, colonizer and the colonized, but
within individual texts and individual subjects – all this has produced
a history of the production of capitalist space which has been at least
as much concerned with the bifurcations, the misdirections, the divaga-
tions from the road to modernity, as with an attempt to trace out its
general direction.

When I left space alone, there were still issues I wish I had
addressed, texts I would have liked to find an occasion to write about;
and among the essays in this book, Andrew McRae's, with its account
of cartographers, chorographers, narratives of vagrancy, the various
radically divergent notions of space jostling with each other in the
Elizabethan period, was especially evocative in reminding me of what
I used to find so compelling about questions raised by the production
of space in the eighteenth century. This Afterword, however, will point
in a rather different direction from the one followed by McRae. His
essay offers an account of space as multiply layered, as a plural noun,
a name for the totality of the divergent discourses by which it is produced. I'm happy enough with the image of space, quoted by McRae
from Lefebvre, as *mille-feuille* pastry; less happy if we forget that one leaf,
however uneven, flaky, fragile, sits on top of all the others. At the end
of his essay, I found myself wondering whether it wasn't committing
itself to an idea of history in which an attention to the sheer plurality
of the competitors does not complicate, as it should, but replace, as I
think it shouldn't, the question of who won and who lost. McRae is
surely right when he argues that the new geography of the Elizabethan
surveyors "did not simply erase a spatiality of community and shared
memory"; but in the long run, not simply, not immediately, the lines
inscribed on the landscape by the relatively powerful cut more deeply,
and do erase those drawn by the relatively powerless.

It's in the spirit then of a rather qualified revisionism that I offer this
Afterword, which for most of its length will focus on two texts, both

written in the 1740s, though one was never published or even completed, and the other reappeared in numerous different versions throughout the second half of the eighteenth century. I've chosen them for a number of different reasons. In the first place they offer me the opportunity to comment on some of the issues raised by McRae's essay and others in this book. Secondly, they each offer radically different accounts of space; one of them, to borrow Raymond Williams's terms, apparently the expression of an unusually "residual," post-feudal but emphatically pre-modern formation, the other – at least at first glance – of a "dominant" ideology of mercantile capitalism. Thirdly, however, they both engage the binary of home and empire that the Introduction represents as central to the scheme of this volume, but engage it so insecurely as to invite reflection on the unevenness of the history sketched in a number of the subsequent essays. We can think of them as envelopes, one addressed to the past, the other to the future; but when we examine the contents, we may wonder whether the envelopes were inadvertently mixed up. In the last section of this Afterword I will attempt to explore this binary further to throw light on the two very different accounts of georgic, as imperial, as domestic, in the essays of Karen O'Brien and Elizabeth Heckendorn Cook.

II

The Life and Adventures of Bampfylde-Moore Carew, the Noted Devonshire Stroller and Dog-Stealer is the first of many titles of a book which first appeared in Exeter in 1745, and by the end of the century had run through at least thirty editions, exclusive of abridged versions published as broadsides or chapbooks. It was published anonymously, though it is sometimes said to have been written by Carew himself, and is described on some of its title-pages as having been "taken from his own mouth." This act of dentistry has been variously attributed to Thomas Price, to the Sherborne bookseller Robert Goadby, and to Goadby's wife.[1] The *Life* describes the travels of rector's son turned gypsy mendicant, born in 1693, who rose, by diligence and devotion to his calling, to become King of the Gypsies, or King of the Beggars, or King of the Mendicants. These three honorifics are used interchangeably, for the society of which Carew is king comprehends not only those believed to be gypsies by race – those who are assumed to be descended from Egyptians – but "every other order of Mendicants, vulgarly called Beggers";[2] and for most of the book the terms "Gypsies" and "mendicants" are each used to include the other. As Anne Janowitz's essay suggests, the notion of the "true," the racialized Gypsy, is still a long time away in the mid eighteenth century. From 1750 onward most editions of the *Life* include a dictionary of "the Language of the Community of Gypsies," which reveals the vocabulary of the mendicants to have been just what Clare, quoted by Janowitz, regarded it as being – a cant dialect, "nothing more than things calld by slang names like village provincialisms," with no apparent trace of "true Romany."

As editions of the *Life* from 1768 onward explain, Carew obtained his kingship under a system of constitutional liberty which is represented as the virtuous opposite of the English constitution as it had evolved under the ministry of Robert Walpole and his successors. In contemporary England, Liberty is heard to lament, "my generous and hardy sons are become foolish, indolent, effeminate, thoughtless; behold, how with their own hands, they have loaded me with shekels."[3] Liberty in England has been corrupted by commercial wealth; she is not so much ironed as gilded. The virtuous constitution of the beggars is a product of their virtuous poverty.

If so far it seems that the community of the mendicants is imagined as a nostalgic alternative to modern, commercial England, this is by no means the whole story. The monarchy of the mendicants and gypsies is absolute, but the crown is elective, not hereditary, and is to be surrendered when the king feels himself, or is felt by others, to be no longer capable of discharging the duties of his office with energy or honor. Only those who deserve well of the community are permitted to be candidates, and on offering themselves for election they are obliged to make a public statement of their principles, to serve as a check on their future conduct. Suffrage is universal, and appears to include the "Cousin Betties," the female order of mendicants. Election is by secret ballot, to ensure that "bribes, even if they were known amongst these people, would lose their effect." So seriously do the gypsies regard their civic duties that, though at other times they are much given to mirth and jollity, they have too much "judgment, prudence, and wisdom" to allow their faculties to be clouded with drink during the period of the election. The king, once elected, is in theory entitled to be kept at the expense of the community; in practice, however, more honor attaches to him if he remains industrious in his calling, and releases his subjects from the obligation of paying taxes in kind.[4]

If it is true, as Janowitz argues, that the " 'Romantic' Gypsy figuring freedom and independence" is a late nineteenth-century invention, some such idea, whether Romantic or not, was clearly in place one hundred years earlier. The *Life* was reprinted so frequently through the last quarter of the eighteenth century that much of what people at the time imagined they knew about gypsies must have been derived from it; and it represented the gypsy life not simply in terms of individual liberty – a freedom to roam, a freedom from the constraints of regular employment – and not simply as a communal life, but as a life lived within a highly organized community, a political utopia founded as much on a modern critique of modernity as on the vision of an imaginary and ideal past. The addition of this report of the Gypsy constitution may account for the popularity of the *Life* in the 1780s and 1790s: no less than seventeen editions appeared in the decades when the reform of Parliament and the suffrage came to be a live political topic and began to gather support among artisans and laborers.

As we shall see, this is not the only place in the *Life* where a notion of modernity interrupts what is, for most of its length, a patently residual text. Though some versions of the *Life* show an awareness of Hogarth's progresses and Fielding's picaresque novels – from 1750 some editions include a comparison, supposedly in the manner of Plutarch, between Carew and Tom Jones – the generic roots of the text reach back far beyond Defoe to the Elizabethan rogue-pamphlets discussed in McRae's essay, and I can think of no other eighteenth-century popular life-narrative of which this is more true. Carew is a perpetual itinerant, changing places and identities in a never-ending search for opportunities to practice his craft as trickster. He never takes casual work or seasonal employment; he learns the trade of rat-catcher, but only to provide him with more opportunities to catch conies. Most of the book describes a series of deceptions practiced by Carew on the gentry and nobility, who are invariably delighted to be taken in by such a skillful – and genteel – conman. At one point the *Life* goes so far – so far back in popular tradition – as to invite us to believe that Carew's friend the noble Lord Weymouth was in the habit of traveling round the West Country dressed as a beggar, in order to test the hearts and dispositions of his aristocratic and gentle neighbors.

Most of Carew's adventures take place in Devon, Somerset, and Dorset; for most of the book he crosses and recrosses these counties, practicing his art in towns and villages whose names crowd the pages, place after place after place, as if in a gazetteer and yet not at all like one. The production of space is the last thing that concerns the author of this book, at least as long as Carew stays within the country of the south west. Successive actions – though the phrase assumes a match between the sequence of events in the life and the *Life* which at times is patently missing – successive actions sometimes occur in adjacent villages as if in the course of a single expedition, and sometimes in places up to a hundred miles apart. Between one place and another there are no routes, no directions, no distances, no differences; place-names are used not to signify places that differ from each other in character, in size, in architecture, in economy, but simply as a means of distinguishing one incident from another: Carew did this here, that there. There are no places between places; no sense that to go from A to C you must pass through B: A, B and C simply happen, and the reader must consult a map to know how they lie relative to one another. The heroes of picaresque are endlessly preoccupied with how to get from place to place – not just what directions they must take, but what means of conveyance they can make use of. Does Carew walk, does he ride, does he thumb a lift? We are almost never told. Though the earliest title-pages describe him as a "stroller," his feet barely touch the ground: he just turns up, here or somewhere else, and might as well be navigating by the roadless maps of John Speed for all the use he seems to make of the veins and arteries in the landscape.

In that part of the text, by far the larger part, which describes Carew's travels in the West Country, the *Life* displays a notion of travel analogous to that described by McRae, in his account of Elizabethan chorography, as "gliding," a notion by McRae's account already residual by 1600 or so. There is no geography in that part of the text which is situated in the West Country, and no commerce except between mendicant and mark, whose economic transactions are represented as, primarily, social transactions, in which the opposed interests of each party are dissolved in their mutual enjoyment of Carew's knavish tricks. But within the envelope of one idea of space is concealed another, much more modern, sense of how space is divided, measured, and put to use. On various occasions, Carew voyages beyond the three counties. In one of (I think) only two dateable episodes in the book – or in any of its later versions – he travels to Edinburgh to witness the '45, and accompanies the Jacobite army down to Derby.[5] At other times he goes to London, to Newcastle, to Wales and Ireland; to France and the countries that surround the Baltic; and, on three occasions, to North America. It is the accounts of the Atlantic voyages that are the most surprising, for Carew, in leaving the Old World, finds himself in a new genre.

The elaborate descriptions of the places Carew visits in the New World are given on the pretext that, as a professional mendicant, he carefully studied them in order to represent himself, back in the West Country, as a penniless voyager far from home, or as a much-traveled, broken-down sailor. But we are offered no comparable account, indeed no account at all, of the different places in the Britain that from time to time he pretends to hail from, and it's safe to assume that the author has borrowed the descriptions of North America from promotional literature and from other published accounts of the geography and economics of the colonies. The description of Newfoundland offers us something approaching a commercial map of the island: space is marked by distances, compass-bearings, latitudes; the climate, the quality of the soil, the off-shore sandbanks, the convenience of the ports, are all the subject of comment; two pages are devoted to a minute account of the process of drying and salting cod. The interpolation of all this into the *Life* invokes concerns and interests quite different from those of the reader invoked by the rogue-narrative, and this is still more the case in the descriptions of the American colonies between Maryland and Massachusetts, and especially of the towns and cities there. Philadelphia, for example, is minutely described and mapped: the navigable portions of the Delaware and the Schuylkill are measured, and the depth of the anchorage at the city's quays is fathomed. The convenience of Philadelphia's situation between these rivers is explained, the position of wharfs and warehouses is described, together with the success of the ship-building industry. The streets are named and measured; the areas allotted to individual dwellings are computed, the houses valued, and so on. The city – and the same is true of the other settlements visited by Carew – is produced entirely as an economic rather than as a social space, or as a space in which social exchange is presumed to be entirely a function of commercial exchange.[6] Each time Carew returns from America, however, this new economic geography is erased from his memory or from the memory of the text, and he resumes his wanderings, not from place to place, but from place-name to place-name. In short the *Life* is fractured between a notion of England, and of the West Country especially, as spaceless – as if those emancipated from the commercial nexus have no need to know how space is articulated by those who live by trade – and a description of colonial space as fully commercial, and so as minutely and carefully accounted for, laid out as if in a commercial map that, for all that it might concern Carew, has yet to be drawn for England.

III

Such a map, however, was being drawn even at the moment when the *Life* first appeared. In the late 1730s and throughout the 1740s, John Dyer, the poet of *The Fleece*, one of the formal georgic poems discussed above by Karen O'Brien, worked sporadically on the grand project of his life, the production of what he described as a "Commercial Map of England." The manuscript of what may be all that ever became of this project consists of some eighty pages, divided into two main parts.[7] There are fifty or so pages of notes, for the most part arranged alphabetically by county, and partly drawn from Defoe's *A Tour through the Whole Island of Great Britain*; and there are the beginnings of an essay, running to twenty-five pages of which two are lost, entitled "A Plan of a commercial map of England and a discourse on the uses of it," dated 1749 and apparently written when Dyer was abandoning hope of finding a patron for the project.

The map, as it emerges from the manuscript, was to produce a description of Britain entirely as a scene of commerce. Dyer's big idea was to mark by symbols the raw materials, the manufactures and the agricultural products associated with each town and region. This would have had various advantages. In the spirit of Thomas Proctor, the Jacobean advocate for improved communications quoted by McRae, Dyer imagined that by consulting the map, merchants who dealt in particular commodities would have been able to discover whether there was a nearer source of supply, or one more conveniently situated on the road or river network, than those they customarily bought from. Mining engineers, by studying the pattern of collieries across the country, would have been able to estimate where future excavations were likely to be profitable. Entrepreneurs would have been able to identify places badly supplied with particular commodities, and calculate the likely success of opening new channels of internal trade, if necessary constructing new roads and navigations ("Plan," ff. 44, 33, 32, 38).

Dyer notes for example that if a proper road were to be made between Aberystwyth and Leominster, this would make Aberystwyth the most convenient port to London for trade with Ireland. Such a road, which might be constructed, he suggests, by the army, or by criminals, would enable Leominster to exchange its hops and cider for Irish wool ("Plan," ff. 47–9); it would

cut it's way through Copper and Lead mines; and also invigorate the languid Flannel Trade which lies scattered over that mountainous Countrey: These would be followed by a Fishery of Herrings ... and many other Trades; for one Trade creates another. ("Plan," f. 49)

The map would also reveal new opportunities for extending the network of inland waterways; an examination of the maps of the midland counties would suggest, for example, the convenience of a navigation linking the Soar south of Leicester with the Cherwell or Evenlode, and so joining the three great rivers of England, the Trent, the Thames, and (via the Avon) the Severn.[8] By describing the present commercial geography of Britain, Dyer believed he could influence its future. To reinforce the point, he intended to fill the margins of each map with large-scale plans of "some Ports, Rivers, Roads, &c.," not as they were but as they would be, after "Supposed improvements" ("Plan," f. 32).

It seems likely that this emphasis on communications, on how the geography of England could be redrawn for "the better circulation of our Trade" ("Plan," f. 32), would have produced, had the project found a patron, a new way of organizing the atlas, as much by region as by county. The manuscript contains the draft of a specimen map. It is without the symbols Dyer intended to add, but contains a few words – "coal," here and there, "mineral springs" – to mark the position of exploitable resources. It describes an oblong tract of land roughly coextensive with Worcestershire; unlike earlier and other contemporary county maps, however, which for the purposes of each individual map usually represent the contiguous counties as uncharted blanks, this map follows the roads and rivers to destinations across administrative boundaries. The oblong includes a significant slice of west Warwickshire, but excludes the projections of Worcestershire north west toward Tenbury and south east beyond Evesham, apparently leaving them to appear on the neighboring maps. Perhaps what Dyer had in mind, however tentatively, was something like the regional economic geography advocated by William Marshall in the 1790s, rather than a geography in which economic divisions give way to what Marshall described as "the arbitrary lines of Counties."[9] Dyer's region, however, is unlike those defined by Marshall in two ways. First, it seems to be based not on surface geology but on the structure of communications: the organizing feature of the area described is a rough lozenge whose northernmost point is formed by the convergence, at Edgbaston in Warwickshire, of two Roman roads, one running north east from Worcester, on the Severn, the other north west from Bidford-on-Avon, also in Warwickshire. To the south, the lozenge is closed at the confluence of the two rivers at Tewkesbury in Gloucestershire. Secondly, Dyer's is not simply an agricultural region: in the England of the "Commercial Map," the traditional distinctions between agriculture and manufactures, country and town – emphasized

in *The Fleece*, though only to be dissolved in a grand poetic vision of
unity in difference – are never imagined as existing in the first place:
however and wherever produced, commodities are simply commodities, waiting to be moved along roads and rivers in an infinite series
of exchanges.

Thus described, Dyer's manuscript reads like a textbook example of
"the production of capitalist space," and in an intriguingly literal sense;
for Dyer writes as if to construct new lines of communication for the
circulation of commodities, to make better economic use of the space
that is England, is indeed to make more space. By the improvement
of communications, he writes, "may Desarts be render'd populous,"
and "Countreys *virtually enlarged*" ("Plan," f. 49, emphasis added). The
vision of the map is of a nation in which every possibility for economic
exchange is maximized, and in which the traditional oppositions
between agriculture and manufactures, country and city disappear
into a uniform commercial modernity. But as Dyer develops his notion
of "virtual" enlargement, it begins to emerge that in this text, and in
marked contrast with *The Fleece*, he is committed to a vision of the future
of England as little England (and of Great Britain as little Britain, Ireland
as little Ireland),[10] the survival of which appears to depend on the simul-
taneous maximization of internal space and a minimization of the importance of foreign markets. All commerce is imagined as taking place
internally, between one center of population, one economic region, and
another.

In *The Fleece* Dyer looks forward to the construction of a global British
Empire held together not by arms but by trade. "Why," he asks:

> Why to the narrow circle of our coast
> Should we submit our limits, while each wind
> Assists the stream and sail, and the wide main
> Woos us in ev'ry port? See Belgium build,
> Upon the floodful brine, her envy'd power;
> And, half her people floating on the wave,
> Expand her fishy regions. Thus our isle,
> *Thus only may Britannia be enlarg'd.*
> But whither, by the visions of the theme
> Smit with sublime delight, but whither strays
> The raptur'd muse, forgetful of her task?[11]

These lines occur toward the end of Book 3, and the self-denial by
which Dyer restrains his muse's anxiety to explore the sublime vision of
empire, lasts only a few lines; throughout Book 4 he gives himself entirely

to imagining Britain's imperial present and future. In the "Commercial Map," however, he remains committed to a resolutely anti-imperial vision, as if frightened by what history taught was the corruption that waited to ambush and destroy imperial nations. His vision here is of an inward-looking island economy, made tough and sinewy by a tightly-clenched network of roads and navigations; he represents "our Islands" not just as unwilling but somehow as incapable of expanding except by the process of "virtual enlargement," the inscribing of new lines in the spaces between old ones. This, he claims, is "the only way we have of keeping pace with the Powers of Europe" ("Plan," f. 53):

The ambitious Kingdoms of the Continent are enlarging their territories: the haughty dominion of France, above all, is daily increasing; while Great Brittain and Ireland are circumscribed; They are bound about by Seas & Oceans; They cannot augment themselves, no; but they can do better; they can exceedingly People their Provinces and Strengthen their Borders; and where there are numerous Manufacturs and abundant Traffick, the nearness of Towns and villages to each other makes the circulation of Riches brisker, and Assistance readier to the State in times of Danger: Compactness and, I can almost say, Smallness of Territory, has often contributed to Strength and Power. ("Plan," ff. 53–4)

The strength and survival of England, and of Britain and Ireland, by this account, depends entirely on the construction of a nation whose internal unity can only be loosened by venturing abroad.

In other ways, too, we need to read the vision of England's future as described by the "Commercial Map" not as the celebration of the never-ending "enlargement" of commercial possibilities but as an attempt to limit and to circumscribe them. The opposition between circulation and settlement, described for the Elizabethan period by McRae, is still active in Dyer's text. His desire to promote what he calls "the full improvement" of Britain and Ireland is based on the notion that improvement is finite: there will come a point when all the useful lines are drawn, all industries and markets finally settled and linked, in a tight, closed economic system which will resist economic change as effectively as it resists foreign invasion or competition ("Plan," ff. 50–2). He is much alarmed, in particular, by the vagaries of markets and the consequent vagrancy of industries, their tendency "to shift from place to place" ("Plan," f. 50) in search of new sources of power, better access to the arteries of exchange. The aim of the improvements he suggests is as much to stabilize old industries as to promote new ones; trades, by remaining in one place, will promote fixity in the work-force and

the development of occupational castes, as families are enabled and
encouraged to follow a single trade in a single place through succeeding generations. In these days of shifting centers of production and the
enforced flexibility of labor this may seem a benevolent concern, but
that it was not entirely so is suggested by the one moment in the text
where Dyer contemplates the movement of labor with equanimity. The
only entry under "Y" in his alphabetical section, where his notes on
Yorkshire were intended to appear, is a plan for emptying workhouses
of "y[e] weak Lame & old" and packing them off to work in the woolen
and fish-drying industries ("Plan," f. 26). The scheme is alarmingly prophetic of Jeremy Bentham's, fifty years later: "Not one in a hundred is
absolutely incapable of all employment. Not the motion of a finger –
not a step – not a wink – not a whisper – but might be turned to account,
in the way of profit."[12]

   In her essay "Imperial Georgic," O'Brien compares Virgil's vision
of Italy in Book 2 of the *Georgics* with Dryden's translation of it, pointing out that "Virgil is more preoccupied with Italian unity than with
the imperial extension of Rome," whereas Dryden's translation, there
and elsewhere, gestures toward re-imagining Italy in the context of early
English imperialism. There is something of the same contrast at work
between the "Commercial Map" and *The Fleece*. In the poem, it is true,
Dyer represents England as at once the pattern of a modern imperial
economy and as still somehow a colony of Rome: the towns and cities
of England are continually referred to by their Latin names; the regions
of England and Wales are imagined as inhabited by the Silures, the
Brigantes, and so on. Finally, however, the unity of these British tribes
depends on the cooperative labors which together enable the woolen
industry to find markets throughout an extended commercial empire.
In the "Commercial Map," Dyer re-imagines imperial England in the
context of internal Italian unity, a unity which exists apparently in
and for itself. On the strengthening ties between England, Scotland,
and Ireland, as well as between the different regions of England, that
would be achieved by knotting the roads and navigations of our island
into a closer mesh, he writes:

a Child's hand may break the Separated Arrow; but what Arm can bend the
Quiver? therefore were the Fasces carried before the Romans, to repres-
ent the Latians, Tarentines, Estruscans, Ligurians, &c., in unity invincible.
("Plan," f. 55)

   As well as representing himself, in both the poem and the map, as
an advocate for the mercantile interest, Dyer wrote in both texts as a

scholar of Romano-British antiquity; but if, in *The Fleece*, his antiquar-
ianism is finally in the service of a vision of capitalist modernity, as
pastoral is to georgic, this is rather less true of the "Commercial Map."
I am thinking here especially of his fascination with the old network
of Roman roads or of roads supposed to be Roman, which he calls
attention to partly in order to point the contrast between Roman virtue
before it became corrupted, and the vices of modern aristocracy, too
preoccupied with its own metropolitan pleasures to initiate great public
works in the provinces ("Plan," ff. 42–4).

Two Roman roads in particular, Watling Street and the Fosse Way,
were still important commercial arteries in mid eighteenth-century
England. But Dyer's interest in such roads, in his notes, especially, to
the "Commercial Map," goes far beyond his brief as modernizer of
internal trade routes or as spokesman for the profitable as against the
unprofitable classes of society. He seems to see the intersecting lines
inscribed by the once-virtuous Romans as the safest guide through the
maze of modern corruption. He continually calls to attention the places
where ancient roads intersect each other, or cross large navigable rivers:
Streatley, where the Ridgeway and the Icknield Way, both then supposed
to be Roman, meet at the Thames; Dunstable, where the Icknield Way
crosses Watling Street, or Royston, where it crosses Ermine Street;
Cirencester, where the Ermin Way, the Fosse, and Akeman Street all
meet; the Roman borough Tripontium, where Watling Street crosses
the Avon, less than a mile from Catthorpe, where Dyer was curate from
1742 to 1751.[13] These knots in the network are the nodal points of what
John Goodridge, in his enormously well-informed and thoughtful study
of *The Fleece*, has described as Dyer's "mytho-topography,"[14] a system
of geography in which Roman Britain is as present to his imagination
as modern England.

Here, for example, is Dyer's note on High Cross – near Claybrooke,
south of Leicester – where the Fosse crosses Watling Street, a mile from
the brook which becomes the River Soar:

North-E. near Cleybrook y[e] Fosse leads to Lincoln by Ratae & Vernemetum
– and to y[e] N. W. goes directly to Wales by Mandvessedum in Warcs. ("Plan,"
f. 16v.)

He means of course that Watling Street goes to Wales; but what in-
trigues me here is the present tense: the roads run through a terrain in
which the ancient place-names for Leicester, Willoughby, and Mancetter
near Atherstone are as real, as present to him as Claybrooke, Lincoln,

Wales, and Warwickshire. Read from this point of view, Dyer's specimen map of Worcestershire may have strayed into Warwickshire not
so much in order to unite the counties in an extended modern commercial region, but because by looking beyond the county boundary
he could include more of the nodal points of Roman Britain. That this
was what he had in mind is suggested by the fact that, in order to complete the lozenge described above, he ignored the eighteen-century road
joining Alcester and Bidford, which followed a wide curve of the River
Arrow, and substituted for it the abandoned line of Ryknild Street, the
Roman road from Edgbaston that had once joined the two towns. And
when, in the "discourse" on the "Commercial Map," Dyer proposes
a new canal to link the Trent and Thames, he argues that it should
follow the route of the Soar past High Cross, the Roman Venonis ("Plan,"
ff. 41–2). This was an oddly impracticable route: the Soar at this point
is a tiny stream in an inconveniently undulating landscape, and it is
difficult not to suspect that in making this suggestion Dyer was at least
as anxious to tie another strand into his Roman knot as to facilitate
the passage of goods from Hull to Oxford.

In short, in the "Commercial Map" England is imagined at once as
a space to be laid out entirely for the circulation of trade, and as the
unconquered colony of an antique metropolis whose defeat and decay
Dyer had described in his poem of 1740, "The Ruins of Rome." Dyer
had learned well the lesson taught by the decline and fall of an over-
extended commercial empire. The commitment of the "Commercial
Map" to advancing the interests of the nation by promoting those of
commerce is animated as much by a fear of the effects of trade as by
an enthusiasm for trade itself. The notion of commerce as a polishing
agent is never so much as glanced at; commerce threatens the dissolution
and collapse of the nation unless it is carefully policed and confined to
its proper channels. The concern for "the better circulation of our Trade"
is precisely that: a desire to create a closed, watertight system, where
nothing leaks in or out, where commodities move so that people can
keep their place, where England can avoid the fate of Rome only if its
economic improvement follows the blueprint drawn up by Roman virtue.

IV

If the "Commercial Map" represents England as a tortoise, its extremities retracted within itself, safe inside its shell, the England of *The Fleece*,
the final destination of much of Dyer's work on the earlier project, is

an octopus, its tentacles reaching out to embrace every continent on earth. The transformation of map into poem may have represented a change of mind on Dyer's part about where the best interests of the nation lay, though its (hopefully) benign imperialism was not, perhaps, as O'Brien suggests, an immediate reaction to the Seven Years' War, which began when the poem was in its final drafts. The change of ideology, however, may equally have been the result of the change of genre, for, as O'Brien points out, eighteenth-century georgic after Thomson was firmly wedded to an imperial ideology; its mock-epic became less mock, and could no longer find fulfillment within the peaceful confines of a small island. It seems right, therefore, to link the abandonment of English formal georgic to the loss of the American colonies and developing embarrassment over the slave trade; though to O'Brien's general explanation I would add – as perhaps she would have done, given more space – that a genre which claimed to describe agricultural and manufacturing processes, in the context of a general account of the economic organization of an imperial economy, was particularly vulnerable to the development of a science of political economy, and the related attribution to poetry of a more personal register and a sentimental, consolatory function.

If the genre of formal georgic largely disappeared, however, a version of the discourse of georgic – the celebration of rural life and the nation based on an idealized or distanced acknowledgment of the necessity of labor – survived quite comfortably into the next century, by attaching itself to the discourse of sentiment. Among writers mentioned by O'Brien, this involved – in William Cowper and James Grahame, and also, I would argue, in Wordsworth – a retreat to the domestic, the small-scale, to something like the little England of Dyer's map, or the little Scotland of Grahame's *British Georgics* (1809). Perhaps nothing encouraged this more inward-looking, often very regional georgic than the threat of invasion and economic isolation during the Napoleonic wars: Constable's georgic vision, for example, in the middle and late 1810s, of the valley of the Stour, the navigable river which seems to lead not outward to the sea but into the very heart of rural England; or, as Elizabeth Heckendorn Cook argues, Fanny Burney's *The Wanderer* of 1814, a georgic of the New Forest.

It was intriguing to learn, from Cook's essay, how George III as Farmer George was invoked as the patriarchal superintendent of Burney's georgic fantasy of little England. Part of my fascination lay in the fact that of the various versions of himself by which George courted the affection of his subjects, his identity as Farmer George had been the most vulnerable, in the years between his first recovery from illness, and the period in which *The Wanderer* was written, to ridicule, satire, and contempt. In 1789, when Burney witnessed the adulation with which George was greeted in the New Forest, the wounded king was so much an object of national sympathy and guilt that to satirize him was virtually unthinkable. By 1795, however, the year of near-famine, things were very different. In that year James Gillray for example published his caricature "Affability,"[15] in which George and Charlotte, masquerading as a farmer and his wife, seek out a farm-worker busy feeding pigs. Hoping no doubt to demonstrate the easy familiarity with his people he had allegedly demonstrated in the New Forest six years earlier, George subjects the terrified man to a furious interrogation: "Well, Friend, where a' you going, Hay? – what's your Name, hay? – where d'ye Live, hay? – hay?" – all this delivered at point-blank range, and with a crazed stare.

In the main, George's georgic character was satirized as revealing not the bluff freedom but the miserliness associated with the English yeoman, as if the soaring price of food was to be attributed to farmers profiteering under the protection of George's example. Also in 1795, an anonymous London publisher, probably Richard Lee, issued the short pamphlet *Rare News for Old England*, in which, while his subjects starve, the "Farmer General" appears at a country fair with two oxen for sale, and insists that his agent should not let them go at less than a shilling a pound. "What a proof," the pamphlet comments, "of paternal affection and loving-kindness"; the anecdote, it continues, "agrees so well with the uniform conduct of the person it alludes to, that any evidence of its authenticity would be superfluous."[16] In the same year John Wolcot, writing as Peter Pindar, published his verse account of a later journey made by George through the New Forest to his favorite resort of Weymouth. The poem begins by representing the king as something very like Nimrod (see Cook), the mighty hunter, whose carriage and its escort of light horsemen flash through rural England, terrifying wildlife and farm animals, flattening poultry, and forcing old women to shelter in roadside ditches. It is in Weymouth that George assumes the farmer; boasts of the noble oaks he has felled in Richmond Park to make way for cereals, and of the man-traps set at Windsor to protect his poultry; buys bullocks and pigs from local farmers, using his royal authority to beat down the price; refuses charity to a sailor who has lost a leg in George's service, and cannot afford a wooden one; hears with delight of the rising price of agricultural produce, and, when his agent warns him of the complaints of the poor, reproves him for talking politics. Throughout his month in Weymouth, he has his provisions sent down from London, ensuring that the local economy will make nothing from his stay.[17] The growing hostility to Farmer George, and the belief that, by the example he set, he bore much of the responsibility for food shortages and high prices, finally came to a head in London in October 1795, when the king was pelted in his coach by a crowd demanding bread, and was metonymically dismembered when the empty coach, returning to the Royal Mews, was torn to pieces. It says much for the loyalty of Fanny Burney and her New Foresters that their admiration for the image of benevolent Farmer George survived that year.

Equally fascinating in Cook's account of *The Wanderer* is the notion of the novel as a feminine, if not perhaps as feminist georgic. The imperial georgic discussed by O'Brien is inescapably masculine: the not-so-mock epic register, the sometimes belligerent visions of empire policed by the British fleet, the panoramic prospect views of the wealth of the landscape, and the economic organization of the nation, all announce that this is a genre beyond the compass of women writers. If it is right, however, that the georgic, in the extended sense defined by Anthony Low – "an informing spirit, an attitude toward life"[18] – survived the end of the eighteenth century by attaching itself to a sentimental, small-scale, domestic vision of a very little England, it survived as a feminized genre, suitable for appropriation by women precisely because it no longer attempted the large masculine themes of Dryden or Dyer. We can trace the beginnings of this shift in the illustrations to Thomson's *Seasons* that begin to appear in the 1790s, which usually concentrate on the domestic interludes in the poem, and which culminate in Constable's recently re-discovered painting, *The Wheatfield* (1816). I take this to be a version of the tale of Palemon and Lavinia from "Autumn," re-imagined as sentimental-georgic puppy-love between pre-adolescent children.[19]

I want to concentrate, however, on what might happen to the prospect view in this newly feminized georgic. The knotting-together of the pictorial and the georgic, well exemplified in Elizabeth Bohls's fine essay on Edward Long, was a foundational trope of metropolitan formal georgic from *Windsor Forest* onward, and was fundamental also to the masculine character of the genre. As I have argued elsewhere, because women were widely assumed to lack the ability to generalize, to see objects in terms of general categories as opposed to concrete particulars, they were widely believed to be incapable of grasping the principles of pictorial organization, or of the social and economic organization figured in the panoramic prospect. The point is made succinctly enough by Burney's friend Hannah More, writing in 1799. Women, she writes

excel in details; but they do not so much generalize their ideas as men, nor do their minds seize a great subject with so large a grasp. They are acute observers, and accurate judges of life and manners, as far as their own sphere of observation extends; but they describe a smaller circle. A woman sees the world, as it were, from a little elevation in her own garden, whence she makes an exact survey of home scenes, but takes not in that wider range of distant prospects which he who stands on a loftier eminence commands.[20]

It is because women, More goes on to explain, are (or must be persuaded they are) "inferior in wholeness of mind," in "the faculty of comparing, combining, analysing, and separating"; perhaps especially in the "power of arrangement,"[21] that the sphere of their social knowledge is or should be confined to the domestic circle – the immediate foreground, the landscape of their own gardens – and they cannot or should not aspire to occupy the eminence from which men claim to "command" the whole prospect of society.

It may have been with this passage in mind that when Burney required Juliet, her heroine, to "take a general survey" of her georgic paradise, she mounted her not on a lofty eminence, but on a "hillock." And once on that little elevation she sees not the panoramic vista of Thomson, or Dyer, or Long, but two things only: the forest trees, and the sunset. The aged oaks are no longer, as in formal georgic, the raw materials of the naval and merchant fleets, but the symbols of an enfolding, protective patriarchy, "spreading their venerable branches to offer shelter from the storms of life"; the sunset does not beckon her to the distant horizon, but reminds her to count the blessings vouchsafed to her by the beneficent Creator, the "parent of resignation."[22] The view expands her soul as it contracts her earthly horizons; it teaches her to seek fulfillment not in the wide world but within herself. The contracted horizon of feminine resignation could not be more at home in the little England of this sentimental georgic.

NOTES

1 See the article on Carew in *DNB* and the title-pages summarized in the *Eighteenth-Century Short Title Catalogue*. Two editions appeared in Exeter in 1745. From 1749 until 1775 all editions were published in Sherborne,

though usually in partnership with a London bookseller. Thereafter until
the end of the century all editions were published in London, with the exception of two of the four which appeared in 1785, one in Hull, the other in
"London, Bristol, and Exeter."

2 *The Life and Adventures of Bampfylde-Moore Carew, commonly called the King of the
Beggars* (1789), p. 40 n. I quote for my own convenience from the edition
I happen to possess.

3 Ibid., pp. 47–8.

4 Ibid., pp. 46–51.

5 The other such episode is Carew's first trip to the American colonies (see
next paragraph). According to the *Life* (pp. 90–2), Carew heard George
Whitefield preach in Derby near Philadelphia, and touched him for three
or four pounds. If this is true, it must have happened on May 15, 1740,
the only time, according to Whitefield's journals, that he preached in Derby.
See Iain Murray, ed., *George Whitefield's Journals* (1960), pp. 423–4.

6 *Life*, pp. 21–4, 92–5.

7 The manuscript is in the Dean and Chapter Library at Durham Cathedral;
my thanks are due to Roger Norris, the Deputy Chapter Librarian, for
providing me with a photocopy of it, and to John Goodridge, who kindly
allowed me to see his own draft transcription of the text, to be published
in *The Complete Works of John Dyer*, eds. Goodridge and Belinda Humphrey,
2 vols. (Cardiff: University of Wales Press, forthcoming). Except at one point,
where I prefer my reading to Goodridge's, I have quoted throughout from
his transcription, but have silently omitted Dyer's alterations and alternative wordings. For an account of the "Commercial Map," see Ralph M.
Williams, *Poet, Painter and Parson: The Life of John Dyer* (New York, 1956),
pp. 97–101.

8 "Plan," ff. 41–2, and compare with the passage on canals and navigations
in *The Fleece*, Book 3, in Dyer, *Poems* (1761), p. 151.

9 See Marshall, *The Rural Economy of the West of England*, 2 vols. (1796), I: 1.

10 It is difficult to preserve decorum in referring to Dyer's notions of nation-
ality. He turns to discuss the desirability of union between England and
Ireland in the last pages of the "Plan"; before that, it is not easy to know
whether he is discussing England, England and Wales, Great Britain
including Scotland, or the entire Anglo-Celtic archipelago.

11 Dyer, *Poems*, pp. 148–9, emphasis added.

12 Bentham, "Outline of a Work entitled Pauper Management Improved,"
(section 1) in *Annals of Agriculture* 30 (1798): 89–176, this passage p. 145.

13 "Plan," ff. 4b, 6. Tripontium is an important site in *The Fleece* also. See
Dyer's reference to "Tripontian Fields" in *Poems*, p. 61: "Where ever-gliding
Avon's limpid wave / Thwarts the long course of dusty Watling-street."
For more on Tripontium, see John Goodridge, *Rural Life in Eighteenth-Century
English Poetry* (Cambridge, 1995), pp. 131, 199 n. 18. Archaeologists have
now moved Tripontium about a mile and a half further north than where
Dyer believed it to be; it is now separated from Catthorpe by the M6.

14 Goodridge, *Rural Life*, p. 161.
15 Reproduced in Draper Hill, *Fashionable Contrasts: 100 Caricatures by James Gillray* (1966), plate 63.
16 *Rare News for Old England! Beef a Shilling a Pound!* ([1795]), pp. 3–4; though the pamphlet has no publication details, it is included in Richard Lee's advertisement leaves for 1795.
17 "Peter Pindar" [John Wolcot], *The Royal Tour, and Weymouth Amusements* (1795), *passim*.
18 Low, *The Georgic Revolution* (Princeton, N. J., 1985), p. 7.
19 *The Wheatfield*, painted 1815–16, exhibited 1816. The painting is illustrated in Leslie Parris and Ian Fleming-Williams, *Constable* (1991), p. 160–2.
20 More, *Strictures of the Modern System of Female Education*, 3rd, edn., 2 vols. (1799), 2: 26–7.
21 Ibid., 2: 28.
22 Burney, *The Wanderer; Or, Female Difficulties*, Margaret Anne Doody, Robert. L. Mack, Peter Sabor, eds. (Oxford, 1991), p. 676.

Index